IMAGES
of America

PIGEON FORGE

ON THE COVER: In the summer of 1941, before the country entered World War II, men and boys were still hanging out at the local garages in Pigeon Forge, Tennessee. These repair shops were servicing some of the last prewar production automobiles. Wayne L. Ogle's garage was on the south side of present-day Old Mill Avenue between the Parkway to Pigeon Forge and River Road. In this photograph, dated July 11, 1941, are, from left to right, Harold Quarrels, Wayne L. Ogle, Jess Ogle, and Darrell Pickel. (Courtesy of Rena O. Ogle.)

IMAGES
of America

PIGEON FORGE

Veta Wilson King

ARCADIA
PUBLISHING

ISBN 978-0-7385-8611-3

Published by Arcadia Publishing
Charleston, South Carolina

Printed in the United States of America

Library of Congress Control Number: 2010921320

For all general information contact Arcadia Publishing at:
Telephone 843-853-2070
Fax 843-853-0044
E-mail sales@arcadiapublishing.com
For customer service and orders:
Toll-Free 1-888-313-2665

Visit us on the Internet at www.arcadiapublishing.com

*To my family for assistance and support and
to the many persons sharing historic photographs*

Contents

Acknowledgments		6
Introduction		7
1.	Ironworks and Early Farming Community	9
2.	The Great Smoky Mountains Change a Destiny	57
3.	Roadside Cottages and Smoked Hams Beckon Tourists	83

ACKNOWLEDGMENTS

Publication of this book has been a way to preserve the town's heritage, since there are so few visible remains of historic sites. Beautiful two-story white farmhouses, rolling fields, and unspoiled riverbanks can be enjoyed through photographs of days gone by in Images of America: *Pigeon Forge*. Thousands enjoy our mountains and our busy family fun resort. This book will permit a glimpse of the pioneers who farmed in one field and rented tiny cottages in the other and who established the town people see today.

I am thankful to God for his goodness and guidance. I wish to thank my family—Donnie, Tyler, and Allison—for their patience and assistance, and my niece, Gina Wilson Flynn, for her encouragement to end my procrastination and begin this project. I also thank the business owners and individuals in Pigeon Forge who searched through personal family albums and keepsake boxes for old photographs. Pauline Walters-Spencer, Bill Allen, Sarah Ball, Jerry Loveday, Donna Allen, Ruth Ferguson, and Gwendell Cody in particular provided historic information and a number of old pictures as well. I am grateful to the Pigeon Forge Public Library for their resources and to Maggie Bullwinkel, Southern publisher at Arcadia.

Tedious hours have been spent researching Pigeon Forge's history as accurately as possible. The primary sources of historic information have been writings by Beulah D. Linn, Dott L. McMahan, and Joseph Sharp. My only wish is that I could have included other photographs important to Pigeon Forge's history, but the project had to end somewhere.

Enjoy this book the way you would enjoy thumbing through your grandmother's old scrapbooks.

I will lift up mine eyes unto the hills from whence cometh my help. My help cometh from the Lord.

—Psalm 121: 1, 2

INTRODUCTION

There are more than nine million visits to Great Smoky Mountains National Park each year. The formation of this national park shaped the small resort town of Pigeon Forge in East Tennessee. Today the Parkway is lined with colorful businesses for the vacationer: exciting rides, theaters, and shops; families wonder where to begin! Visitors can only imagine the vast wheat and hay fields accessed in earlier times by only a dirt road along the river.

The Cherokees, native to the rugged Great Smoky Mountains, named the Little Pigeon River that runs through the town, according to the late Joseph A. Sharp, former Sevier County historian. Countless numbers of wild passenger pigeons, now extinct, stopped in this wide valley on their migratory flights. Pioneers said they darkened the skies as they flew in, and their great roosting numbers stripped the beech trees of their branches. Sometime after Isaac Love built a bloomary (iron forge) operation on the Little Pigeon River, the area became known as Pigeon Forge.

Sharp writes that there were three forges and a furnace for smelting in place by 1820 by the current Old Mill site. Water from a nearby dam powered the huge trip hammers that beat the pig iron into commercial bar iron. Water also powered the bellows for the air blasts that fueled the great fires. The ore for the manufacturing process was mined at a site near present-day Teaster Lane (once named Ore Bank Road) and carried on sleds pulled by oxen. Sharp states that citizens told of watching the beautiful lights of these forges from nearby hillsides and thinking that the fires of hell could burn no brighter or hotter. The ironworks operated until the Civil War period (2 tons of iron bars were manufactured in 1856). The equipment was sold and taken to Kentucky in 1885. Almost 100 years after the ironworks ceased operations, Henry Butler proudly displayed one of the forge's old trip hammers at his small roadside restaurant, known as Butler's Farm House.

Isaac Love's son, William, constructed the present-day Old Mill in 1830. Carson Brewer writes in a 1973 *Knoxville News Sentinel* article, "The 40-foot-long, 14-by-14 inch yellow poplar sills they laid down still support the building . . . The heavy wooden door of the Old Mill at Pigeon Forge bears nail and tack prints where messages were posted," leaving evidence that the mill was a community meeting place. A more modern means of carrying news came when William K. Love, the mill's builder, became the first postmaster in 1841 and the place name Pigeon Forge was made official, according to an April 1986 *Mountain Press* newspaper article by former county historian Beulah D. Linn.

A sawmill, also powered by the river, was later built around 1885 where the forge had been; it operated until 1900, according to Brewer. A large storage room for the Old Mill was added where the sawmill and forge had been. The Old Mill General Store is there today.

Pigeon Forge's namesake industry was not the town's earliest history. According to Linn, the earliest white settlers followed the Great Indian War and Trading Path, a trail from Virginia to the Overhill villages of the Cherokees. One branch of the path led by the mouth of Walden's Creek, where Col. Samuel Wear, Sevier County's most prominent early settler, constructed a fort in or before 1783. Colonel Wear may have established the first white settlement on the site as he provided refuge during the last Native American raids of the 1790s. In 1808, settlers built a log meetinghouse. Shiloh Church served as both a Methodist church and a school.

Large-acre land grants were being issued in the 1800s, and in 1841, the Sevier County Turnpike Company was formed to construct a road from the top of the Smoky Mountains through Pigeon Forge to the southern boundary of Sevierville. "In 1859 the Sevier County Court appointed a committee to adopt a plan to build a wooden bridge at the Trotter ford," Linn writes. John Sevier

Trotter owned the Old Mill site near the bridge at this time, and Union army uniforms were made at the mill during the early 1860s. Henderson Chapel Baptist Church organized in 1860 and the Pigeon Forge Methodist Church in 1880. The Pigeon Forge First Baptist Church building was constructed in 1914. Pigeon Forge Academy was built circa 1869. By the early 1900s, this farm community had businesses such as a farmer's supply store, a blacksmith, a bottling plant, and a small cannery supporting agriculture.

It was not until the establishment of Great Smoky Mountains National Park in 1934 that Pigeon Forge's destiny changed. Motor car garages replaced the blacksmith shop. Roadside and riverside cottages offered a night's rest, and country hams and mountain honey enticed passersby. In the late 1950s, officials in Sevierville and Gatlinburg began plans for building an airport along the wide, flat valley north of the Great Smoky Mountains. Pigeon Forge landowners with large-acre farms found the only way to avert the airport was to incorporate. In 1961, Pigeon Forge became a city, with three commissioners—Winfred Whaley, Xan Davenport, and Wade McMahan—and less than 300 residents.

With its train robberies and cancan girls, Rebel Railroad offered entertainment at the present site of Dollywood. Fort Weare Game Park was the county's own zoo, and a market-savvy potter operated a studio in a former farm barn. Fairyland once presented a museum-type attraction of storybook characters, and places such as Hillbilly Village and the Smoky Mountain Car Museum were among the town's first amusements. There was a drive-in theater, drive-in restaurant, skating rink, and bowling alley. More roadside cottages and small inns opened, and family-style dining enticed vacationers on their way to the mountains. Pigeon Forge farmers continued to grow fields of beans and corn beside the early vacationing businesses until the 1980s. The 1982 World's Fair in Knoxville spurred a building boom in Pigeon Forge. In 1986, Dolly Parton and the Herschend family opened Dollywood, which joined the many other attractions that gave the town its identity of an action-packed family resort. Pigeon Forge has expanded to include outlet shopping, mountain crafts, top-rated condominium resorts, camping facilities, and a wide range of dining places.

Changes happen fast in Pigeon Forge today. Since its early days of solid millhouses and iron forges, this area has continued to grow. The Great Smoky Mountains have and always will influence the town's destiny. In the shadow of these mountains, only time will reveal just how far the town will grow.

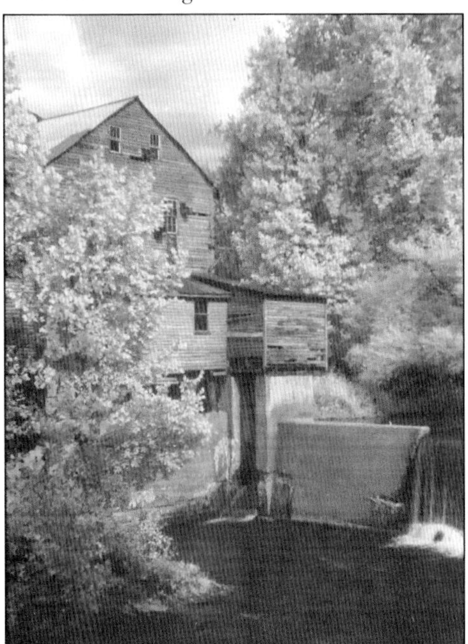

The Old Mill has been in continuous operation since its construction in 1830, with the exception of a few days of severe weather and when it was in bank receivership during the Great Depression. This was according to former owner and operator Kathy Stout Simmons. At first, there was a large breast wheel on the outside of the mill that powered the operations. It is unclear what became of the original wheel but in 1889, two water turbines about 2 feet by 3 feet and made of cast iron were installed to take the place of the wheel, according to the Old Mill's historians. They are about 10 feet under water in a water pen under the mill floor and were initially installed to provide adequate power for a white flour mill, also added in 1889. The present-day outside wheel was purchased by Simmons's father, Fred Stout, who bought the mill from the bank in 1933. It is now used to power the grain elevators. The turbine or tub mills provide power for the huge corn-grinding millstones. (Courtesy of Jerry Loveday.)

One

Ironworks and Early Farming Community

Sometime after the days when settlers sought refuge at Col. Samuel Wear's fort near the north end of modern Pigeon Forge, a small cluster of businesses emerged around the ironworks and the sizeable corn-grinding mill operation. The chief product from the forges was bar iron, but there were also molds for manufacturing kitchen utensils and farming implements. Buhrstones (millstones) imported from France by the mill's builder, William Love, ground thousands of pounds of corn. Love charged a one-eighth toll on the corn being brought to mill. The earliest local enterprises included a blacksmith shop, a water-powered sawmill, a coffin-making business, a bottling plant, a cannery, farmer supply stores, and general merchandise stores. All these centered around the Old Mill. One dirt road led farmers by the business center and ran primarily to the southeast along the Little Pigeon River. A short-lived railroad line running through the town hauled both a few passengers to Knoxville and tanbark to the tannery near Mill Creek. Pigeon Forge Academy was built in 1869 on a site adjoining the present Pigeon Forge Methodist Church. Students attended a few short months of free school, then had the opportunity for subscription school (for a fee) after Christmas. Other small one-room schools were nearby. The first churches included Shiloh Methodist, Henderson's Chapel Baptist, Middle Creek, Pigeon Forge United Methodist Brethren, and Pigeon Forge Baptist. With its schools, churches, and tiny business area, Pigeon Forge was becoming a profitable farming community in this fertile river valley as the 1800s led into the 20th century.

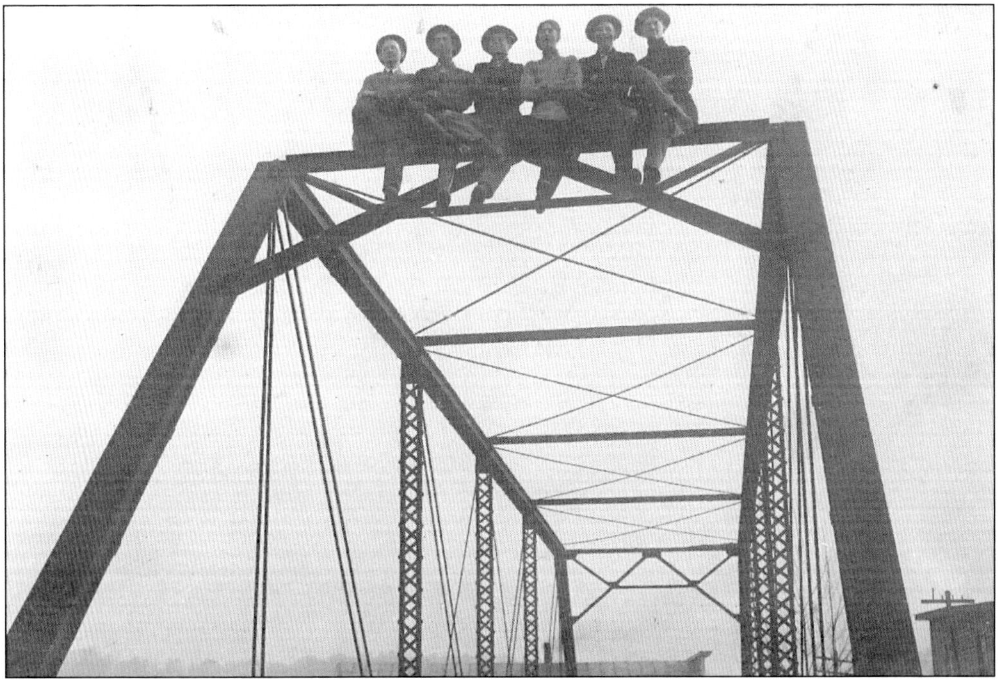

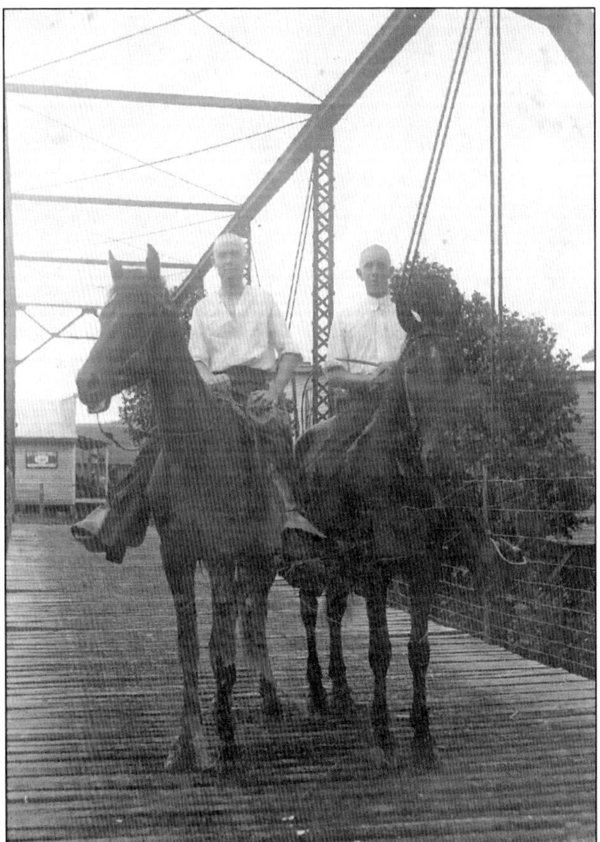

Men bravely sit on top of the steel trusses that frame the Old Mill Bridge. This bridge was constructed after the wooden covered bridge was destroyed in an 1875 flood. (Pauline Householder photograph; courtesy of Jerry Loveday.)

Jim Trotter (left) and James Stanley Householder, son of Joseph and Liza Householder, ride across the wooden floor of the bridge by the Old Mill. This steel structure could not withstand the ravaging flood in April 1920. Mountain storms caused the Little Pigeon River to overflow its banks, and it washed away the dirt on either side, leaving the mill standing only on its pillars. (Pauline Householder photograph; courtesy of Jerry Loveday.)

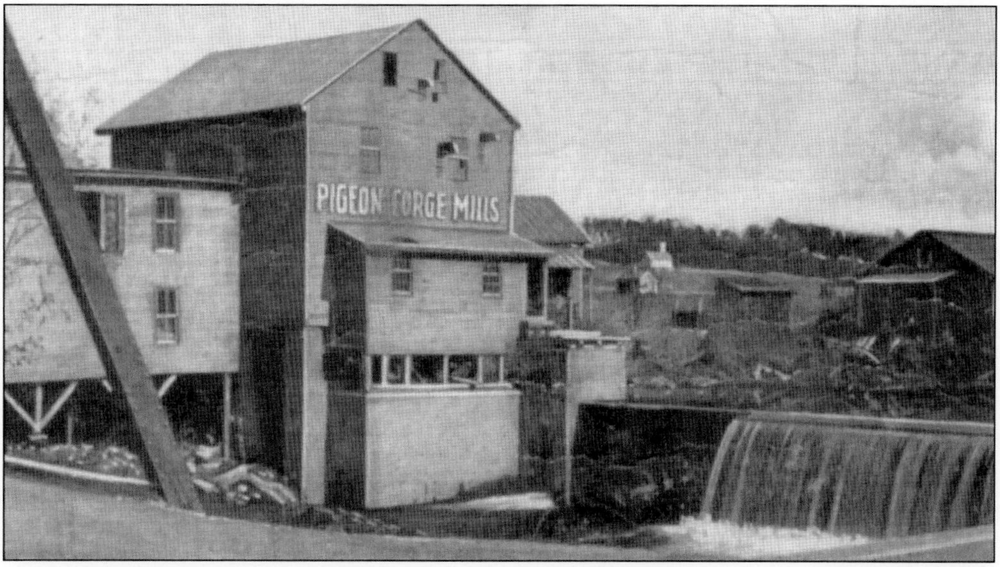

This 1917 Old Mill photograph shows the steel truss of the bridge crossing the Little Pigeon River. The Pigeon Forge First Baptist Church, the railroad depot, and the canning factory's night watchman building are seen in the background. Also pictured is a warehouse for the mill. Corn is being ground by the use of underwater turbine or tub mills. (Courtesy of the Dott L. McMahan collection.)

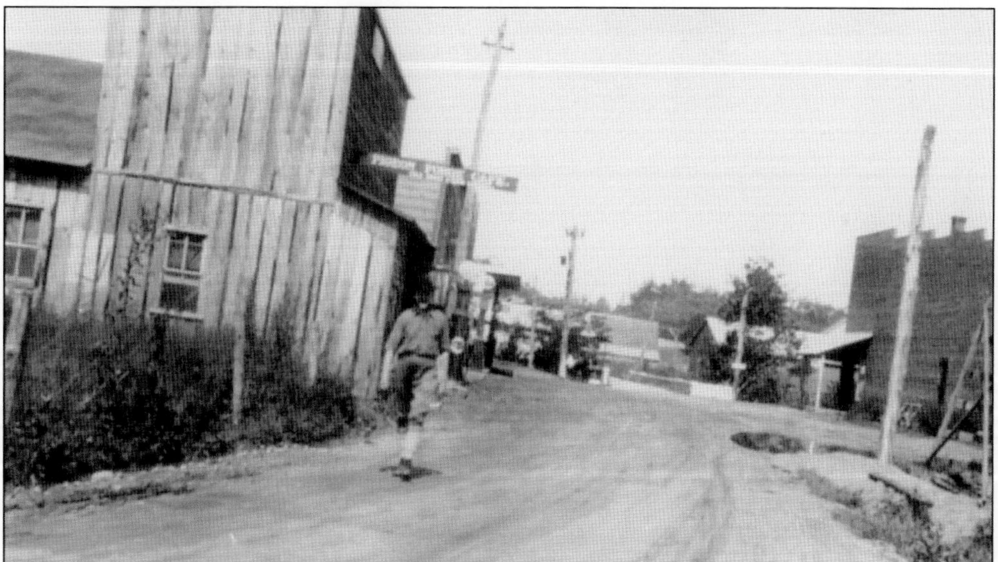

This sparse collection of businesses was the center of Pigeon Forge's primary commercial activity in the 1920s. The picture faces east toward the concrete bridge by the Pigeon Forge Mills (currently the Old Mill). On the left is Tebo Watson's restaurant, Pigeon Forge Café; his garage with the gas pump is in front. Beyond the garage is Watson's barbershop. The tall building front past the barbershop is Shirley Butler's feed building; beyond that is Butler's General Store and gas pump. Butler's original store building still stands across the river in this photograph. Ashley Butler's large barn is in the distance. The brick building at right houses Stott's Store Company. (Courtesy of the Dott L. McMahan collection.)

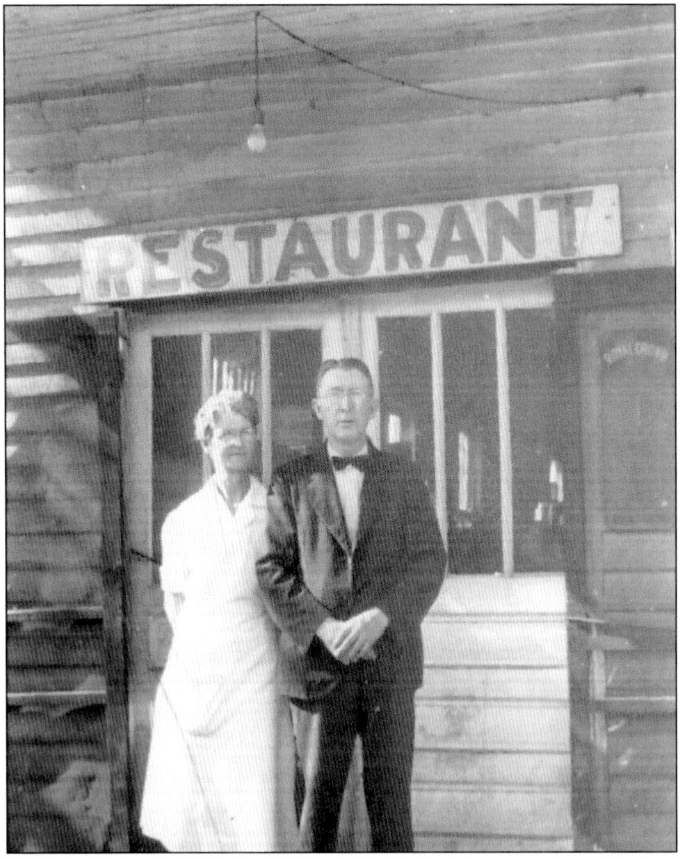

Tebo Watson and wife Becky Fleming Davenport Watson stand at the entrance to Watson's store, restaurant, and barbershop in the 1920s along present-day Old Mill Avenue. From the Mill Creek area and the daughter of G. W. Fleming, Becky was clerk in the store, serving coffee, soft drinks, and sandwiches. Her first husband was Andy Davenport, and after his death, she married Watson, the storekeeper, who was from the Oldham's Creek community. (Courtesy of the Dott L. McMahan collection.)

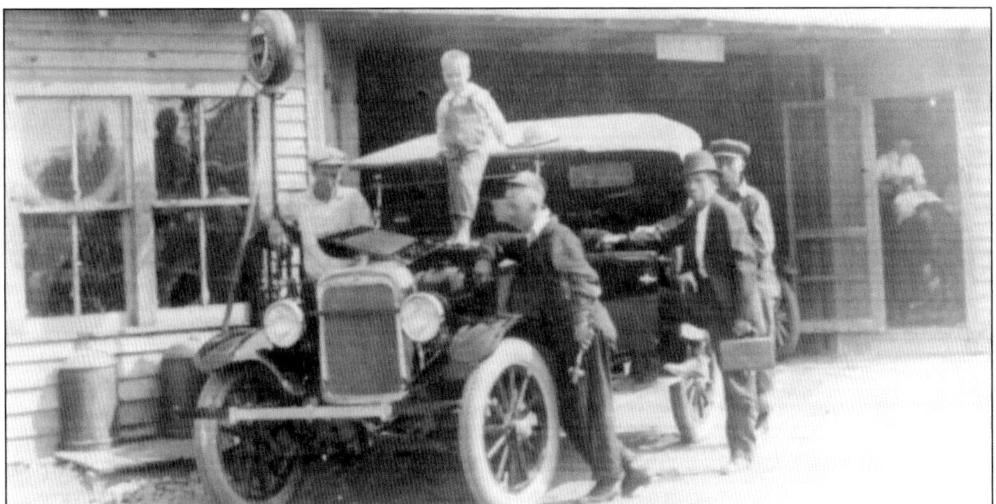

This old automobile sits in front of Tebo Watson's store. One source states that Otis Townsend operated the garage and gas pump here. Watson is seen at right working at his barber's chair. Dr. Stephen V. Gibson is the man with the pill satchel, and David Butler is the child standing on the car. Dr. Gibson practiced medicine in Pigeon Forge in the early 1900s. (Courtesy of the Dott L. McMahan collection.)

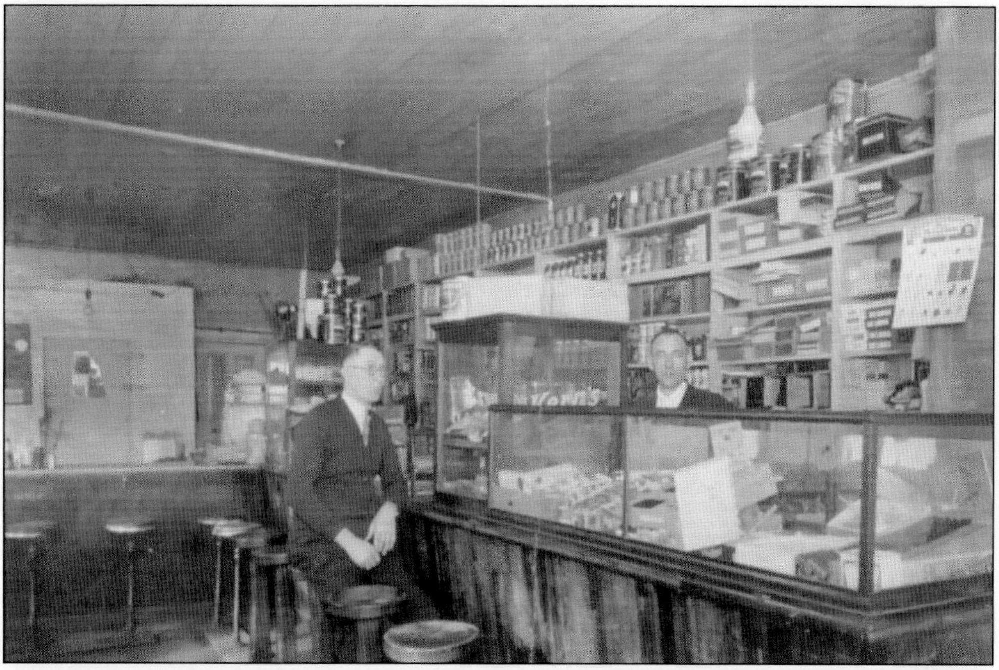

Tebo Watson (left) and West Seaton are pictured inside Watson's store on what was then known as Middle Creek Road. This store was one of the first to have electric lights, generated at a small power plant at the Old Mill in Pigeon Forge, and there was a gas pump out front. (Courtesy of the Dott L. McMahan collection.)

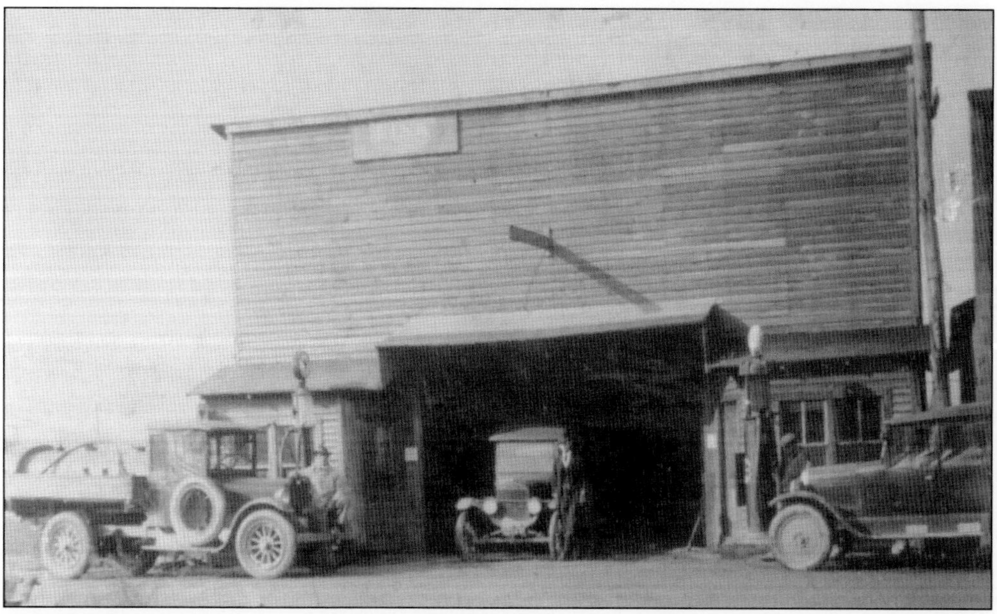

Arlie Roberts operated this garage in the Old Mill section of Pigeon Forge. It sat on the south side of present-day Old Mill Avenue near Stott's Store Company. (Courtesy of the Dott L. McMahan collection.)

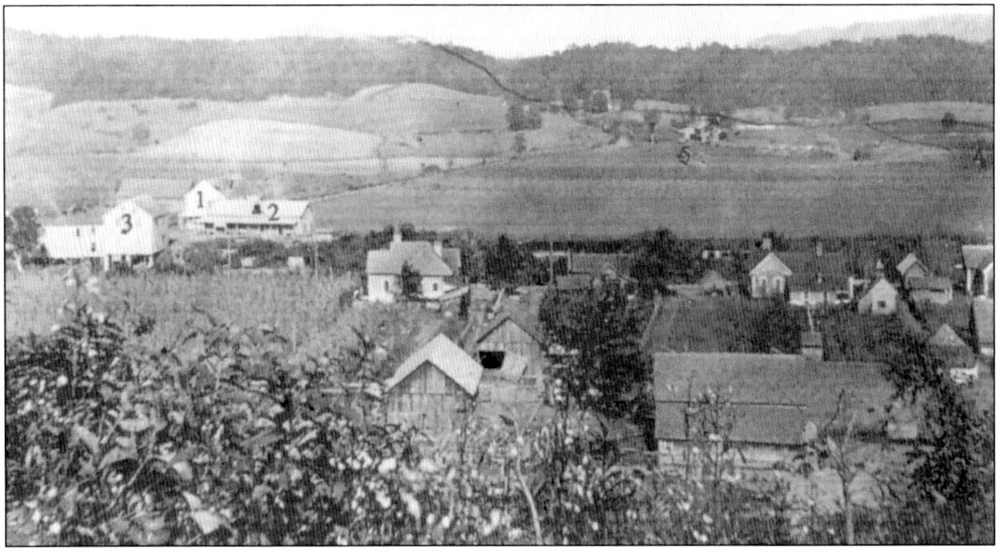

Isaac Perman Franklin mailed this photograph to his fiancée, Leona Southard, in the state of Washington around 1913. He wanted her to know of the town where she would live when they married. The two had met when Franklin, a Mill Creek native, moved to Washington to live and work. The places he identified are as follows: 1.) a community store, 2.) Hiram Franklin's store, 3.) the Old Mill, 4.) the construction site of the Pigeon Forge Cannery, and 5.) the future home of Pigeon Forge School. (Franklin family collection; courtesy of Ersa Rhea Noland Smith.)

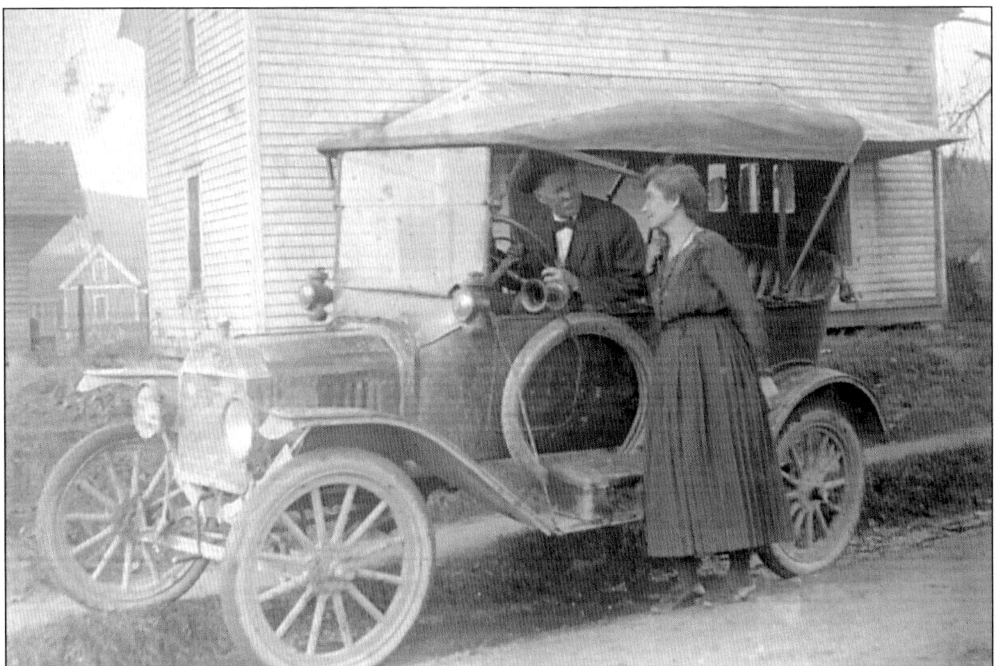

George Washington Fleming is pictured on River Road, around 1923, in front of his home in the taxi he drove in Pigeon Forge. He is pictured with his second wife, Elizabeth Thomas Fleming. The Flemings lived here before the Quarrels family, then moved to Ogle Drive. (Courtesy of C. L. Fleming.)

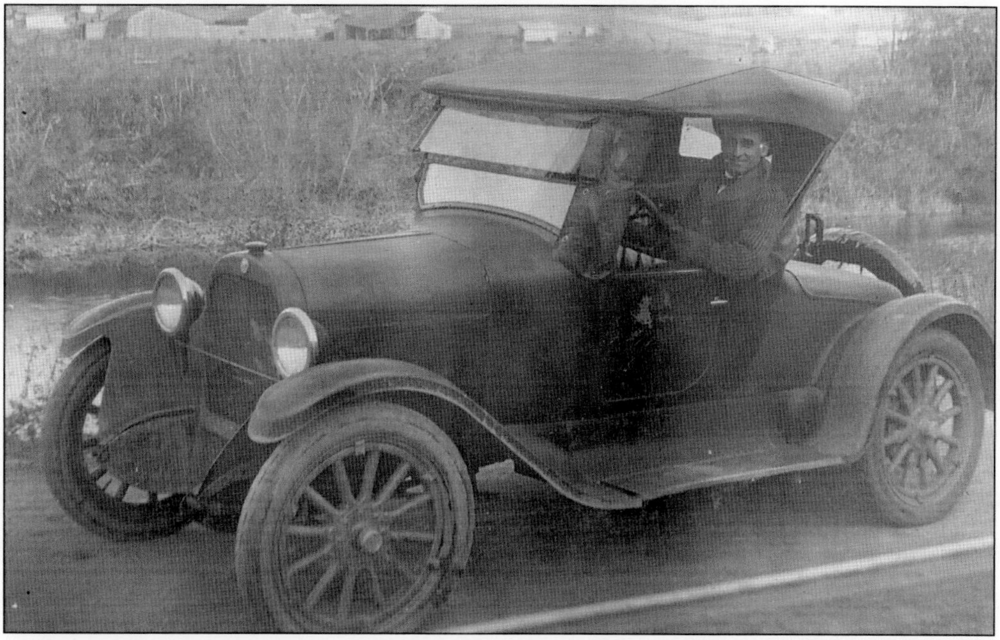

Dr. John Ogle travels the Pigeon Forge area roads in this classic Metz automobile. He practiced medicine in Pigeon Forge beginning in 1911 and moved his business to Sevierville in 1929. (Courtesy of Jerry Loveday.)

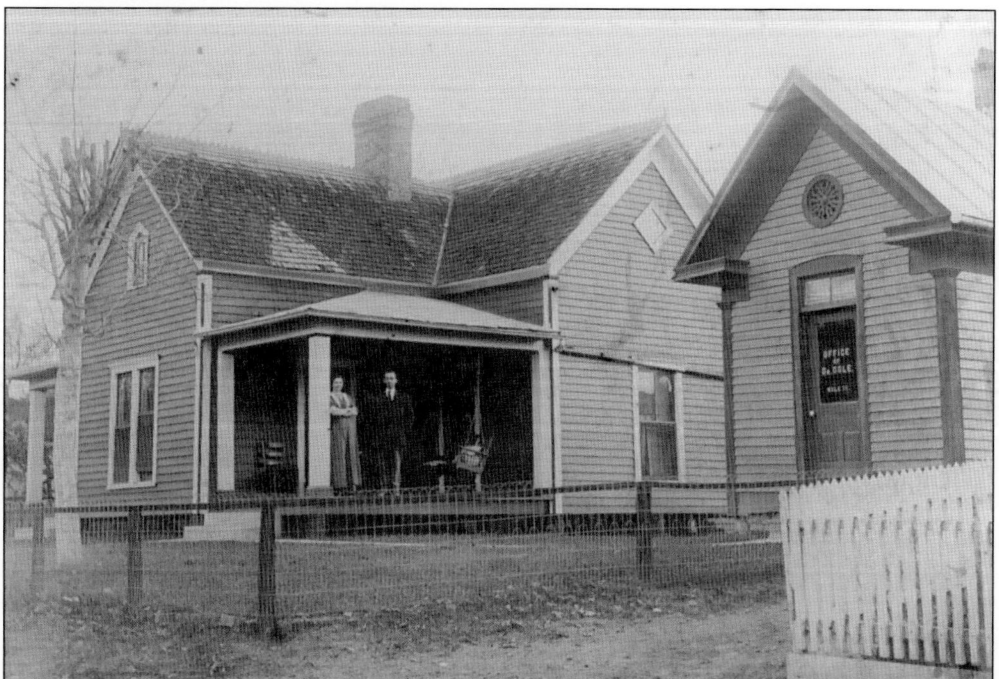

Dr. Ogle's home and office sat along River Road near the Old Mill. He is pictured here with his wife, Blanche. The doctor met Blanche Wayland when he practiced medicine in the nearby Harrisburg community. The two married on November 15, 1911. (Courtesy of Jerry Loveday.)

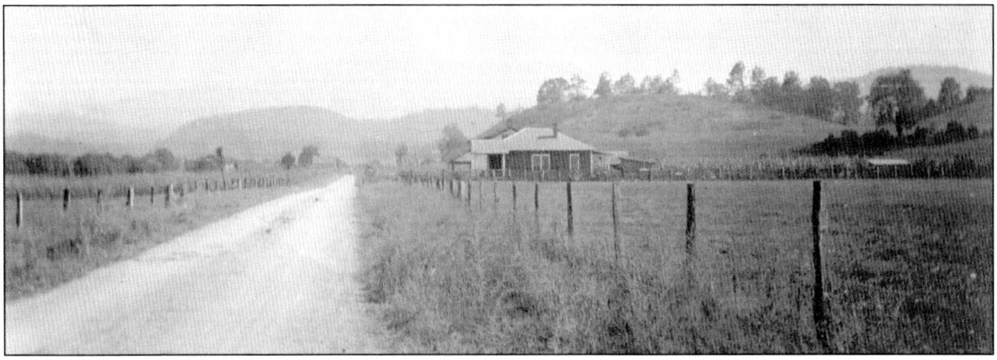

Pigeon Forge was a sparsely developed community in this 1920 photograph taken facing Mount LeConte in the Great Smoky Mountains. The Householder home is pictured at the right. It sat in an empty field south of the present-day First Baptist Church and was moved back when the new divided Highway 441 was constructed. No electric poles were visible along the highway then. (Courtesy of Great Smoky Mountains National Park.)

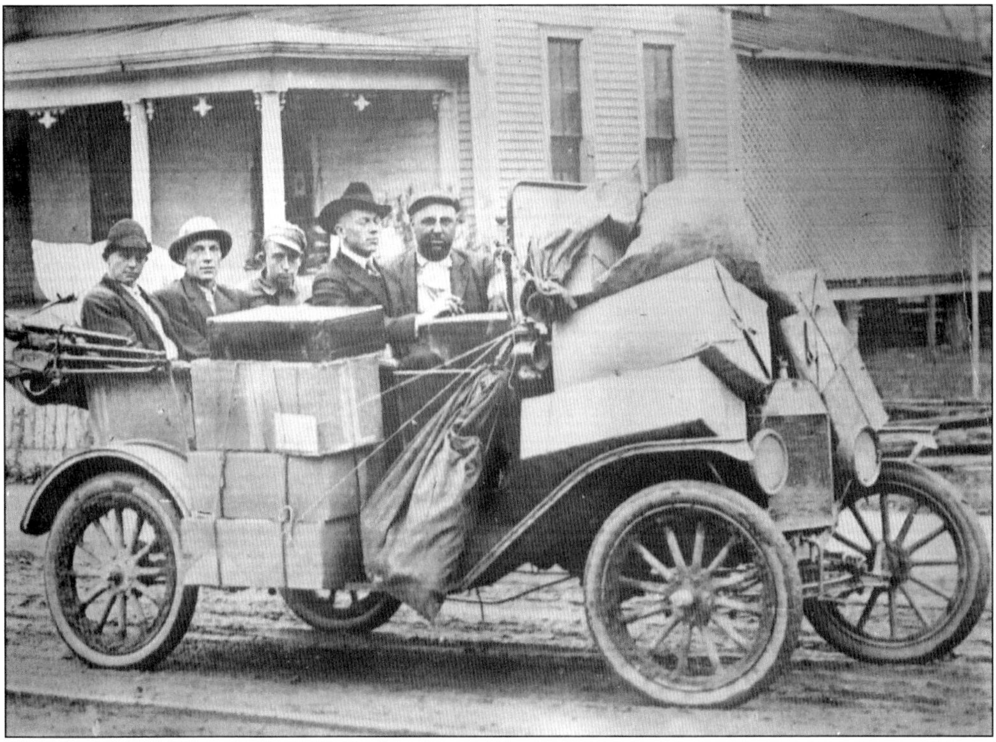

The first automobile to carry the mail along the 12-mile route from Sevierville to Gatlinburg is pictured here at a stop in Pigeon Forge to pick up more mail and passengers. The driver and passengers are unidentified. Dott McMahan wrote that in 1915 a star mail route (a route where mail is delivered by a contract carrier) was established between the two towns. Sam Robertson (likely the driver here) bought a new Ford on September 1, 1915, and carried mail and passengers for over four years. The following, in chronological order, provided their own transportation and followed Robertson as mail carriers: Walter Enloe, Gar King, Everett Trentham, A. T. Householder, and John Rellie Ogle. Tiny post offices moved from store to store throughout Pigeon Forge over the years, the last place being Louise Ogle Rader's store, which she operated with Veryl Whaley Smith. (Courtesy of Jerry Loveday.)

A hammer used in the town's ironworks is almost as tall as little Mary Wear in this 1937 photograph taken at the home of Robert Wear where the hammer sat. The forge by the Old Mill operated in the early to mid-1800s and gave the community its name—that and the passenger pigeons roosting along the river where the ironworks sat. (Courtesy of Great Smoky Mountains National Park.)

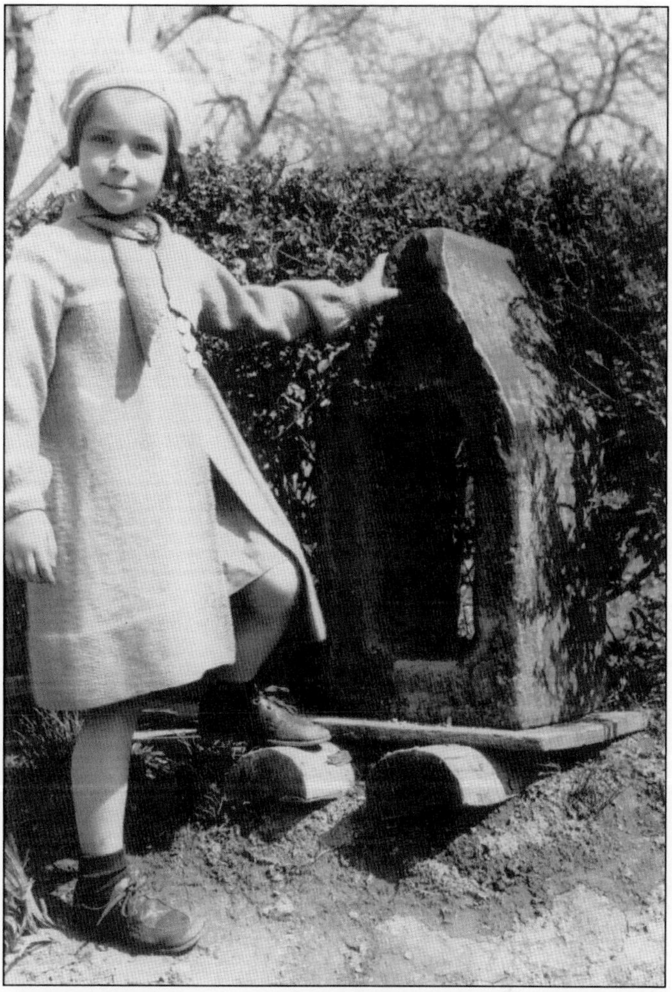

This winding mountain road was the way people traveled from Pigeon Forge to Gatlinburg around 1930. After Great Smoky Mountains National Park was established in 1934, plans were made to develop this Tennessee gateway to the park into a north- and southbound highway on either side of the Little Pigeon River. (Courtesy of Great Smoky Mountains National Park.)

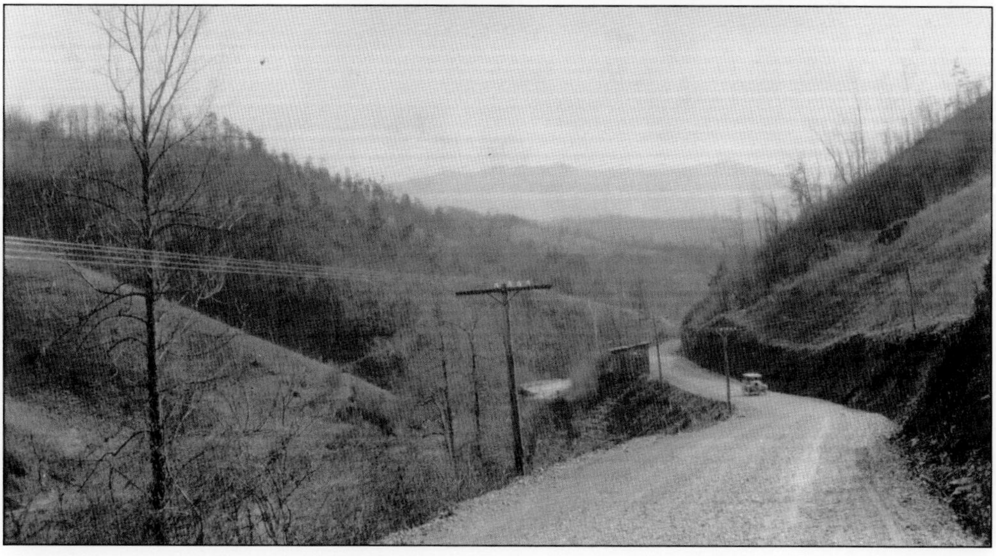

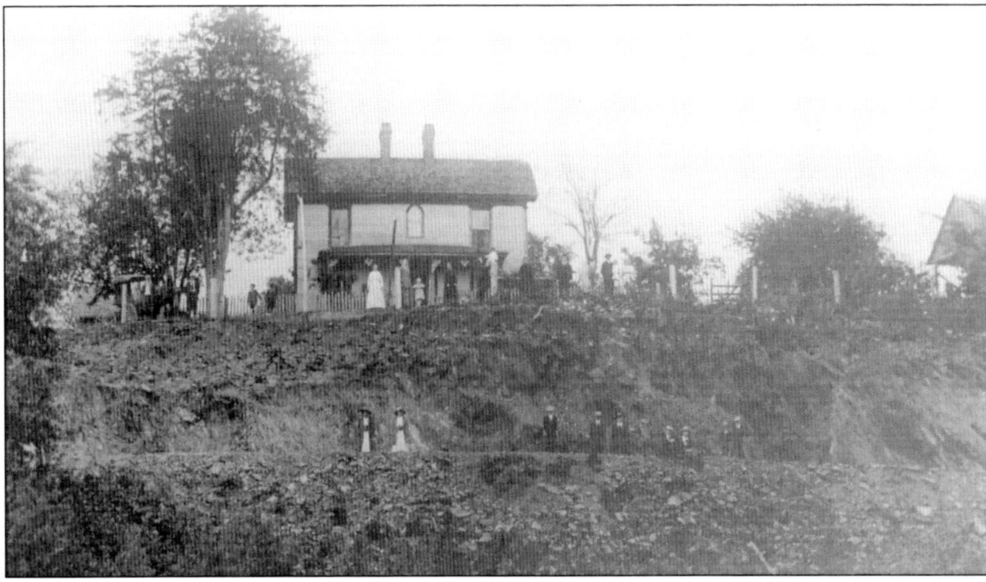

Family members stand by the porch and down along the railroad tracks in front of Henry and Elizabeth Gobble's house by the Little Pigeon River near present-day Dollywood Lane. The Gobbles moved into this home in 1888, and it was later owned by Andrew T. (Andy) and Carrie Gobble Householder, their son-in-law and daughter. Before being razed to make way for a condominium development, the home was owned by Beulah D. Linn, the great-great-niece of Henry Gobble. Beulah's mother was Ellen Gobble Duggan, daughter of Eli Gobble. (Courtesy of the Dott L. McMahan collection.)

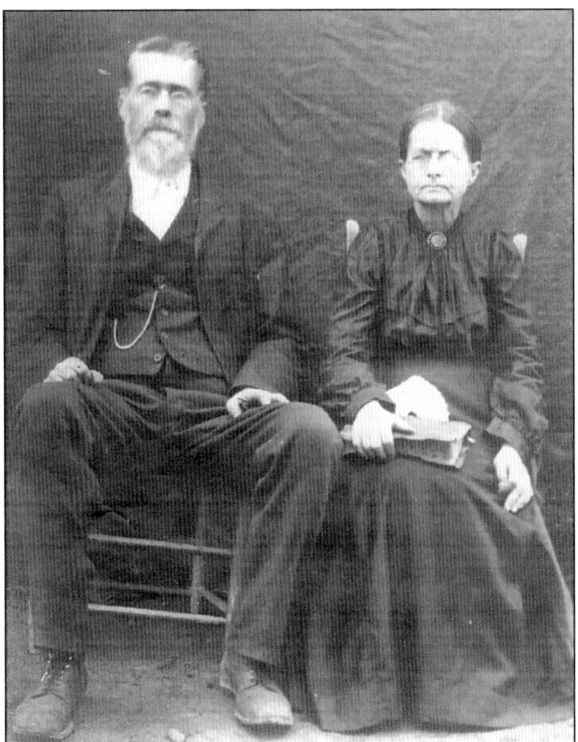

Ma and Pa Gobble posed for this photograph around the late 1800s. Henry Gobble was born on July 17, 1842, and died on August 18, 1908. He is buried in the Pigeon Forge Community Cemetery, and his gravestone inscription reads, "He hath done what he could." His wife, Elizabeth or Lizzie, was born on October 30, 1844, and died on May 3, 1921. Henry and Elizabeth were the parents of James (Jim) Lewis, Julia Alice, John Calvin, Robert A., Carrie, and Charles H. (Courtesy of the Dott L. McMahan collection.)

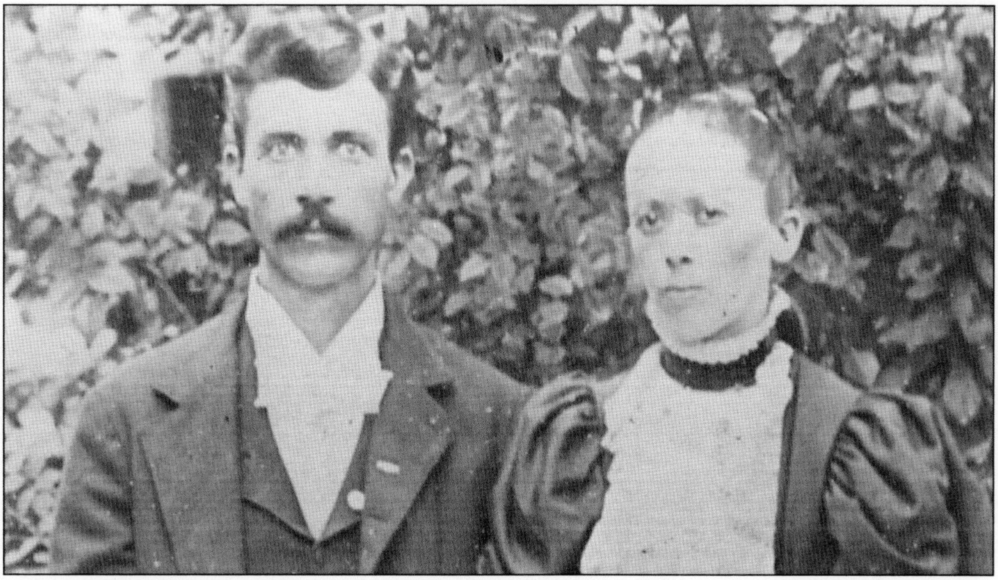

George Washington McMahan is pictured with his wife, Julia Alice Gobble McMahan. The couple was married on March 8, 1898. George was the son of John Marshall and Martha Caton McMahan. Julia's parents were Henry and Elizabeth McMahan Gobble. (Courtesy of the Dott L. McMahan collection.)

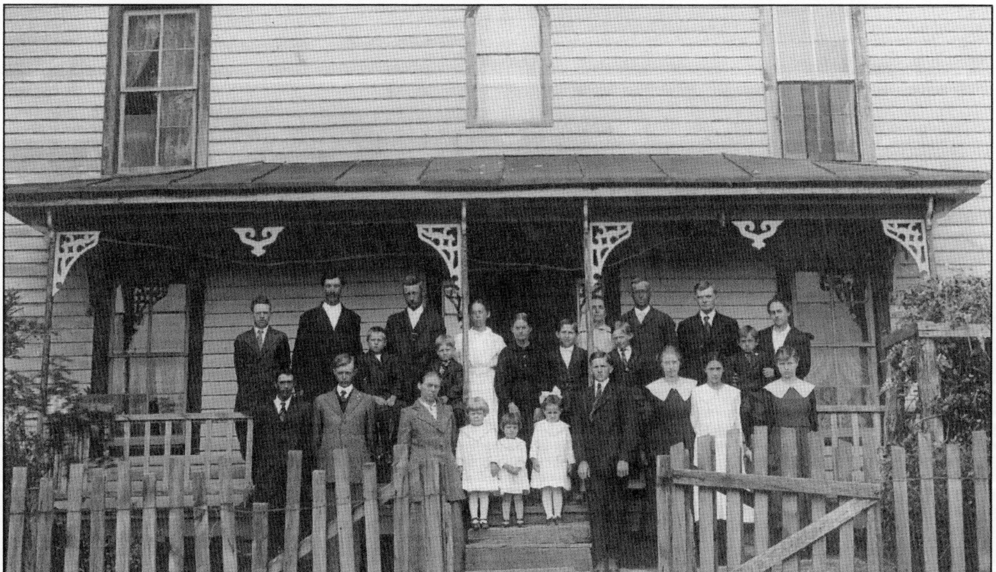

The Henry and Elizabeth Gobble family poses for this photograph around 1918 in front of their home by the Little Pigeon River. From left to right are (first row) Dott L. McMahan, Clyde Gobble, Ellen Trotter Gobble, Mary Gobble Hutchens, Mildred Householder Ogle, Florence Gobble Flynn, Trotter Householder, Eunice Goble, Ada P. McMahan Law, and Hazel Goble McFalls North; (second row) Raymond Gobble, George W. McMahan, Lewis Gobble, James "Jim" L. Gobble, Mayford Householder, Julia A. Gobble McMahan, Elizabeth McMahan Gobble, Hubert Gobble, Rebecca "Becky" Gobble, Elmer Gobble, John Gobble, Andrew "Andy" Householder, Henry Householder, and Carrie Gobble Householder. (Courtesy of the Dott L. McMahan collection.)

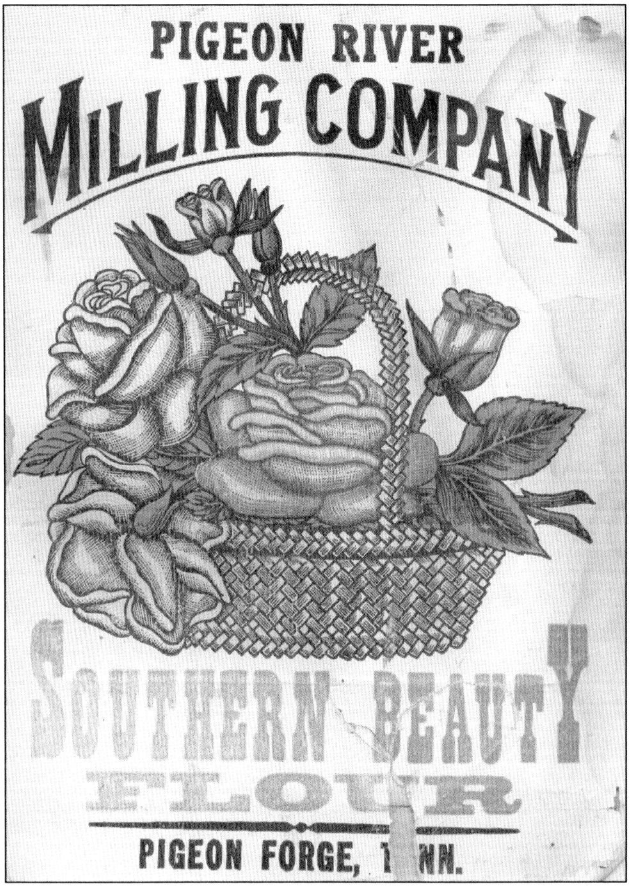

This Pigeon River Milling Company white flour bag was used for the Southern Beauty brand flour sold at the Old Mill. (Courtesy of the Old Mill.)

A team and farm wagon made tasks lighter for those working the fields in earlier times. George Washington McMahan stands with his team in 1923. This was at his farm located between those belonging to his father, John McMahan (on the south side), and his father-in-law, Henry Gobble (on the north side). (Courtesy of the Dott L. McMahan collection.)

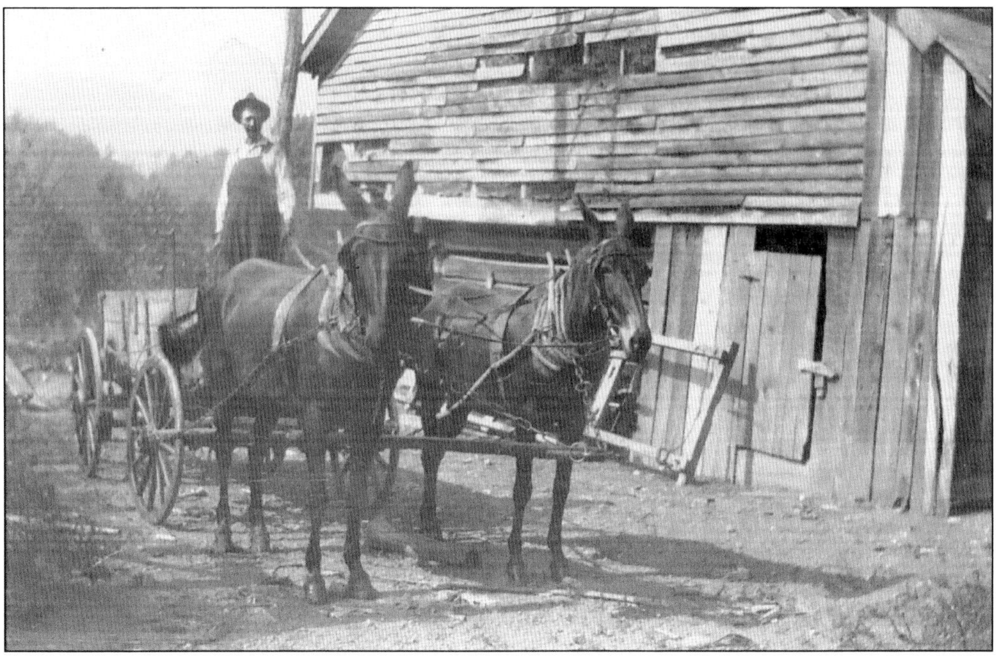

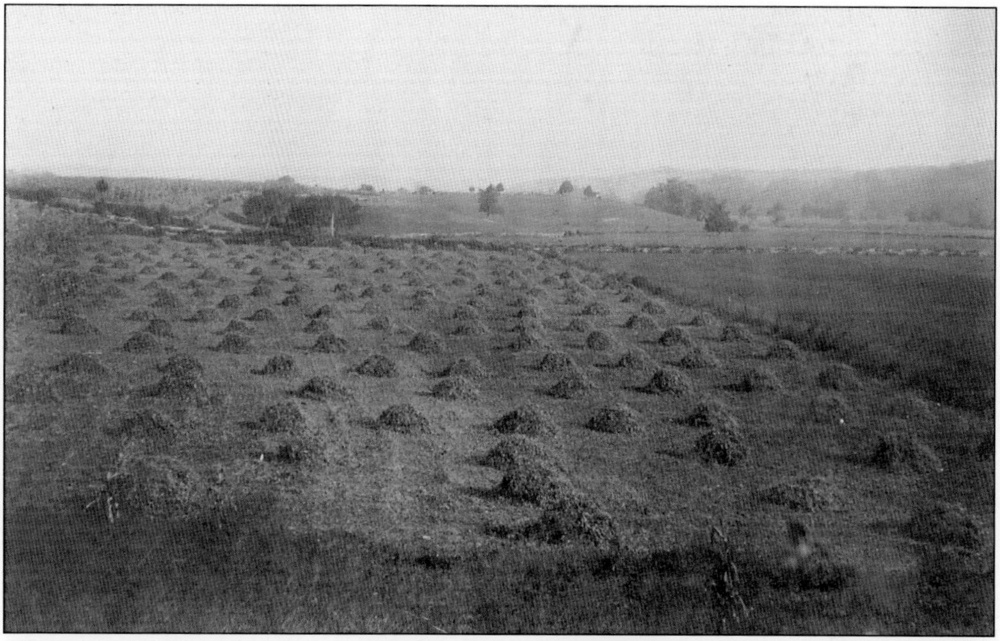

This farmer's field is located in the flat lands of the Pigeon Forge area. Both wheat and hay (timothy, lespedeza, alfalfa, and clover) were grown for production and for family use. Dott L. McMahan writes that when Pigeon Forge was a farming community, there were 15 farms, with as much as 6,000 bushels of wheat being grown. (Pauline Householder photograph; courtesy of Jerry Loveday.)

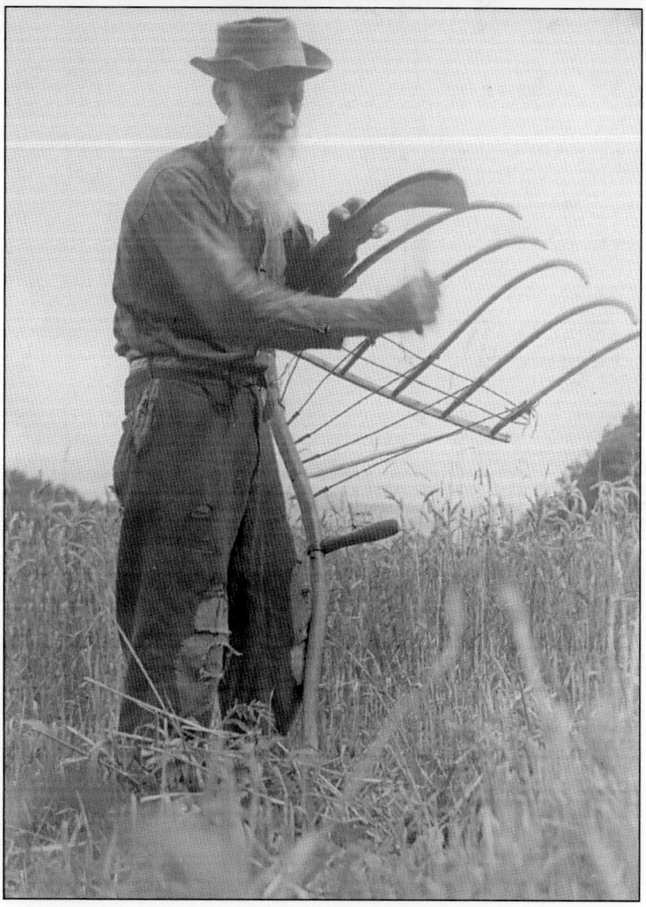

Old-timers said that George Lamon, at age 83, could cut as much wheat with his cradle as the younger men of the area. He lived on a farm along the road between Pigeon Forge and Gatlinburg. This photograph was taken in the 1930s. (Carlos C. Campbell photograph; courtesy of Sarah Ball.)

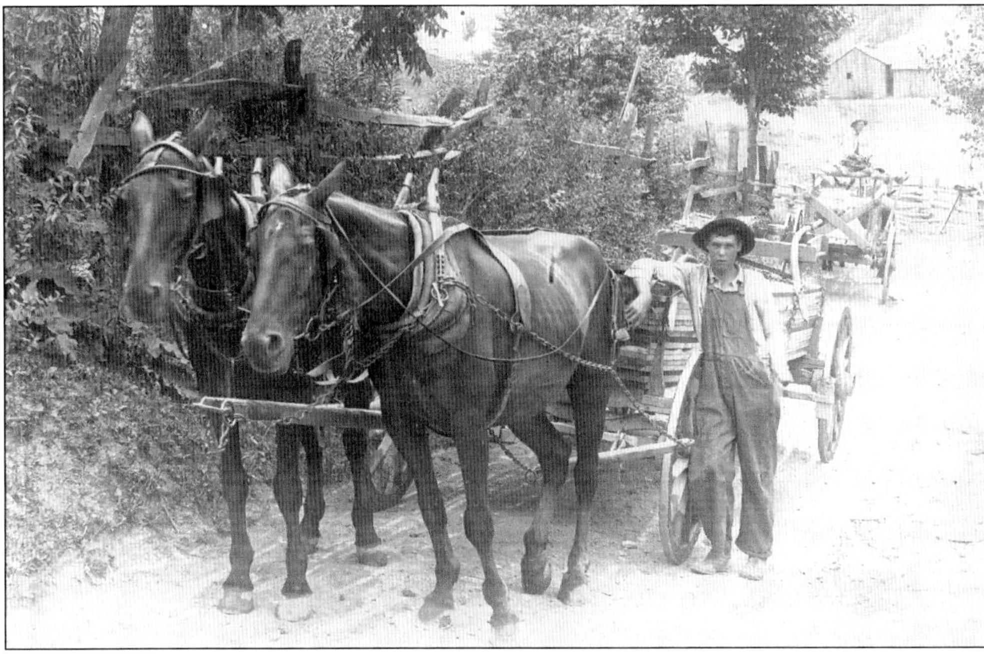

Bill Hatcher, son of Lewis Hatcher, is pictured with his team and wagon. The Hatcher family rented and worked farms both in Pigeon Forge and on Cove Mountain. (Courtesy of Clara Quarrels Killian.)

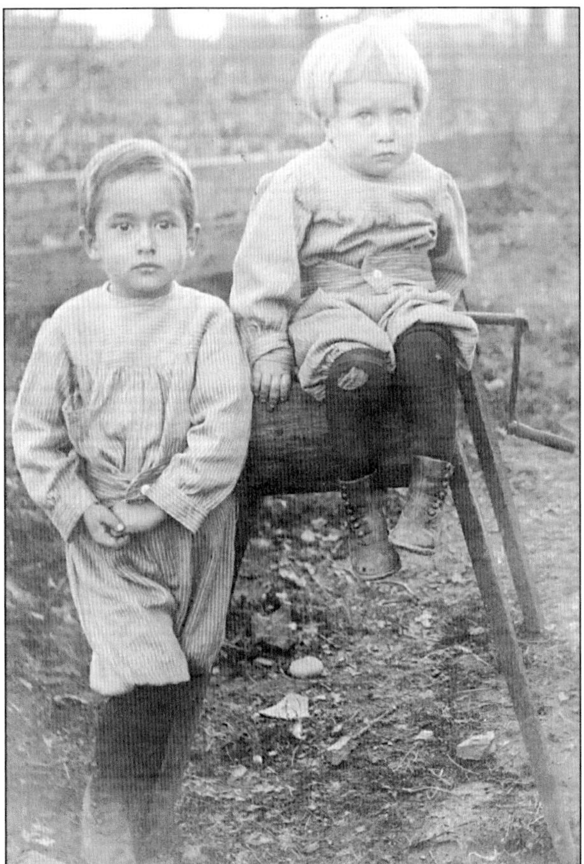

Mayford Householder, seated on an old grinding stone rack, is pictured with his brother, Henry (left). These boys lived on the farm that once belonged to their maternal grandfather, Henry Gobble. Their parents were Andrew (Andy) T. and Carrie Gobble Householder. Mayford was born in 1911 and died in 1934. Henry was born in 1909 and died in 1977. (Courtesy of the Dott L. McMahan collection.)

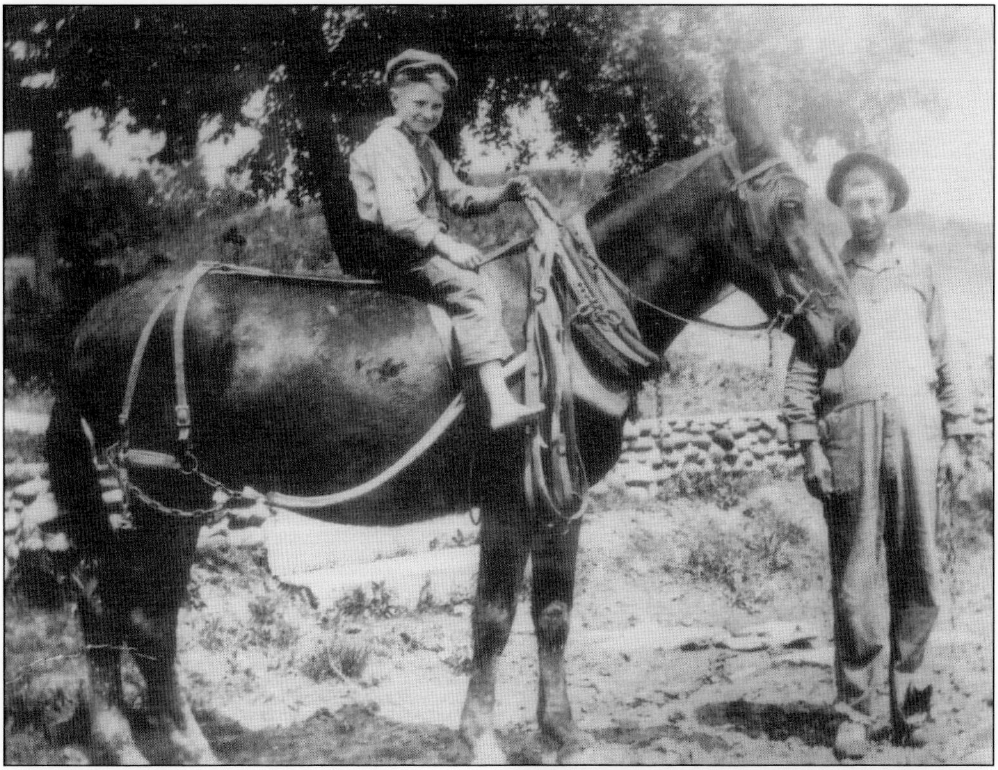

George Washington McMahan stands with his nephew and Old Teebe. It is unclear whether this is nephew Mayford or Henry Householder. (Courtesy of the Dott L. McMahan collection.)

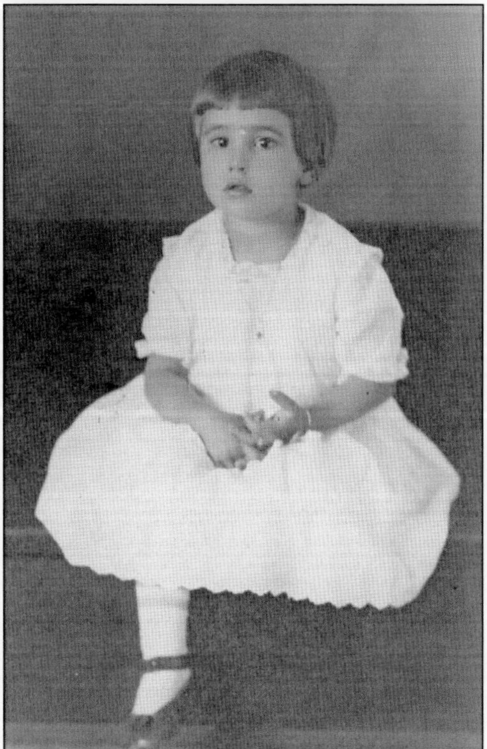

Mildred Householder is pictured here sometime around 1918. She was born on July 4, 1914, and died on March 16, 2008, at age 93. Her parents were Andrew (Andy) T. and Carrie Gobble Householder. In her adult years, Mildred served as manager of the U.S. Post Office at Pigeon Forge for almost 40 years. She married John Rellie Ogle, and they had two children, Michael and Margaret. (Courtesy of the Dott L. McMahan collection.)

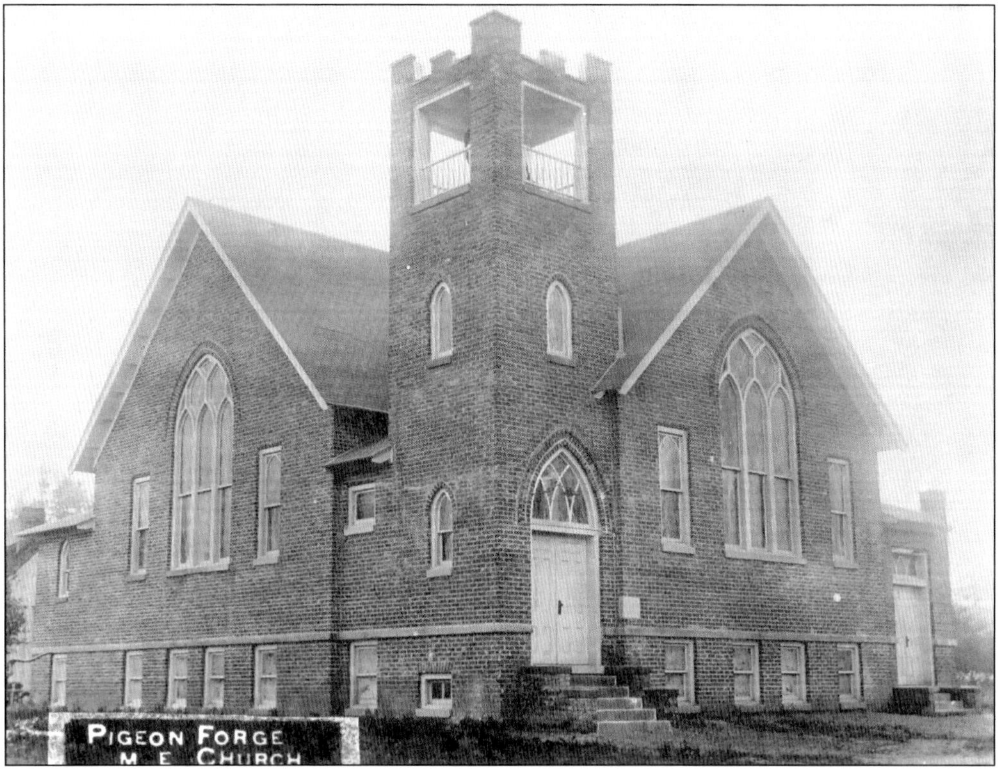

The Pigeon Forge First United Methodist Church building was dedicated on July 2, 1922; it sits at the corner of Methodist Street and River Road. It replaced a smaller church destroyed by fire after being struck by lightning on June 19, 1919. In the interim after the fire, services were held in the school building next door. (Courtesy of Henrietta Franklin Sharp.)

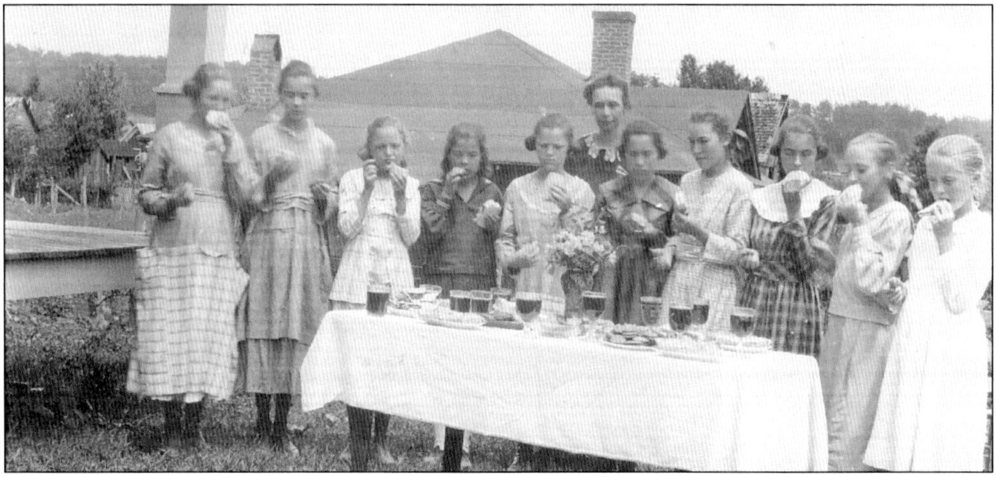

Young girls participate in a church tea at the home of Thomas and Rebecca Trevena, which sat on present-day Ogle Drive, the road leading out to the Methodist Cemetery. Facing in the opposite direction from the cemetery is the home of Tebo and Becky Watson. Pictured from left to right are ? Stott, unidentified, Ruby Wynn, Martha Davis (?), Bessie Stott, unidentified, Iva Stott, Perna or Leona Trevena, Nina Wynn, and two unidentified girls. (Courtesy of the Dott L. McMahan collection.)

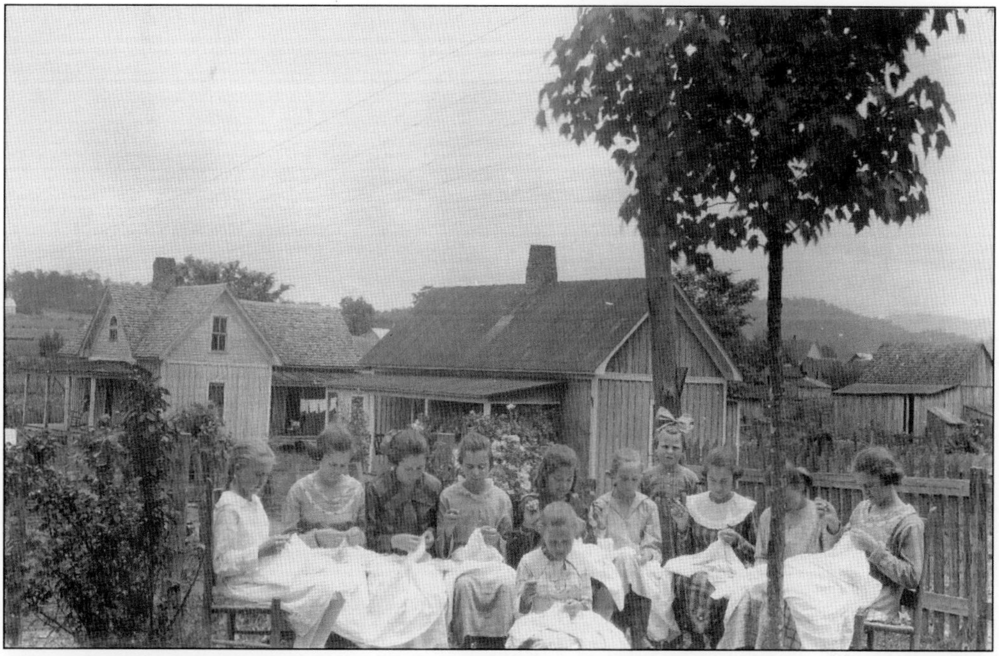

This sewing bee is at the home of Thomas and Rebecca Trevena. Pictured from left to right are unidentified, cousins Bessie and Iva Stott, unidentified, Martha Davis, unidentified, Lucy Trevena, Nina Wynn, Leona or Perna Trevena, Blanche Stott, and Ruby Wynn (center, front). The houses in the background are the homes of Ted Householder, along present-day Ogle Drive, and George Washington Fleming, which sat where the southbound lane of the Parkway is today near the junction of Ogle Drive. (Courtesy of the Dott L. McMahan collection.)

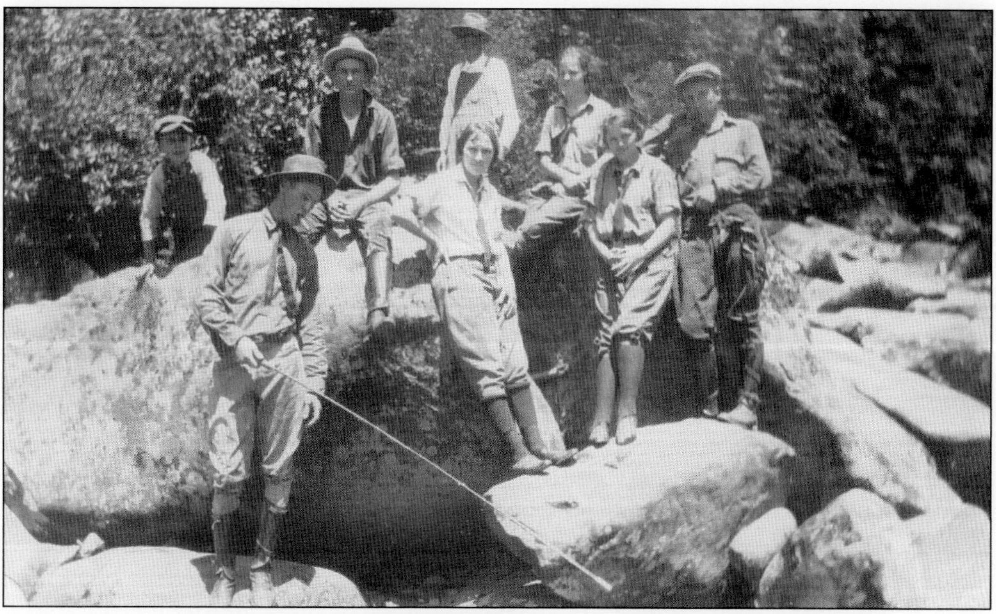

Pigeon Forge residents and church youth groups have been taking outings in the Great Smoky Mountains for years, long before the national park was established. Here is one such group enjoying nature in July 1924. (Courtesy of the Dott L. McMahan collection.)

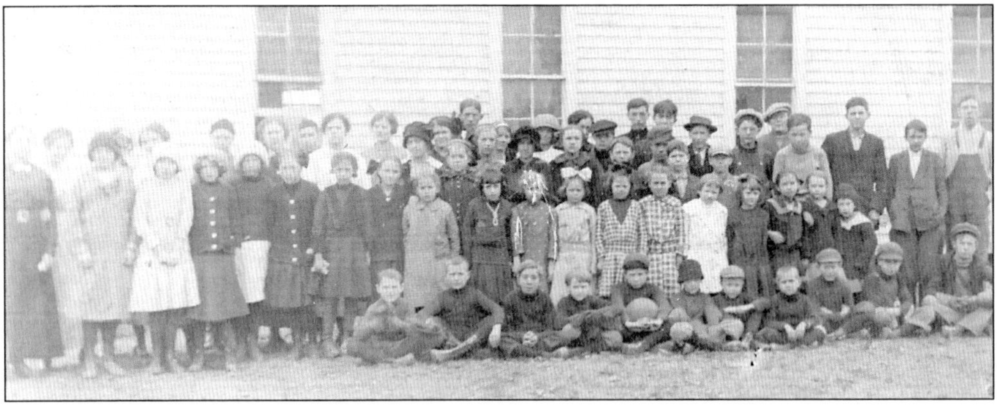

This Pigeon Forge Academy school group photograph is dated 1914. The building was located on River Road near the Methodist church. The teachers were Adra Craig and Sophia Longmire. Craig was later married, first to Judge Ben Robertson and then to Rodney Griffiths. Students in this photograph include Henry Butler, Alice Patterson, Charlie Dixon, Jim Large, Print Dixon, Ben Trotter, Clyde Gobble, Blanche Stott, Bessie Stott, Edna Roberts, Leona Trevena, Florita Butler, Nina Wynn, Bernice Stott, Cora Bull, Ola Large, Myrtle Butler, Bertha Walker, Zula Stott, Eunice Gobble, Emma Householder, Perna Trevena, Ernest Marshall, Dott McMahan, Wesley Lamon or Lawson, Frank Mullendore, Emma Andes, Sam King, Anna Roberts, Deis Shultz, Russell Huff, Stella Stott, Hazel Gobble, Roger Ward, Pink Cogdill, Jim Trotter, and Gifford Lamon. Ada McMahan is the sixth child from the left on the second row. (Courtesy of the Dott L. McMahan collection.)

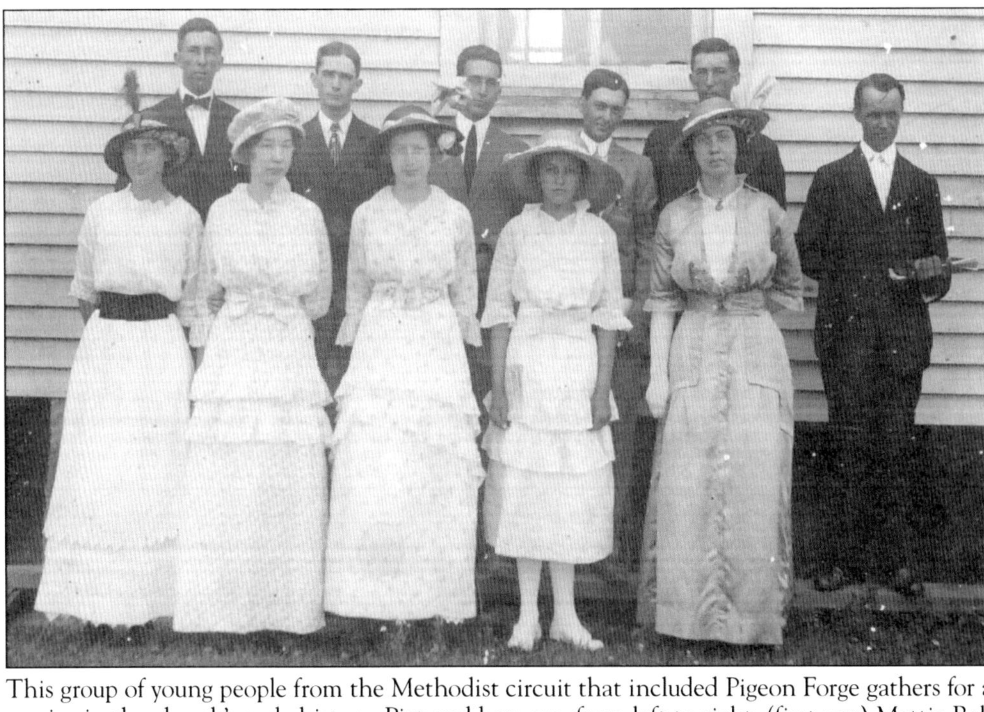

This group of young people from the Methodist circuit that included Pigeon Forge gathers for a service in the church's early history. Pictured here are, from left to right, (first row) Mattie Bell Butler, Georgia Webb, Euncie Gobble, Cora Bull, and Ida Lawson; (second row) ? Tarwater, Dave Householder, three unidentified, and Preacher Willie Bull. (Courtesy of the Dott L. McMahan collection.)

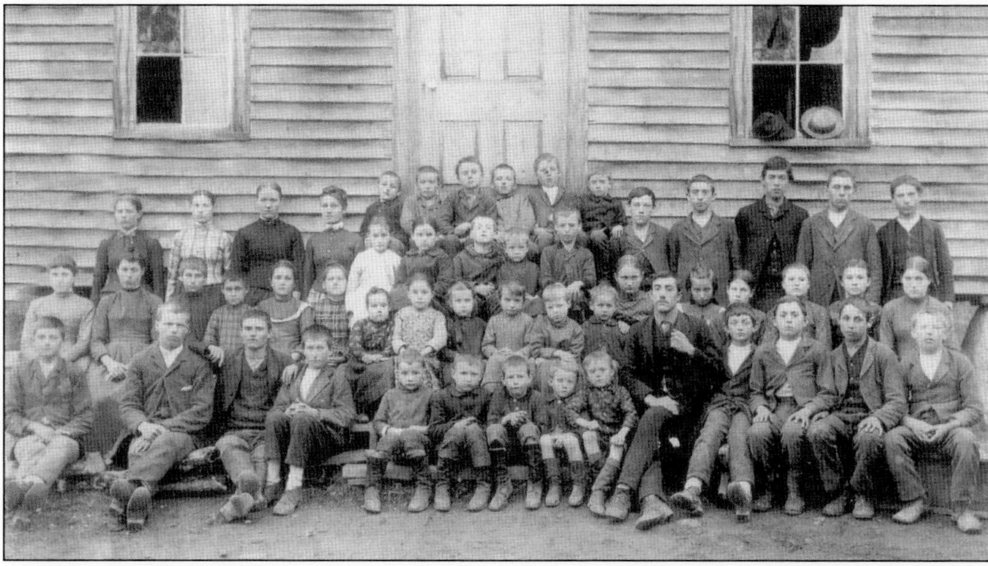

Pine Grove School was located at the north end of present-day Pigeon Forge. When this photograph was taken, many small communities had their own identities outside the main section of town. As the area grew, communities like Pine Grove lost their place names and became part of Pigeon Forge. George W. Montgomery is fourth from the left in the first row. (Courtesy of Pigeon Forge Public Library.)

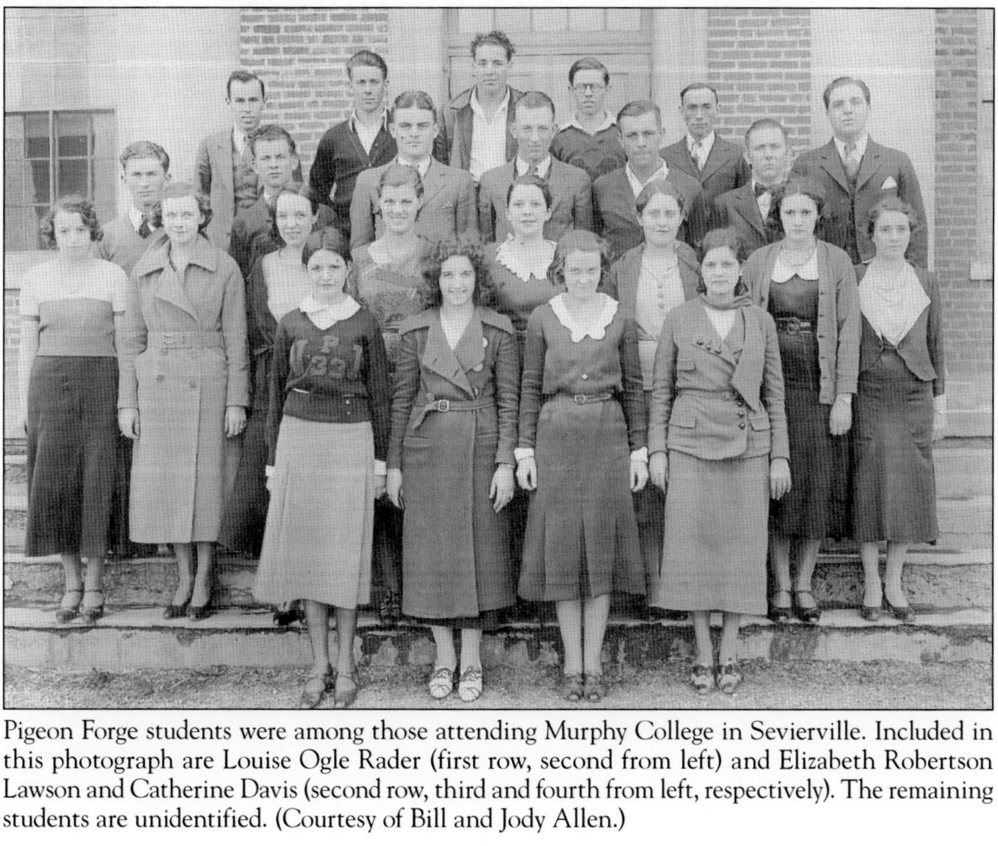

Pigeon Forge students were among those attending Murphy College in Sevierville. Included in this photograph are Louise Ogle Rader (first row, second from left) and Elizabeth Robertson Lawson and Catherine Davis (second row, third and fourth from left, respectively). The remaining students are unidentified. (Courtesy of Bill and Jody Allen.)

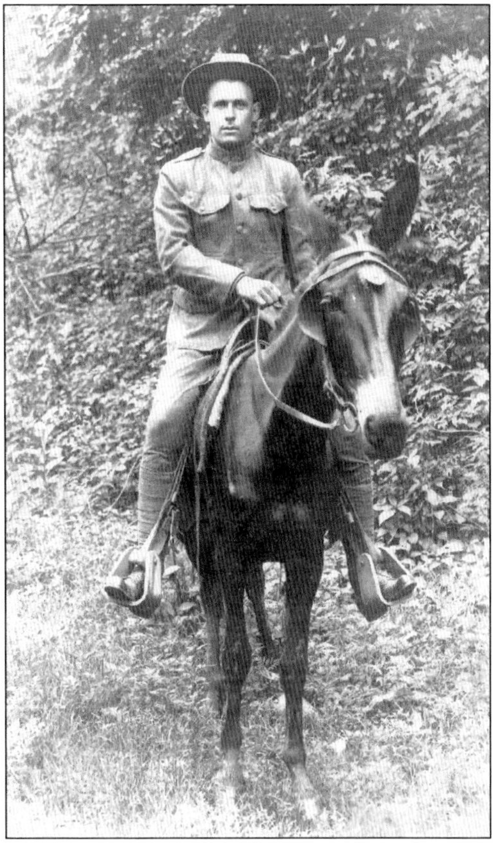

John Houser, of Dixie Avenue, was an infantryman in World War I. He was the son of Elder James and Martha Jane McCarter Houser and was married to Lillie Cardwell. Houser's father was a preacher of the Primitive Baptist faith. (Mattie Houser Clabo collection; courtesy of Mary Lee Carver.)

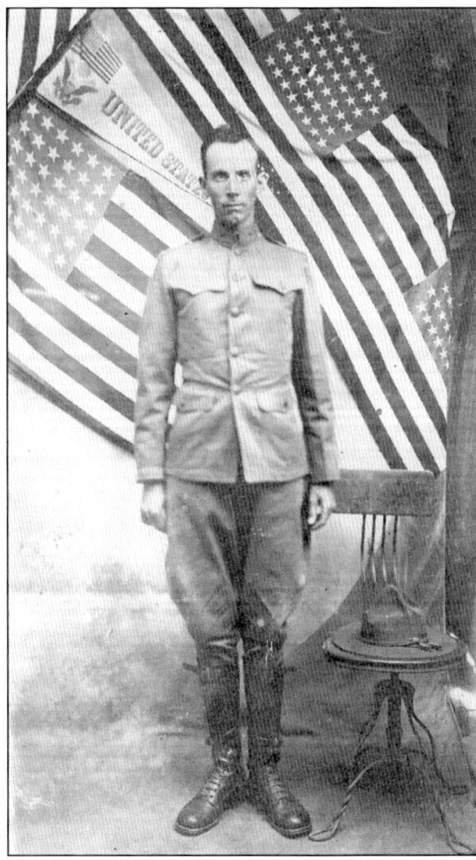

Eli Alvin Wilson served in World War I. He was wounded when the Allies broke Hindenburg's front line. Another soldier from Boyd's Creek serving with Wilson at the time suspected he would not survive. Wilson did and returned home with both shrapnel and vivid war memories. (Courtesy of Wilda Lamon.)

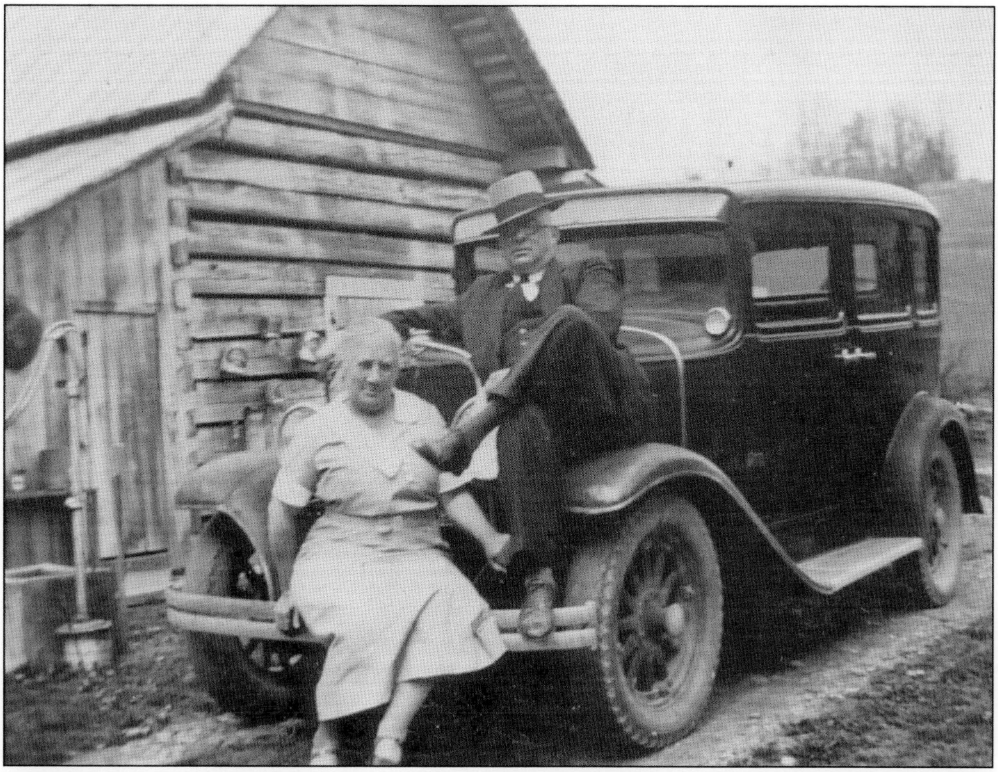

John Robertson is pictured here with his wife, Emma McMahan. He operated a taxi service in the area in the community's early years. The Robertsons lived in the late 1800s and early 1900s. Emma was the daughter of John M. and Martha McMahan. John was the son of Rev. Robert C. and Mary Jane (Mollie) Emert Robertson. (Courtesy of the Dott L. McMahan collection.)

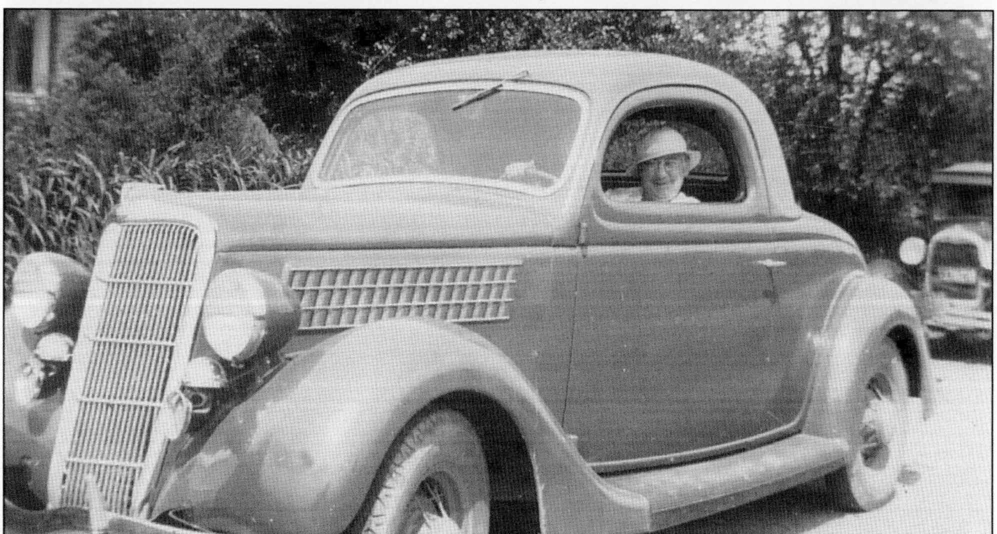

Emma McMahan Robertson, along with D. D. Bulter, cochaired a food supply committee in Pigeon Forge to conserve food during World War I, according to Beulah D. Linn's book *Reunion at the River.* (Courtesy of the Dott L. McMahan collection.)

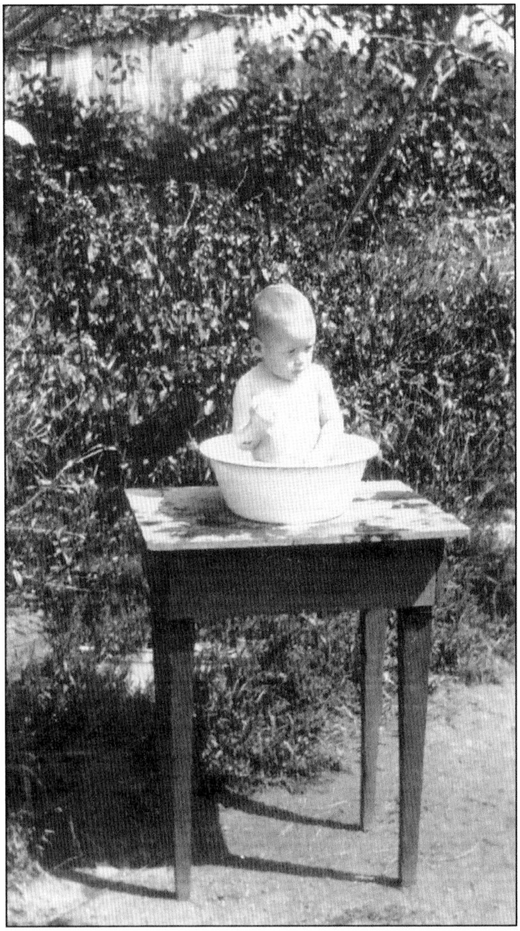

In the early 1920s, there was a different perception of a sponge bath. A wash pan full of water was sufficient for the babies. (Courtesy of the Dott L. McMahan collection.)

Three McMahan sisters pictured here are, from left to right, Sarah Iota, wife of Dr. J. Walter; Leah Emma, wife of John Robertson; and Laura Alice, wife of Thad Trotter. They were the daughters of John M. and Martha Caton McMahan. (Courtesy of the Dott L. McMahan collection.)

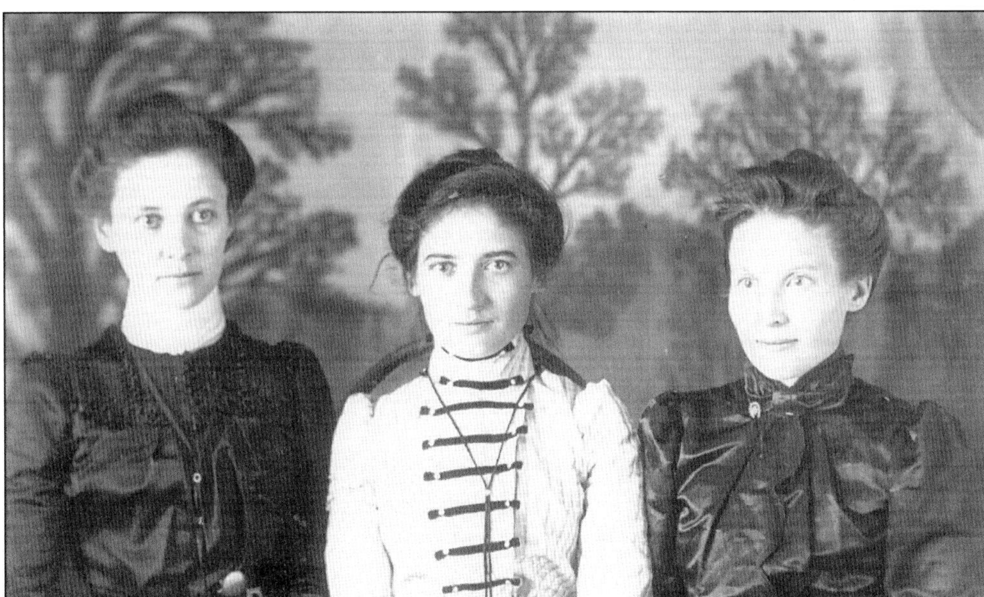

Ruth and Mary Emory were the two daughters of John T. and Hattie Davis Emory. Their home sat on River Road near the old Anen Jones garage at the end of String Town. (Courtesy of the Dott L. McMahan collection.)

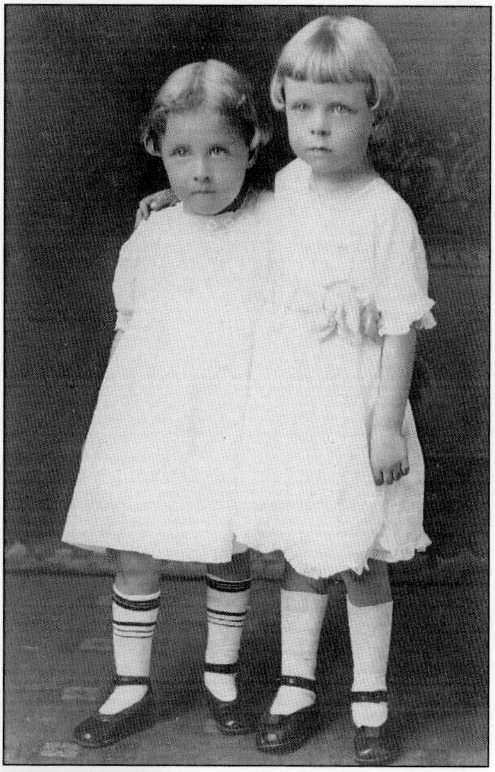

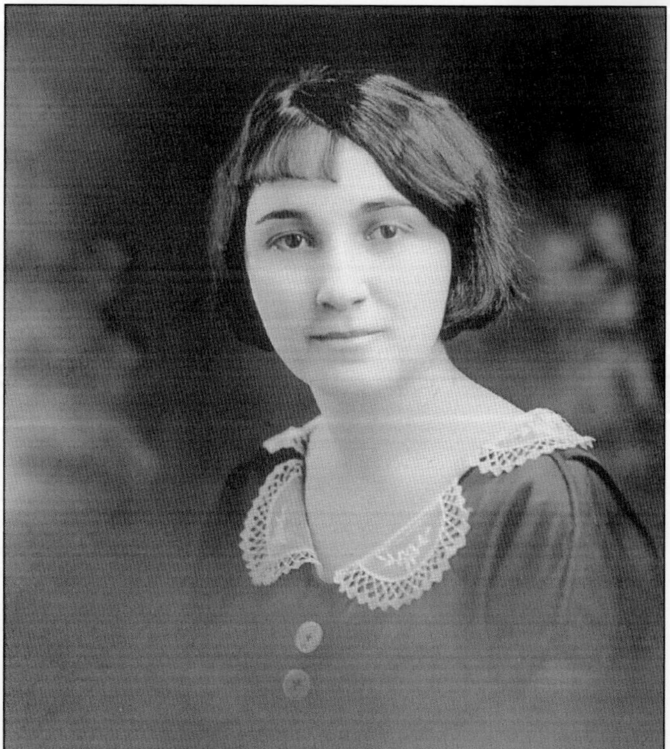

Mary Butler Henry lived to be 100 years old. Her family cultivated numerous acres of farmland in the heart of the town. Many young people learned to appreciate the beauty of music under her instruction. (Courtesy of Pigeon Forge Public Library.)

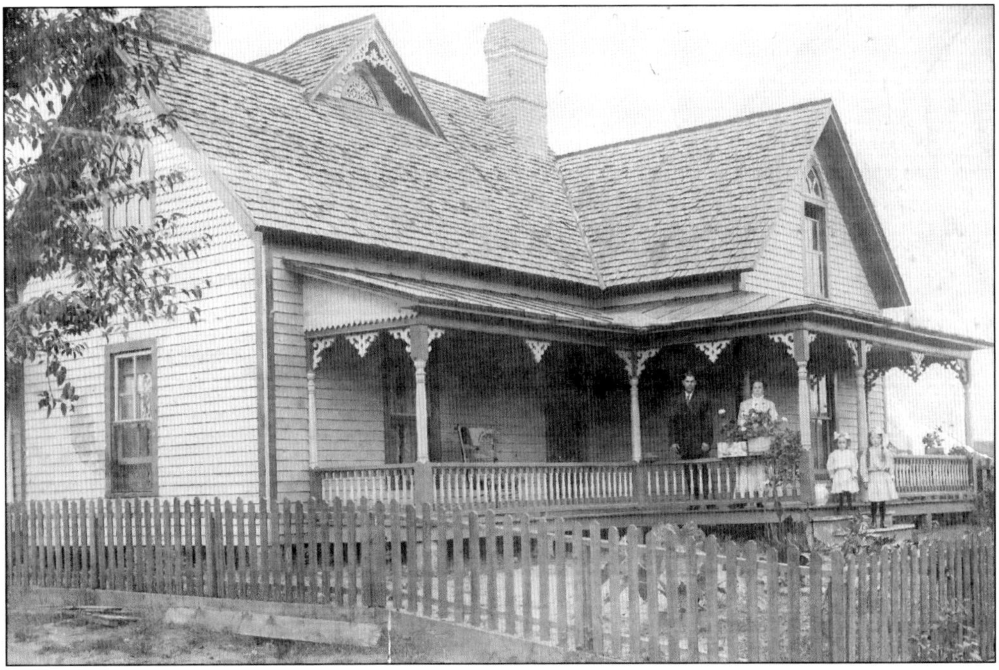

This Victorian home was built in 1896 and purchased by Vic and Ruby Allen in 1934, the year their son William Wynn was born. It sat facing River Road in String Town between present-day Tennessee Mountain Lodge and Colonial House Motel. (Pauline Householder collection; courtesy of Jerry Loveday.)

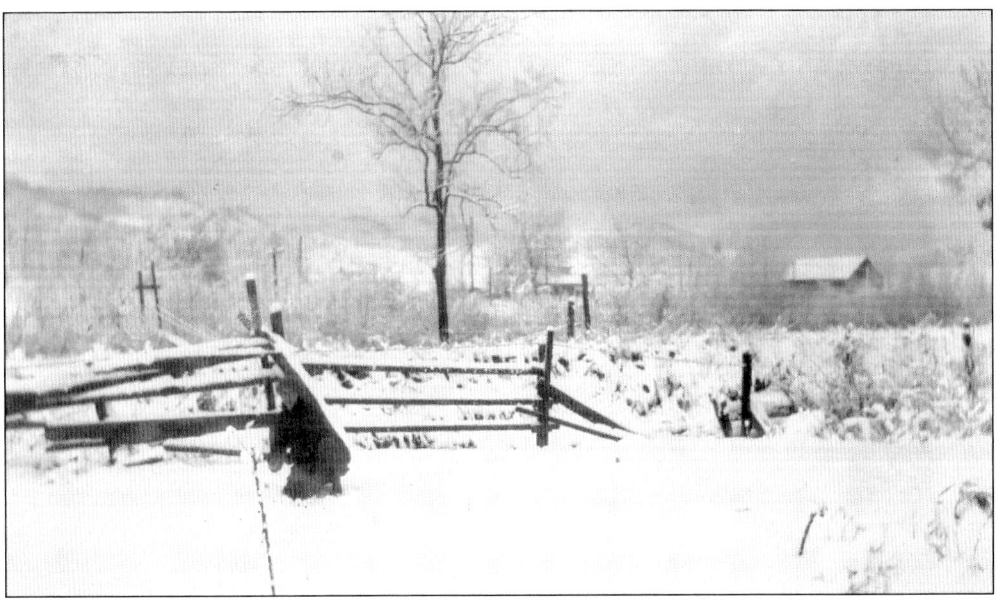

This winter photograph was taken in December 1923 in a field south of the George McMahan home. Around 1939, fire destroyed the two-story home in the background, located on the adjacent Jehu Conner farm. The swinging bridge led to the McMahan farm. In the shadows is Ada McMahan Law. (Courtesy of the Dott L. McMahan collection.)

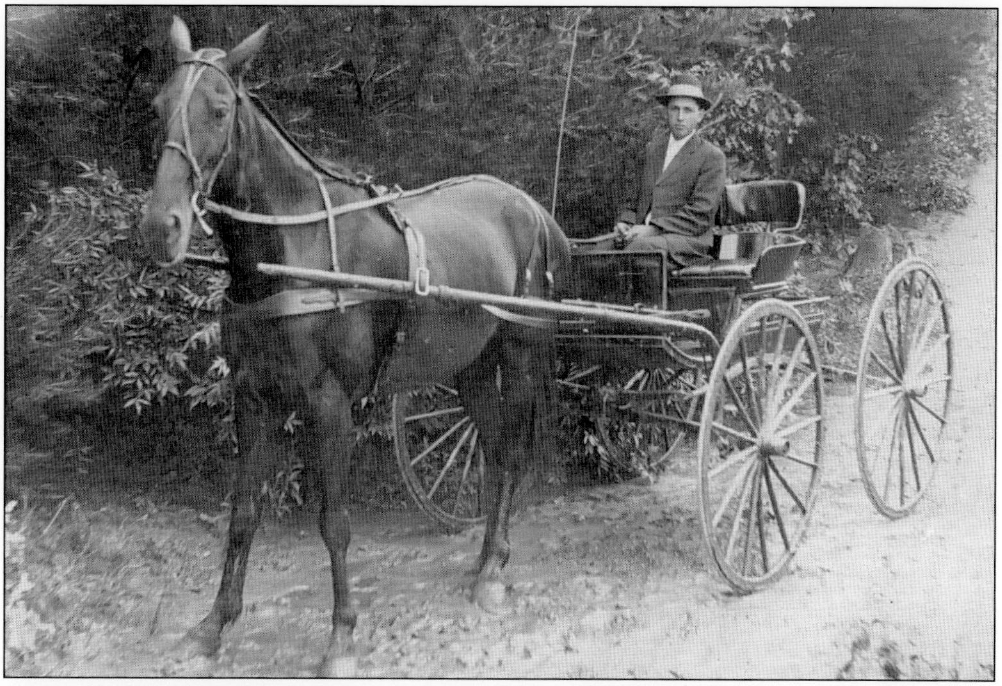

George Fleming drives his one-horse buggy in style in 1912. His home was near the entrance to the Mill Creek community. (Courtesy of Henrietta Franklin Sharp.)

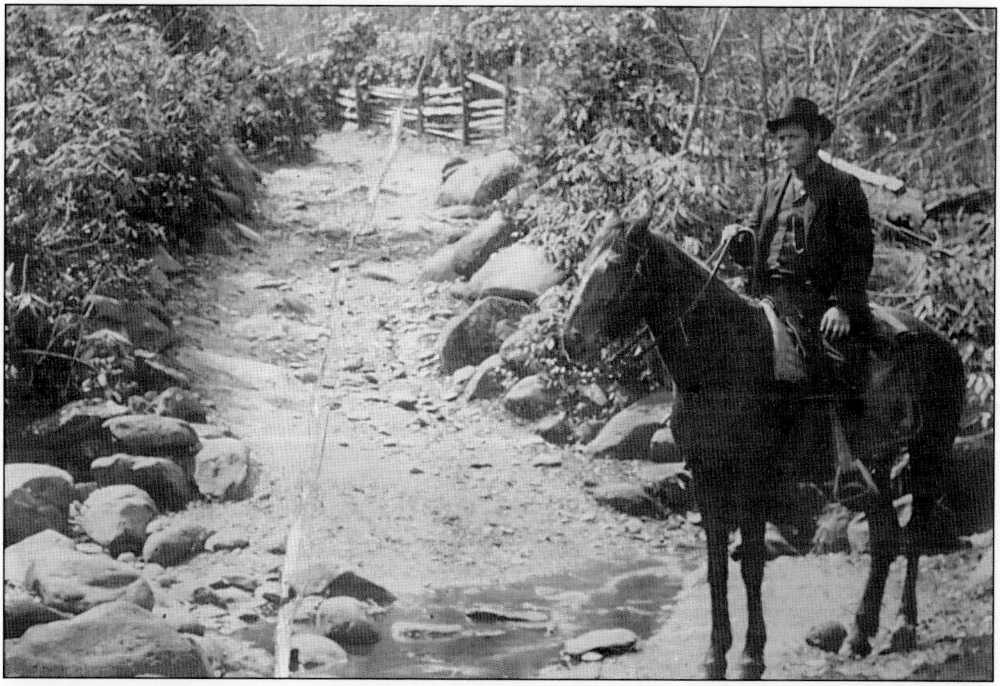

Andrew Davis Martin carried the mail through the mountains of Greenbrier along Mail Route No. 14. He later moved to a home at the north end of what is now River Road in Pigeon Forge. Martin purchased the Old Mill in 1930 and operated it only a few years before the Great Depression caused him to lose it. (Courtesy of Sarah Ownby Ball.)

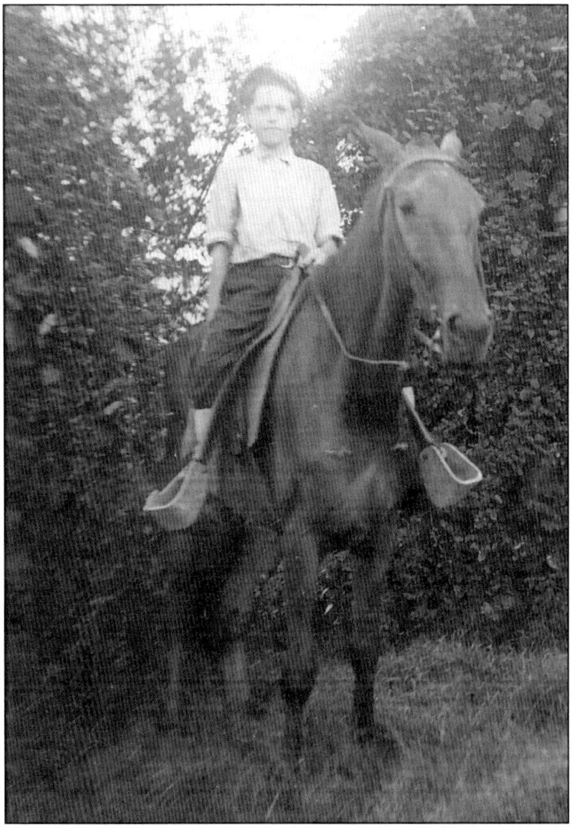

Raymond Gobble, son of James Lewis and Mary Ellen Trotter Gobble, travels horseback. Other Gobble children were Eunice, Clyde, Hazel, Lewis, and Mary. (Courtesy of the Dott L. McMahan collection.)

This one-horse buggy hauled the mail and mail carrier James (Jim) Gobble. He had a route from Pigeon Forge to Middle Creek and Oldham's Creek (Boogertown). Other mail routes from Pigeon Forge in these early years were run by Jim Emert to Wear's Valley and by Andy Householder to Gatlinburg and the Glades. (Courtesy of the Dott L. McMahan collection.)

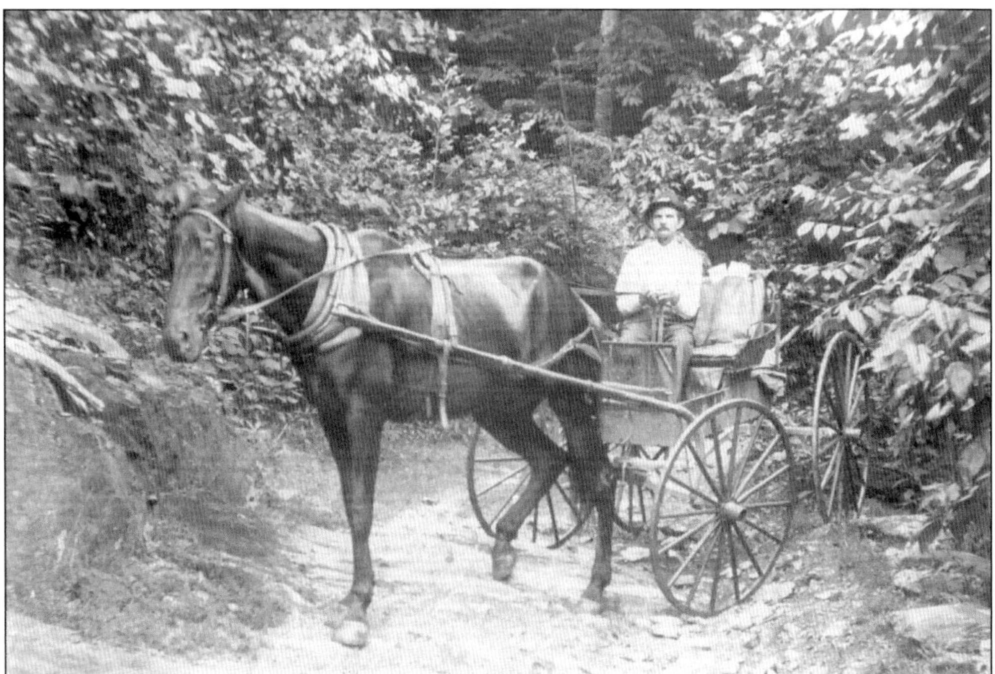

Mary Wynn Trotter, wife of Oliver, is pictured at right with an unidentified girl on the Old Mill dam. The Old Mill was the site for Pigeon Forge Milling Company, Inc., home of Silver Star flour. From 1921 to 1929, businessmen organized the Pigeon Forge Power and Light Company near the Old Mill. It provided service to homes and businesses along the river. (Courtesy of Bill and Jody Allen.)

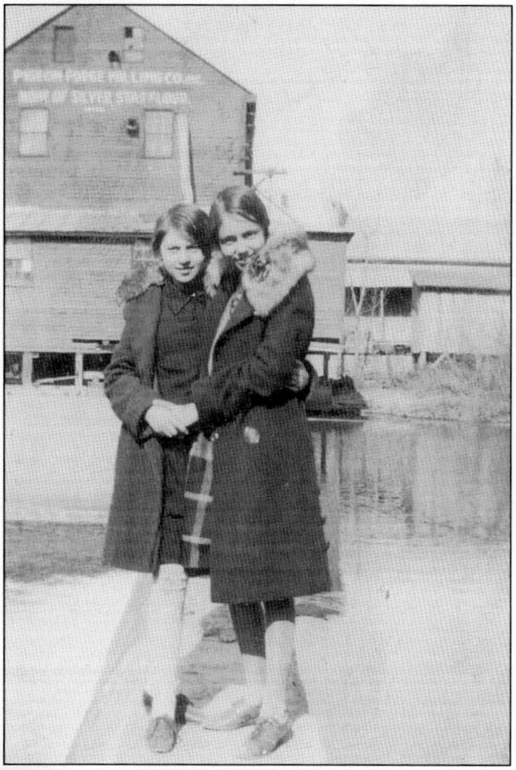

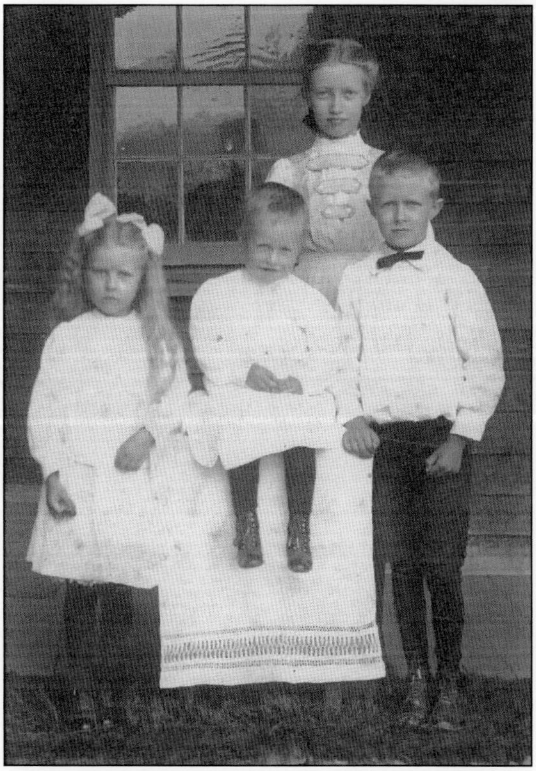

In this photograph are the children of James (Jim) Lewis Gobble and Mary Ellen Trotter Gobble. From left to right are Hazel, Raymond, and Clyde; standing behind is Eunice. (Courtesy of the Dott L. McMahan collection.)

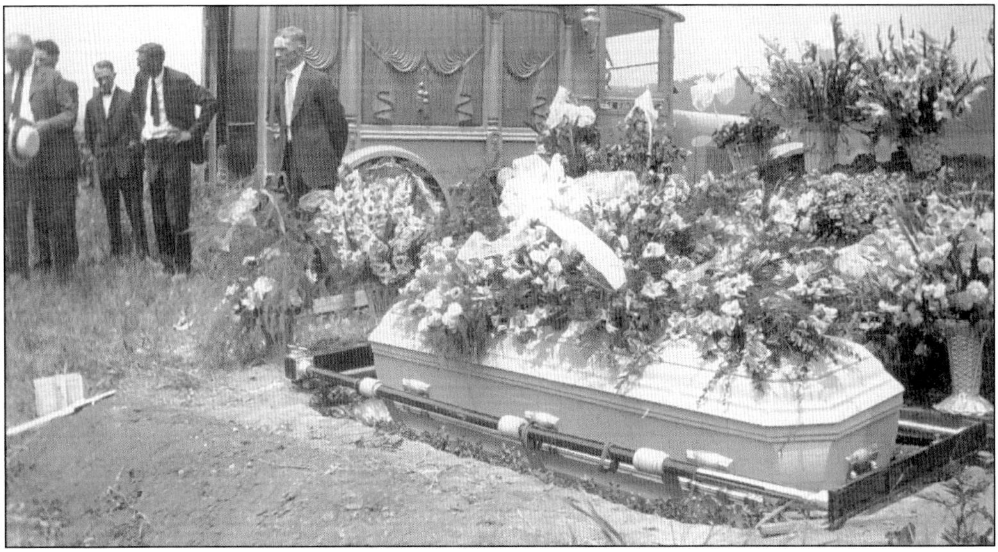

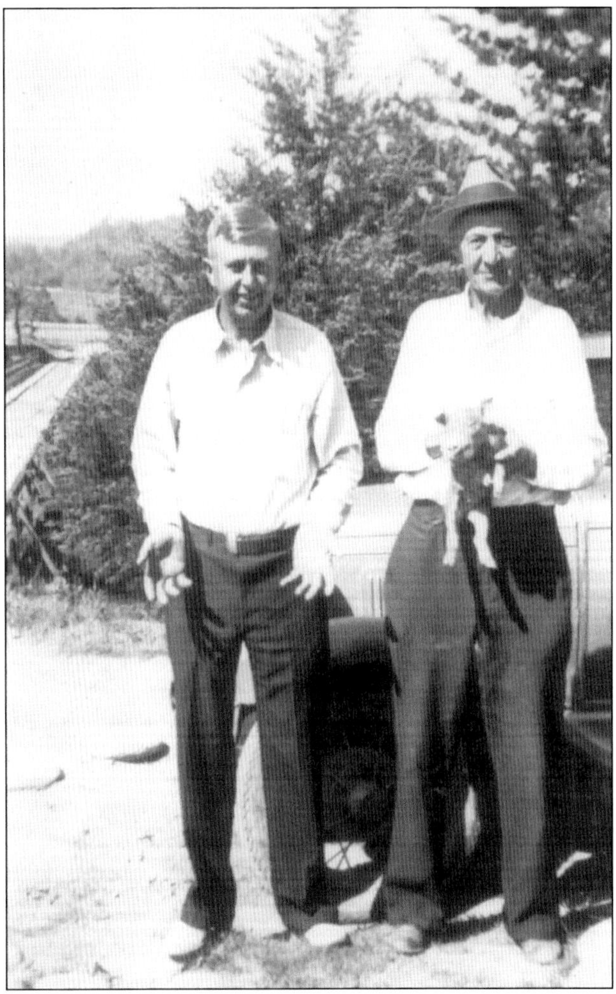

Rawlings Funeral Home in Sevierville conducted the funeral for John Marshall McMahan, who died on January 27, 1926. Mourners stand in the Pigeon Forge Community cemetery on present-day Ogle Drive. Mary Trotter donated the cemetery land before 1897. According to Dott McMahan, Trotter said while walking over her property and looking down on the houses along the river, "What a beautiful place for a graveyard." (Courtesy of the Dott L. McMahan collection.)

George Washington McMahan, right, shows off a piglet from a new litter of pigs. Standing to the left is his son Dott Linwood McMahan. The younger McMahan was born in 1899; he died in 1980. His father was born in 1871 and died in 1944. Note the wooden McMahan Bridge spanning the Little Pigeon River near the McMahan farm. (Courtesy of the Dott L. McMahan collection.)

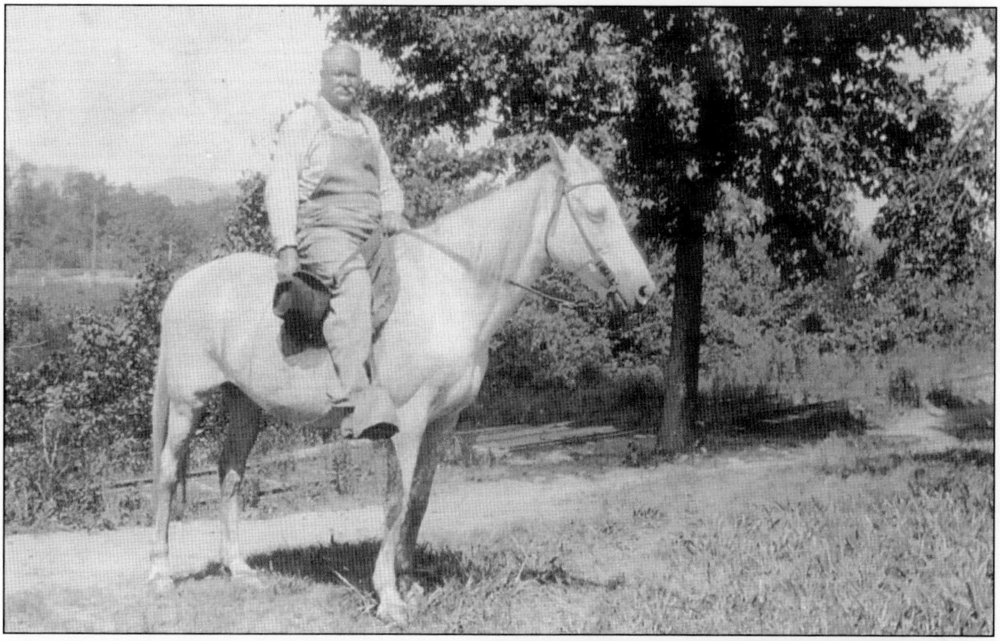

John Marshall McMahan is pictured by the Pigeon River Railroad tracks. These were an extension of the Knoxville, Southern, and Eastern Railroad that entered Pigeon Forge from lower Middle Creek and ran along the river south to McCookville. McCookville was a community along the highway between Pigeon Forge and Gatlinburg. (Courtesy of the Dott L. McMahan collection.)

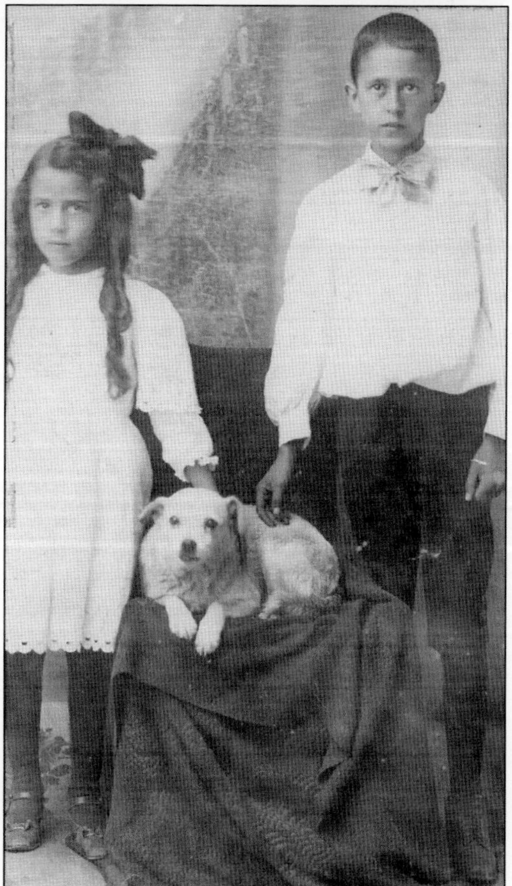

Ada Pearl McMahan stands with her older brother, Dott Linwood. Ada (December 5, 1903–October 3, 1985) moved to Blount County to work with her uncle, Dr. J. Walter McMahan. Dott (June 13, 1899–April 12, 1980) spent years collecting old Pigeon Forge photographs and researching Pigeon Forge's history. He loved to raise unusual chickens. (Courtesy of the Dott L. McMahan collection.)

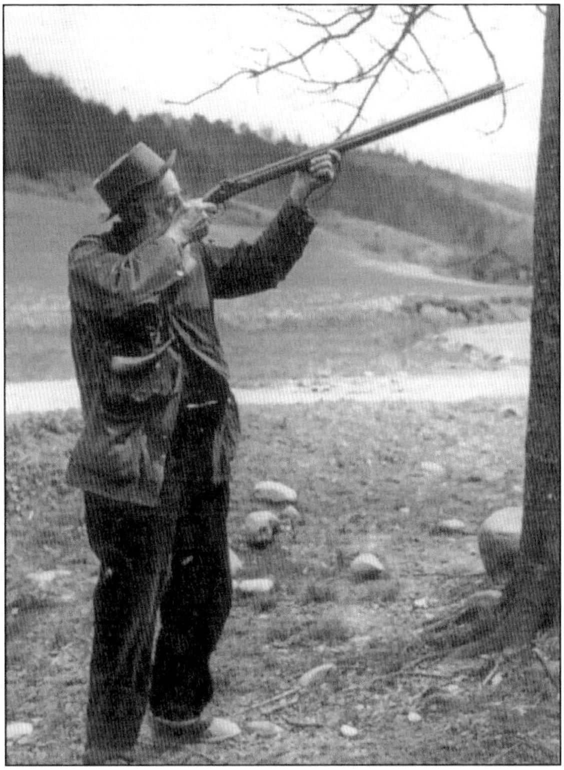

George Lamon was a true mountain pioneer who lived just outside Pigeon Forge on the highway to Gatlinburg. (Courtesy of Tennessee State Library and Archives.)

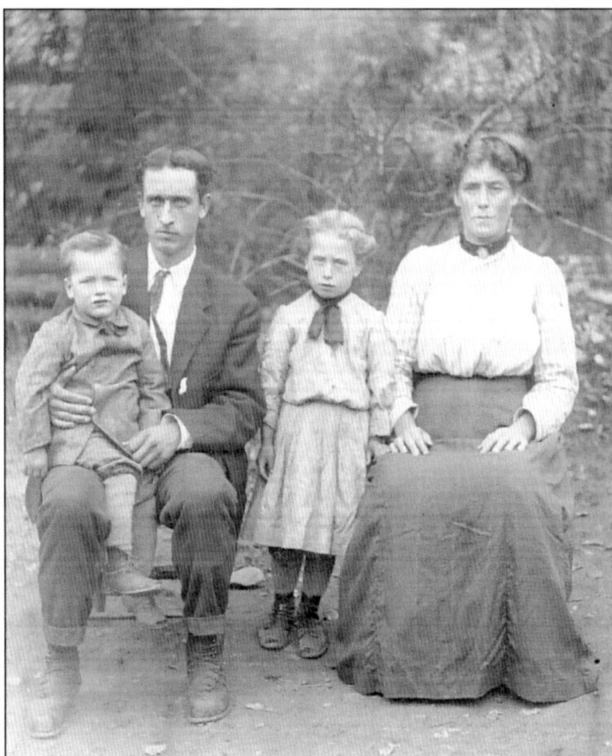

James and Ida King Franklin are pictured with their two children, Sherrod and Mary Frances. James was the son of Lawson Franklin of the Big Ridge community. Mary Frances married Carl Smith, and they lived at McCookville, where he operated a mill along the old mountain road between Pigeon Forge and Gatlinburg. They later moved to Caney when their land was needed for a new highway. (Courtesy of Henrietta Franklin Sharp.)

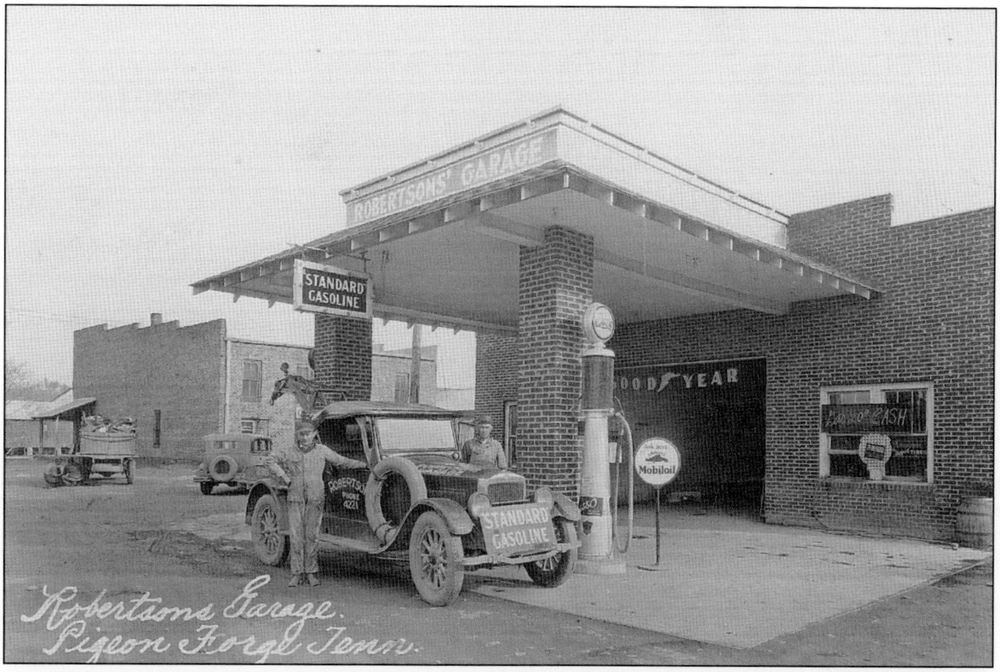

Sam Robertson's garage is pictured in this early photograph with Stott's Store Company in the background. He was one of the first to service automobiles in Pigeon Forge. The business was located on the south side of the current Old Mill Avenue, across from where Paul Sims later operated a garage on the corner. (Courtesy of Pigeon Forge Public Library.)

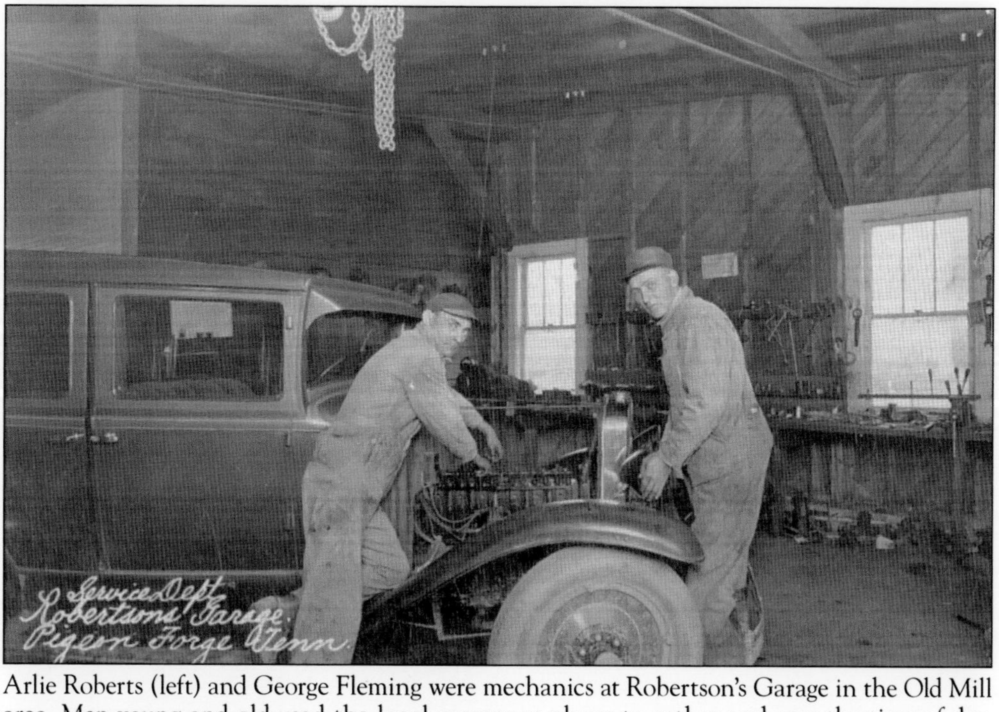

Arlie Roberts (left) and George Fleming were mechanics at Robertson's Garage in the Old Mill area. Men young and old used the local garages as places to gather and pass the time of day. (Courtesy of C. L. Fleming.)

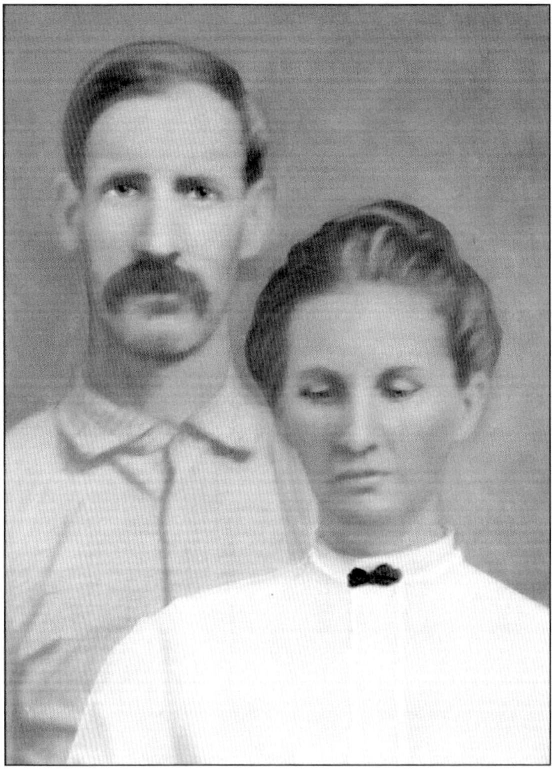

Richard and Nancy Hendricks England and their large family lived in the Pine Mountain community. The Hendricks ancestors traveled from the Netherlands. Richard was the son of Margaret Dennison England and William England, who served in the Civil War in the Union army. (Courtesy of Jo Huskey Harris.)

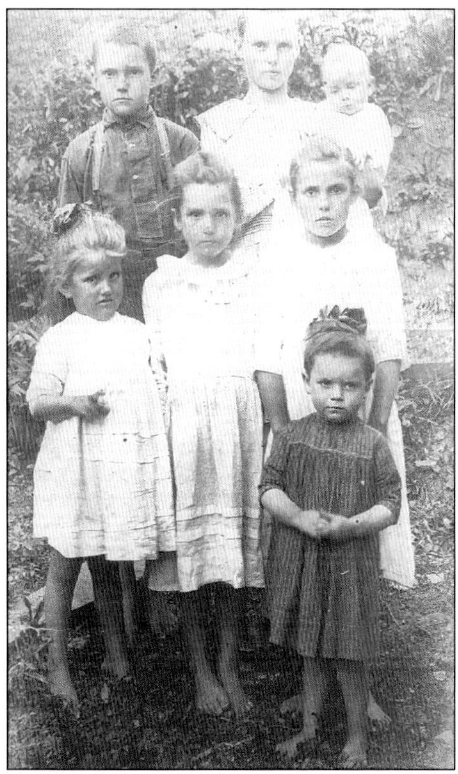

Pictured from left to right is the Lee and Sarah Huskey family: (standing in front) Edith; (first row) Alice, Josie, and Ethel; (second row) Sebern, Della, and Bob. The two younger children, Pearl and Cecil, are not pictured. In their later years, Lee and Sarah lived at Starkey Town near Mill Creek. (Courtesy of Myrtle Ownby Henry.)

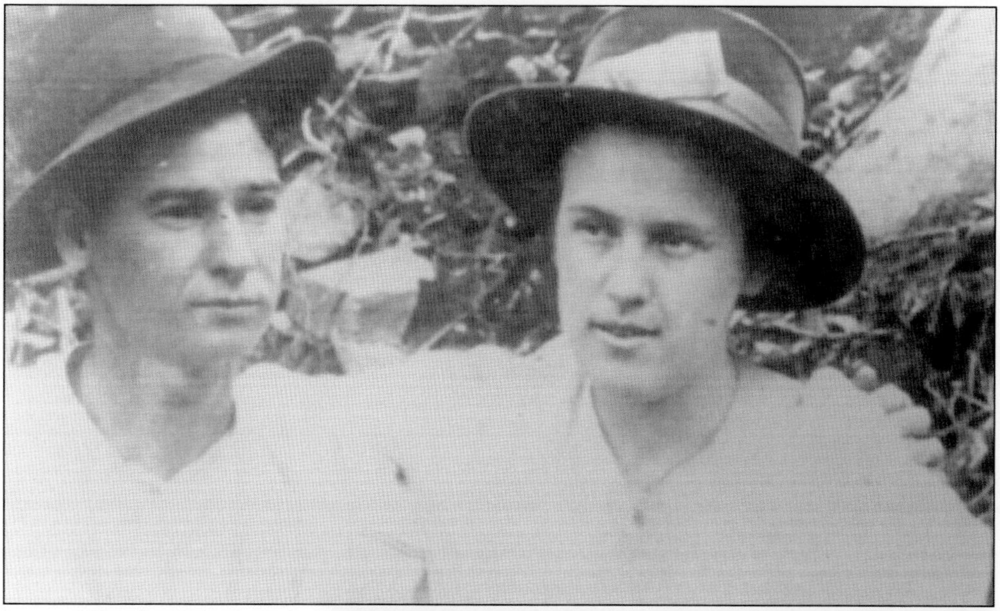

Jess and Beedie Cole moved from the Sugarlands in the Great Smoky Mountains, where he operated a country store, to the present-day Maplecrest area of Pigeon Forge. The couple had seven children, including two sets of twins. (Courtesy of Bill and Jody Allen.)

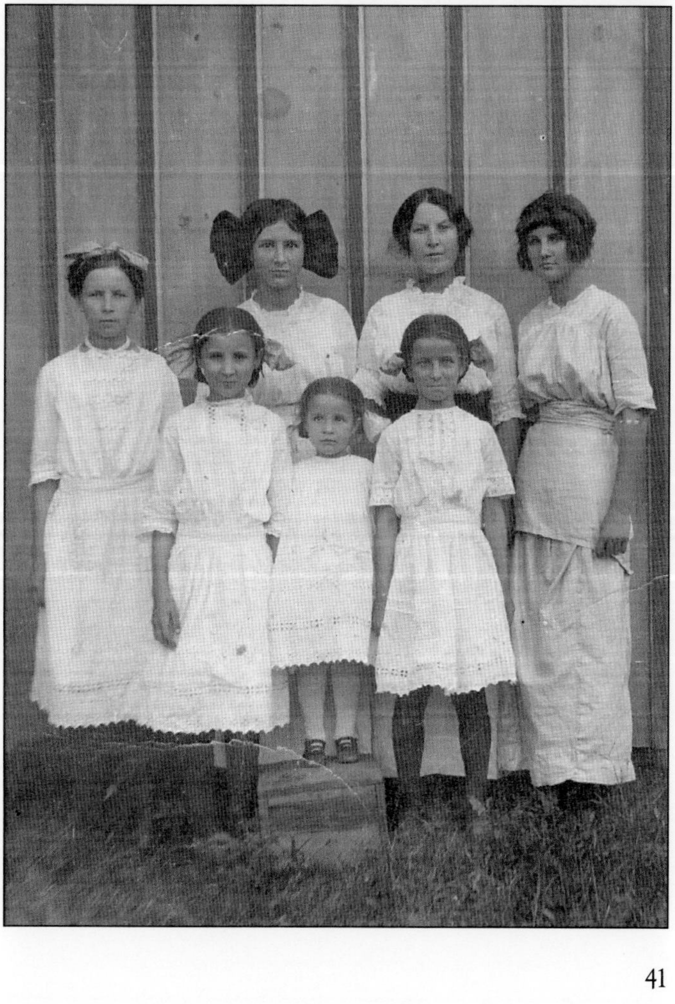

Bob and Mary Alice Wear's daughters pose for this photograph in their Sunday best. Pictured are, from left to right, (first row) Thelma, Annice, and Jean Wear; (second row) Lorah, Audrey, their cousin Annie, and Ina Wear. The Wear family farm was on what is now Wears Valley Road not far from the old Sand Pike area. (Courtesy of Henrietta Franklin Sharp.)

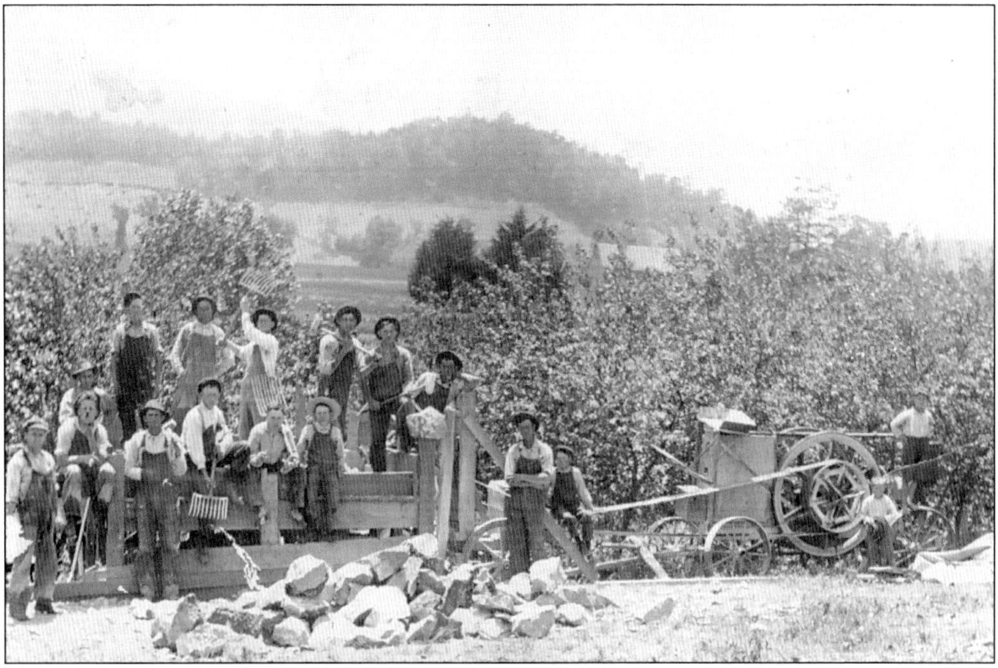

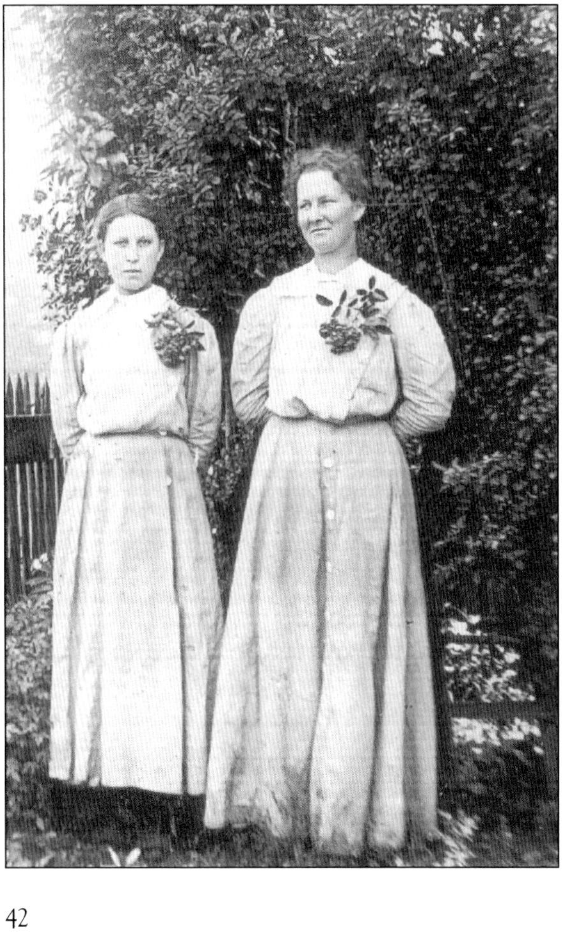

Lafayette Wear, father of Pigeon Forge's Carrie Wear Franklin, is pictured on the first row, third from the left, with this group of bridge builders. The construction location is not known. Wear's son, Sheridan, is also pictured, although it is unclear which worker he is. (Courtesy of Henrietta Franklin Sharp.)

Carrie Wear Franklin (right) is pictured with her sister, Annie. They were the daughters of Lafayette and Martha Sparks Wear. Carrie and her husband, Wiley Franklin, lived in the Mill Creek area. Annie married Bill Powell. This photograph was taken sometime in the early 1900s. (Courtesy of Henrietta Franklin Sharp.)

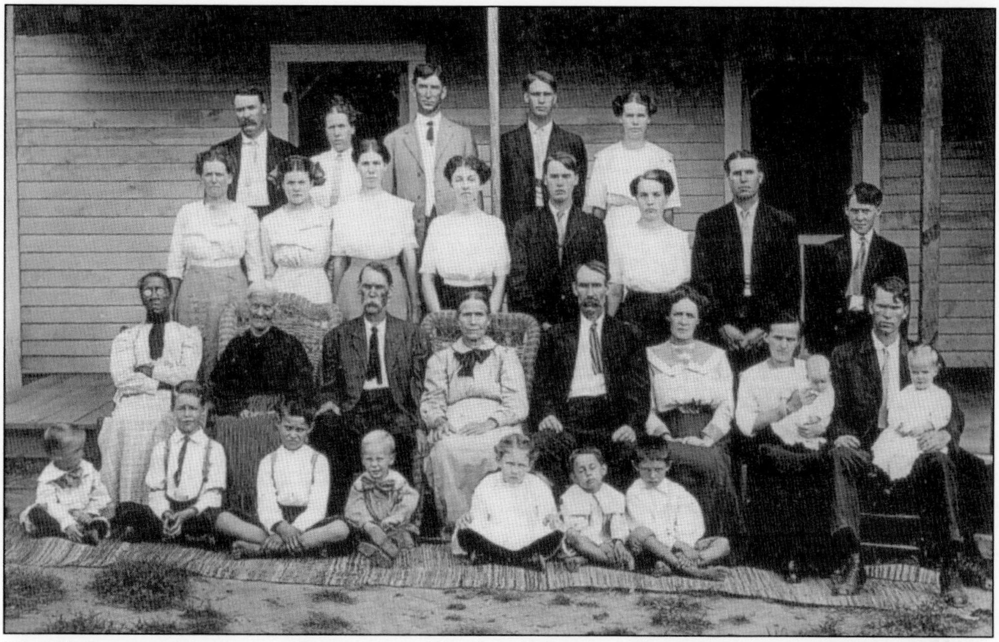

The William and Catherine Benson Franklin family lived in the Mill Creek area of Pigeon Forge. They are, from left to right, (first row) Austin, Ted, Charles, and James Franklin; Grace Ogle; and James and George Franklin; (second row) "Aunt" Jane Franklin, Vina Ann, William, Catherine, William H., Susie, Eda with Cecil, and Luther with Catherine Franklin; (third row) Ida, Stella, Lillie, Nellie and Ben Franklin; Nola Franklin Gobble; and Wiley and Roy Franklin; (fourth row) Hiram Franklin, Vina Franklin Ogle, Calvin Ogle, Perman Franklin, and Julia Franklin Carnes Tarwater. Aunt Jane was left on the steps of the "poor farm" near Sevierville as a teenager, and the Franklin family took her to live with them when it closed. Tom Franklin was manager of this facility for the homeless; it received funds from Sevier County government and was known only as the "poor farm" or the "county home." (Courtesy of Henrietta Franklin Sharp.)

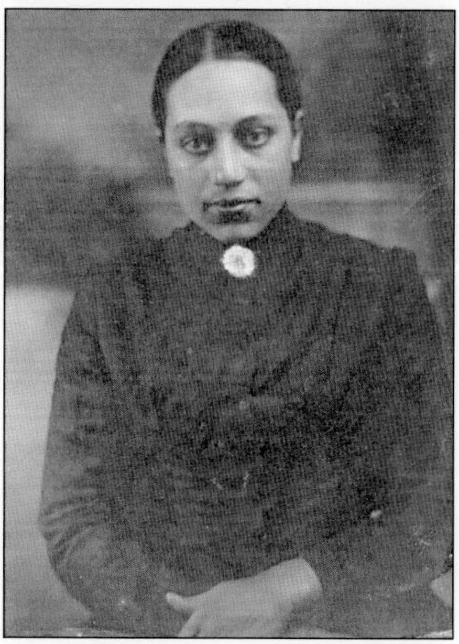

Lizzie Wilson was the daughter of Aunt Jane Franklin, who was an orphan raised by the Franklin family of Mill Creek after age 13. (Courtesy of Henrietta Franklin Sharp.)

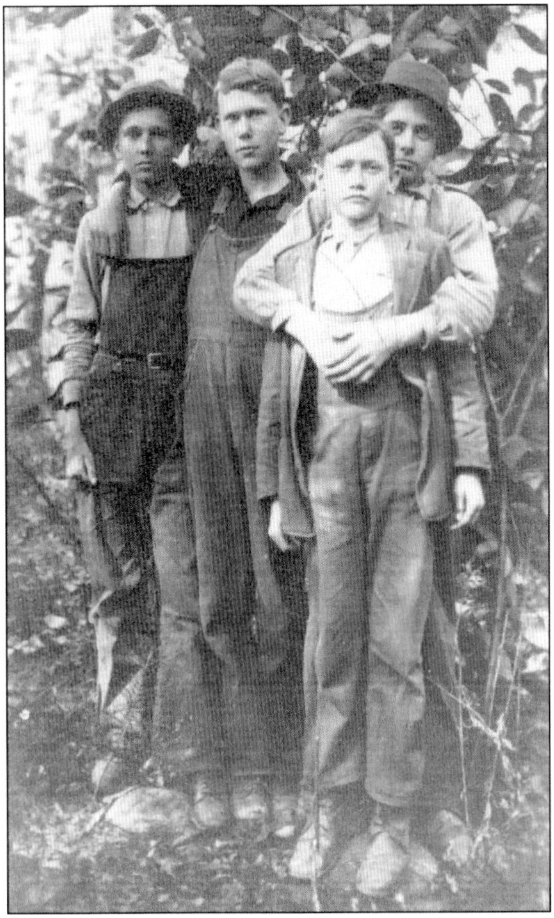

The Quarrels brothers are pictured here. One is William Conway of River Road. Pres. Franklin Roosevelt's National Youth Administration program operated in a building behind his home. At least two brothers operated a garage in Pigeon Forge in 1921. (Courtesy of Clara Quarrels Watson Killian.)

Bill Quarrels of Pigeon Forge, in the foreground, was a tailor for a department store in the Midwest. This picture postcard was postmarked from Kansas in 1912. He mailed it to his sister, Mary, in Oklahoma, writing of the awful snowstorms that had halted rail transportation. (Courtesy of Clara Quarrels Watson Killian.)

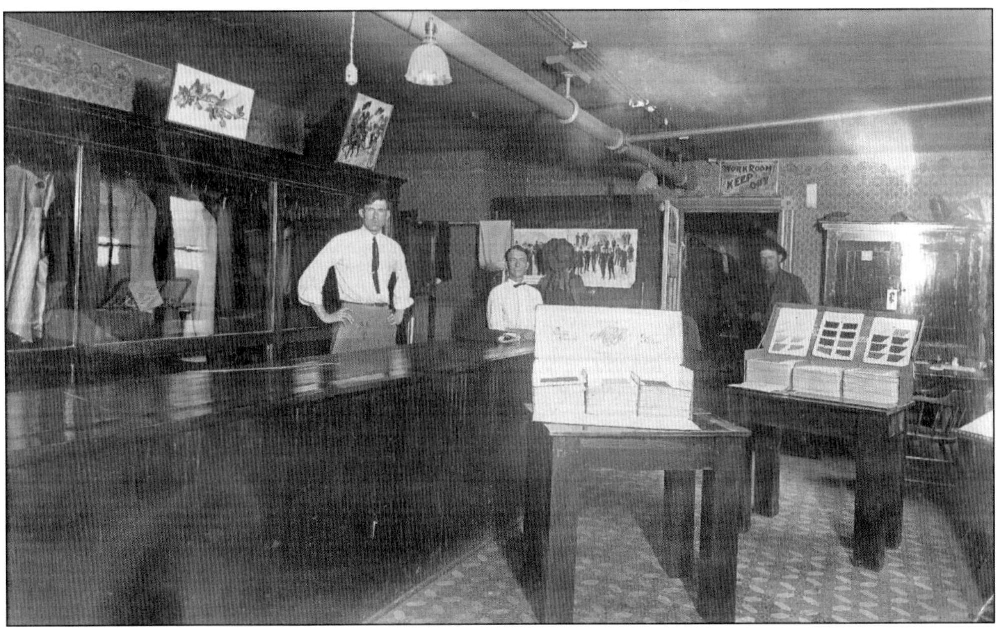

In this photograph, taken in 1913, are four of Dave and Mollie Ogle's children. They are, from left to right, (first row) Carl and Wayne; (second row) Ernest and Ed. (Courtesy of Rena Ogle.)

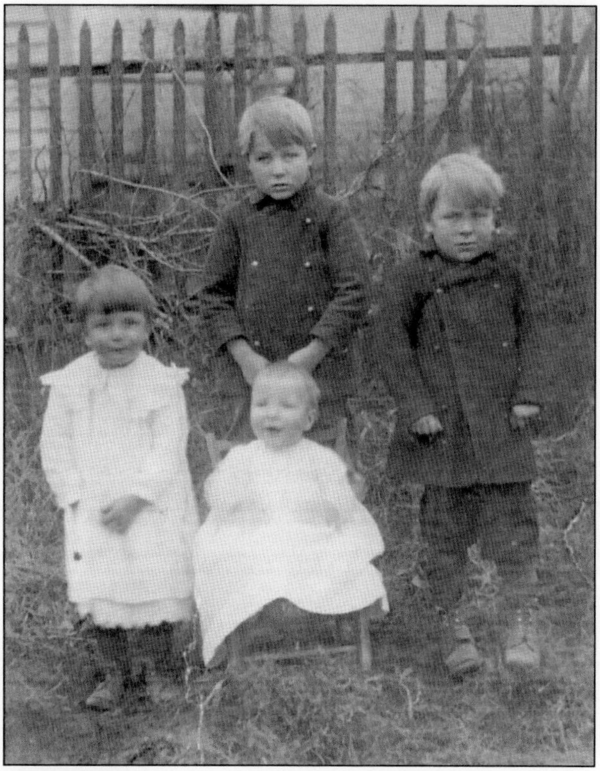

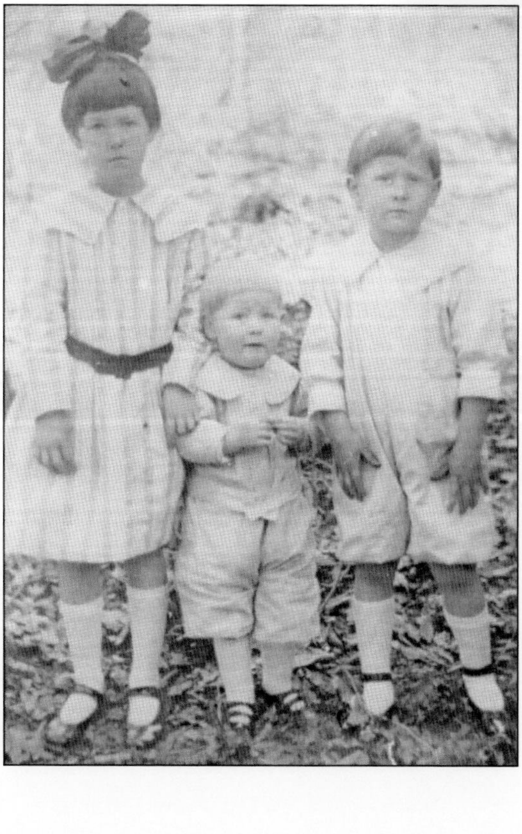

Mattie Sharp (Murrell) stands with her two brothers, George (center) and Fred (right). They are the children of the late George F. and Hettie Houser Sharp. The family lived in Sharp Hollow for a period, then moved to the Kyker farm off the present Wears Valley Road. This photograph was taken around 1920. (Courtesy of Henrietta Franklin Sharp.)

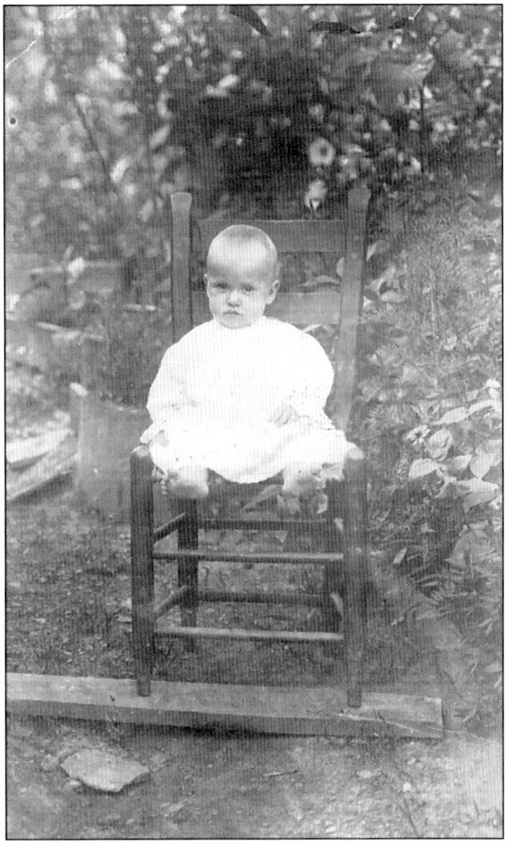

Muncy Houser, born in 1914, is pictured in his child-sized ladder-back chair. He was the son of Robert L. and Nora Ogle Houser and the grandson of Elder James and Martha Houser. The Robert Houser family lived on a large farm in the Mill Creek area. (Mattie Houser Clabo photograph; courtesy of Mary Lee Carver.)

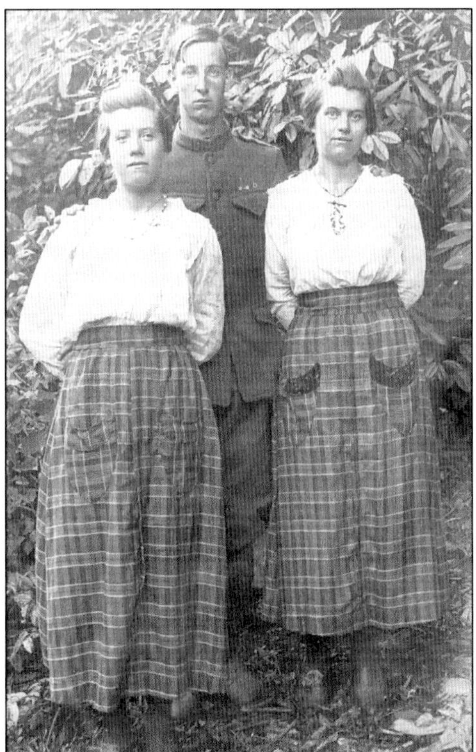

Robert Houser is pictured with his sisters, Mattie (right) and Josie. Their parents were Elder James and Martha Houser. As they married and moved from their Dudley Creek area home, Robert lived at Mill Creek in Pigeon Forge, and Mattie lived a little farther south at Gum Stand. Josie lived at Caney Creek. James was the son of George Easterly Houser, who died at Murfreesboro in the Civil War. The type of uniform worn by Robert is unclear; he never served in World War I, but his brother, John, did. (Mattie Houser Clabo photograph; courtesy of Randy Huskey.)

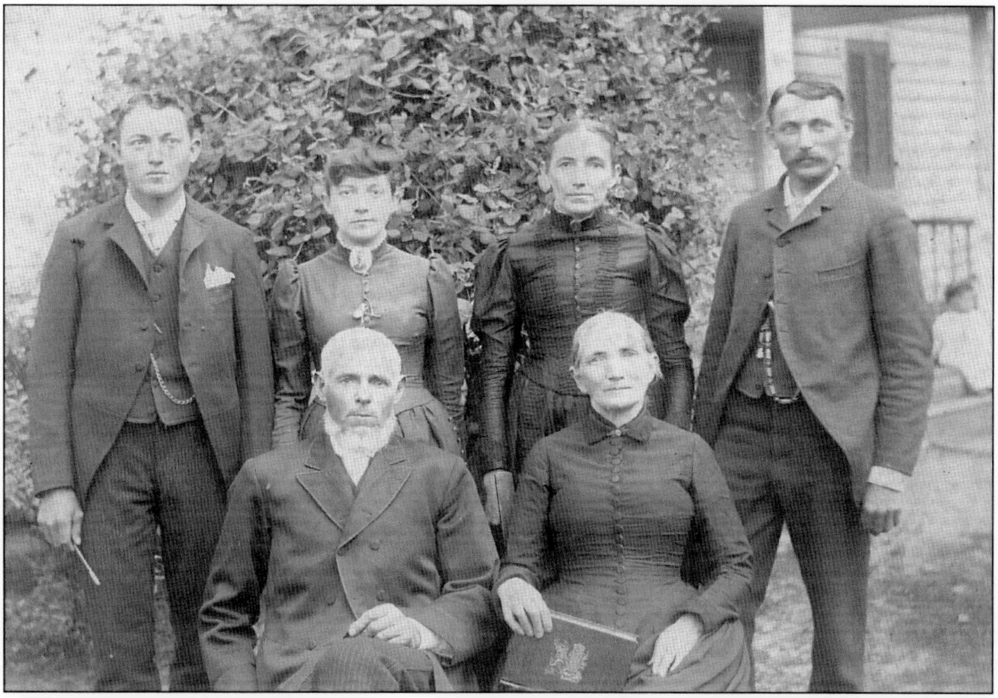

Henry and Martha Emert Butler are pictured with their children, from left to right, Cam (Henry Campbell), Belle Butler Stuart, Sallie Butler Wayland, and Ashley Wynn Butler. (Courtesy of the Householder family.)

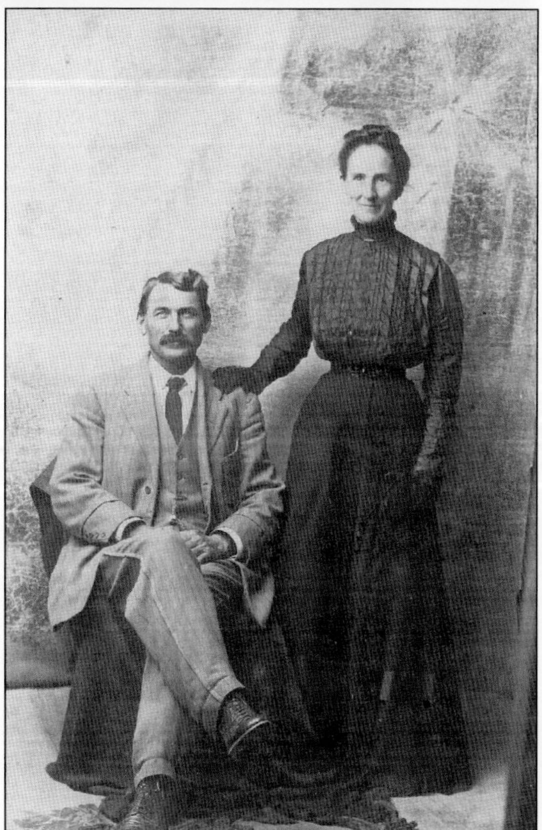

Ashley Wynn and Mary Katherine (Kate) Whittle Butler are pictured in this late-1800s photograph. Both were born around the time of the Civil War. Their children were Dave, Shirley, Mattie, Myrtle, Lela, Mary, Henry, and twins Florita and Juanita. Juanita died at age three. (Courtesy of the Householder family.)

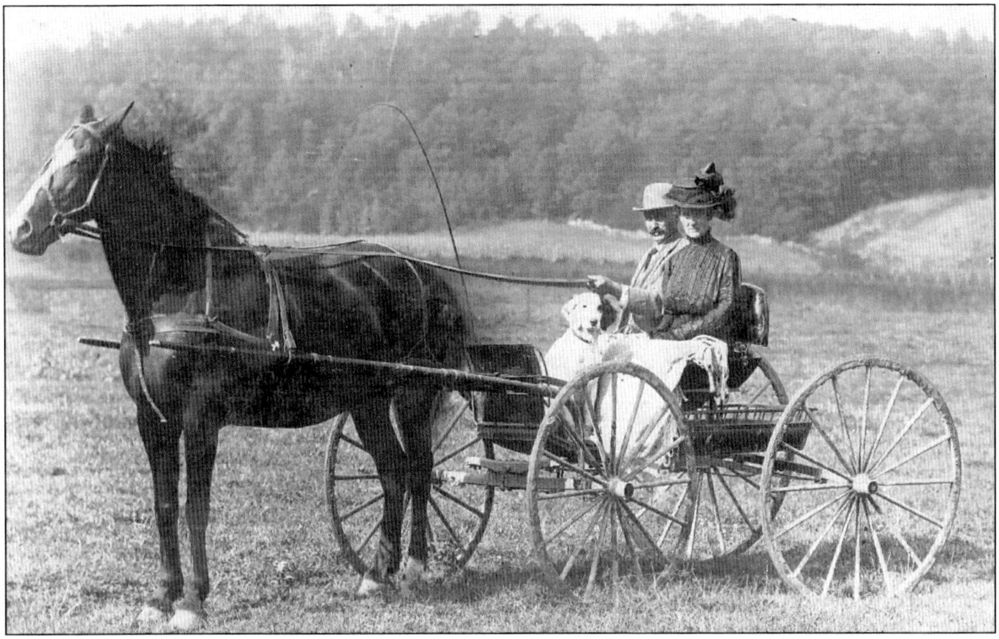

Ashley and Kate Butler take a drive. Butler's Farm, which reached outside the boundaries of Pigeon Forge, included 474 acres. The farmhouse sat near the intersection of Pine Mountain Road and the Parkway. (Courtesy of the Householder family.)

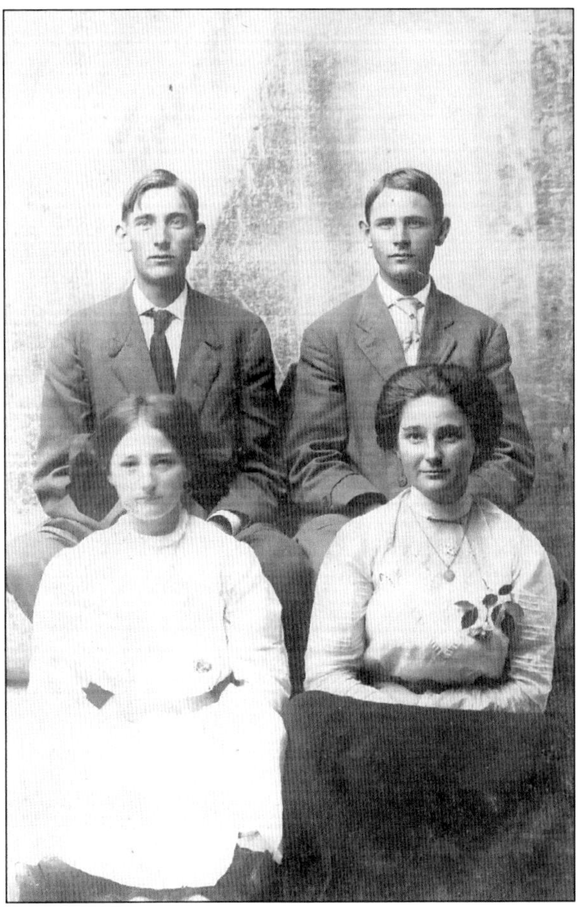

Four of Ashley and Kate Butler's children are pictured, from left to right, as follows: (first row) Myrtle and Mattie; (second row) Dave and Shirley. (Courtesy of the Householder family.)

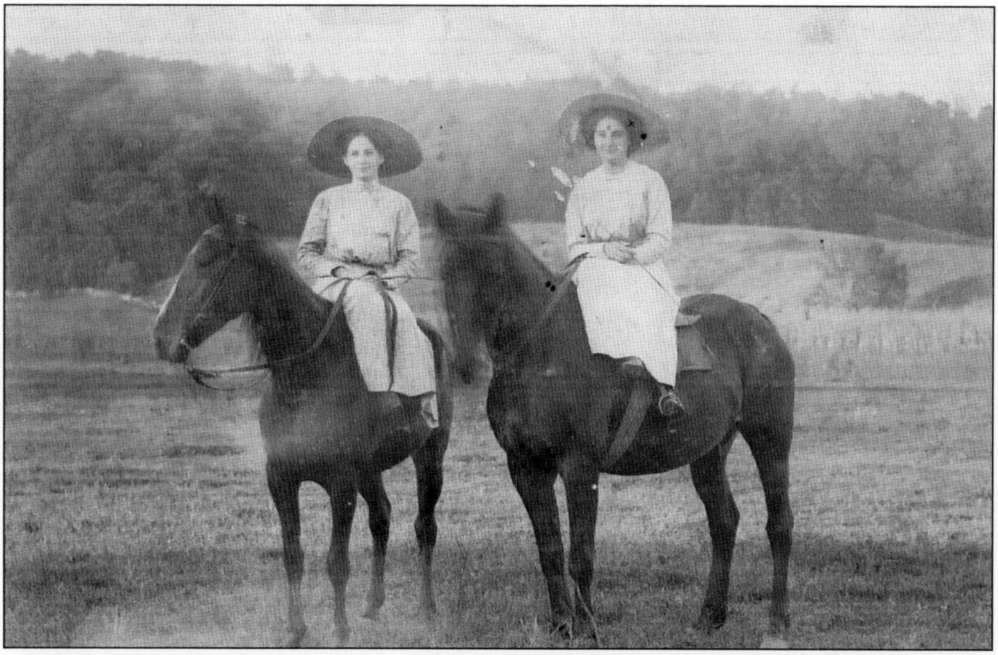

Zula Robertson Large, W. C. Large's mother, rides with Mattie Belle Butler Householder, wife of Dave Householder. Householder is pictured at right. (Courtesy of James Householder.)

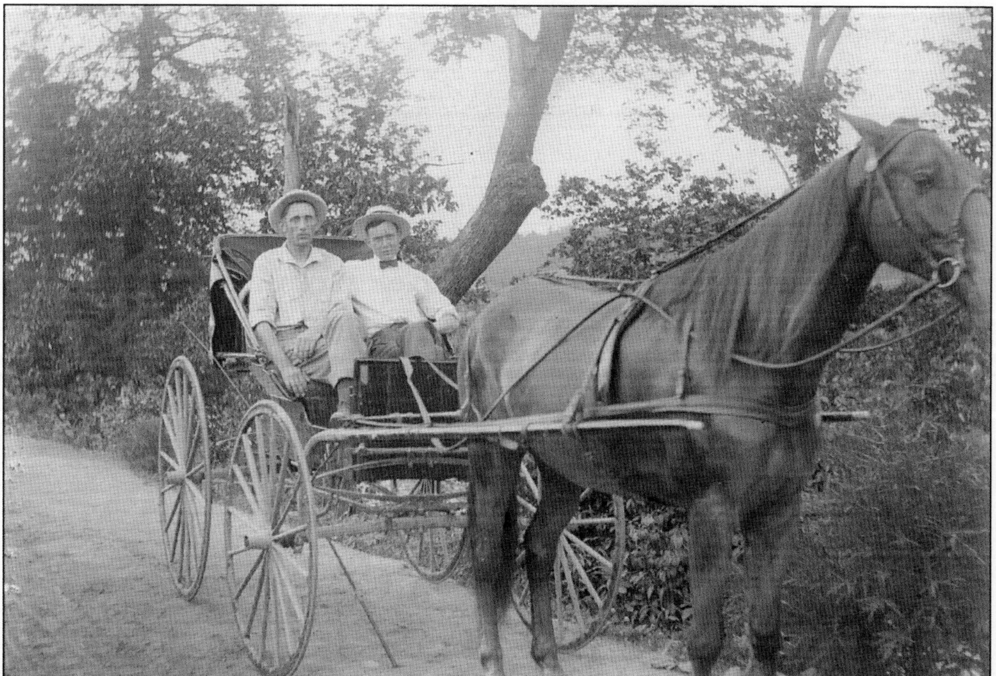

Dave Butler Sr. (left), son of Ashley and Kate Butler, and Jim Trotter (right) are seen riding along this country road. (Courtesy of the Householder family.)

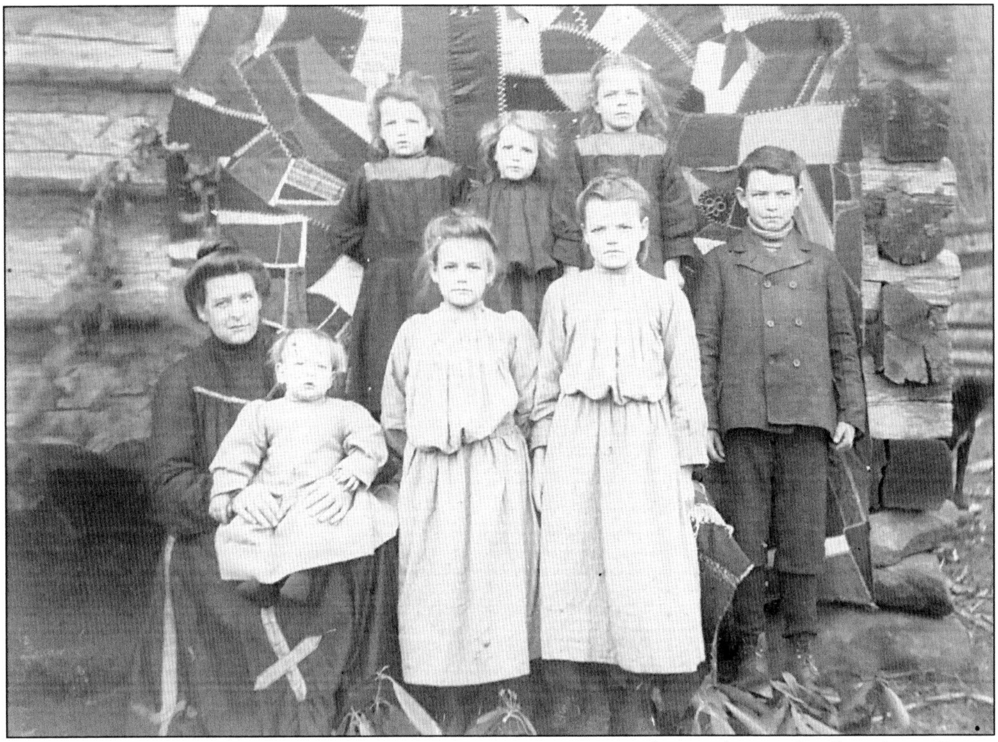

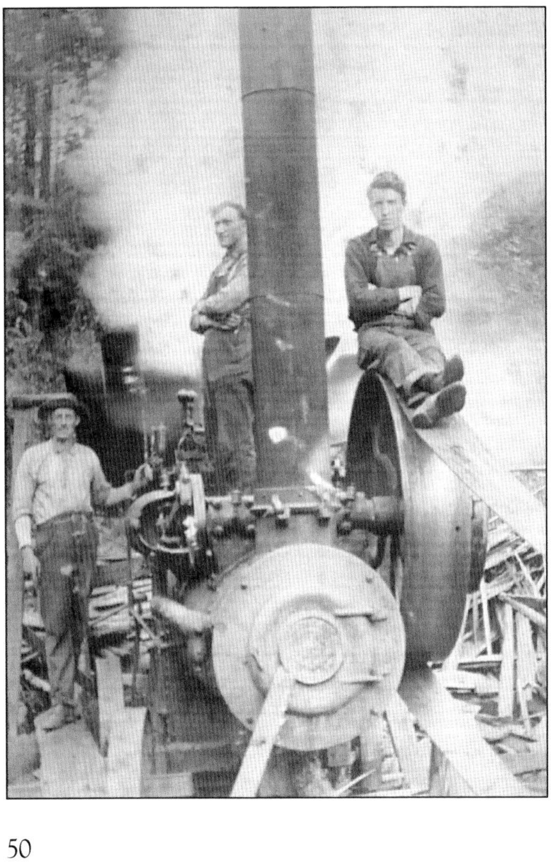

Many descendents of Bill and Sarah "Sally" Whaley from Greenbrier settled in Pigeon Forge after Great Smoky Mountains National Park was established. Pictured in this 1905 photograph are, in no certain order, (first row) Sally Ownby Whaley holding Rex, Lillie, and Minnie; (second row) Lorene, Gertrude, Lucille, and Dan. A patchwork or crazy quilt hangs in the background. (Courtesy of Rena Ogle.)

People from Pigeon Forge and the surrounding area walked into the Great Smoky Mountains to work before it became a national park. Many boarded and only returned home on weekends. Places such as this sawmill owned by West Whaley in Greenbrier, as well as the Wonderland Hotel, lumber operations, and other thriving businesses are hard to imagine today in the wilderness of the mountains. Pictured from left to right are Lonzo Whaley, James West Whaley, and West Whaley. (Courtesy of Rena Ogle.)

As a young adult, Murrell Whaley drove Butler's rolling store over the dusty roads of the Pigeon Forge area and out into the county. He is pictured here (front left) with his parents, Calvin and Mettie, and his sisters, Stella (center) and Lillie. Calvin was the son of John "Dudley" and Nancy Ownby Whaley. (Courtesy of Sarah Ownby Ball.)

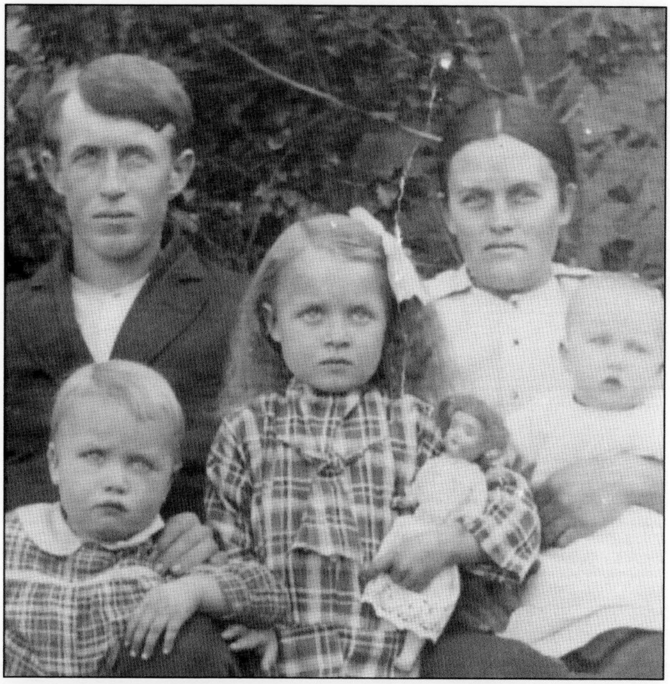

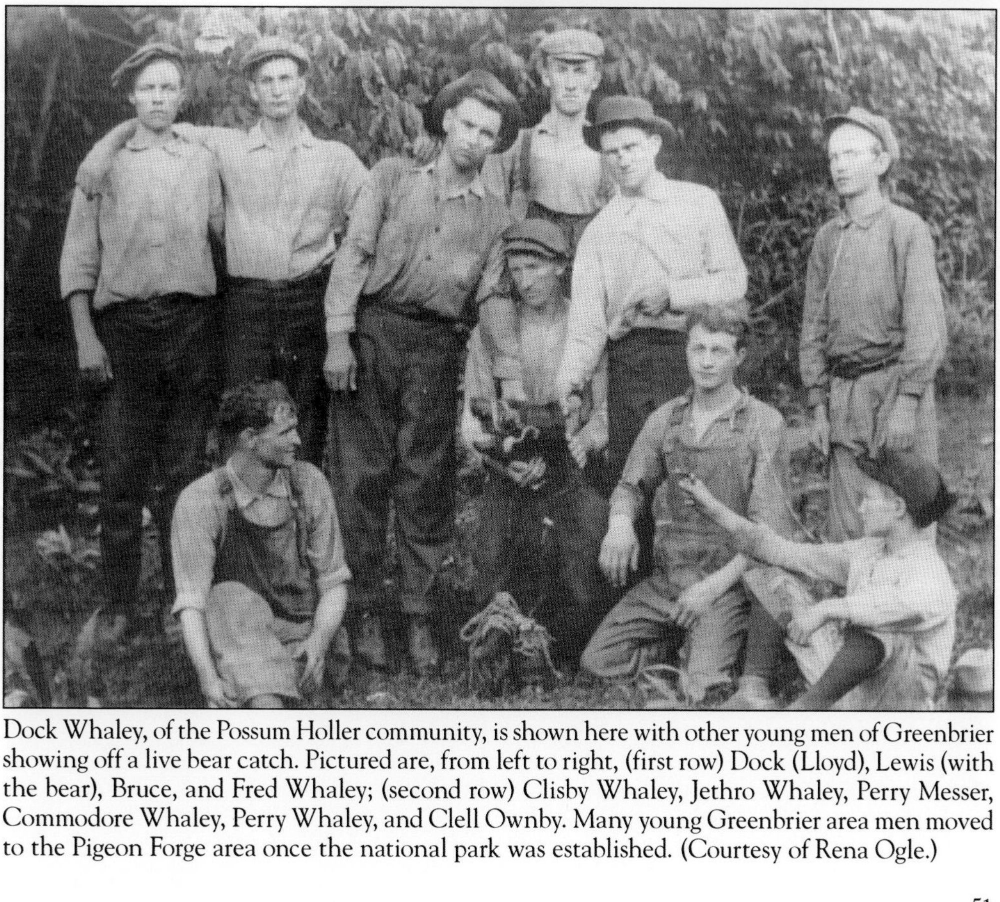

Dock Whaley, of the Possum Holler community, is shown here with other young men of Greenbrier showing off a live bear catch. Pictured are, from left to right, (first row) Dock (Lloyd), Lewis (with the bear), Bruce, and Fred Whaley; (second row) Clisby Whaley, Jethro Whaley, Perry Messer, Commodore Whaley, Perry Whaley, and Clell Ownby. Many young Greenbrier area men moved to the Pigeon Forge area once the national park was established. (Courtesy of Rena Ogle.)

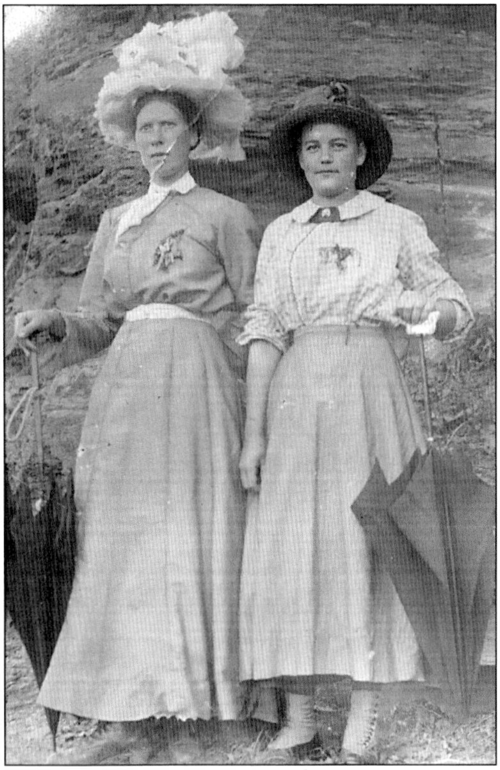

Julia Whaley (left) poses in all her finery with her cousin, Lillie Whaley. These young women lived in Greenbrier in their youth. Lillie married Walter Ownby, also of Greenbrier. In her last years, she lived in Pigeon Forge. (Courtesy of Sarah Ball.)

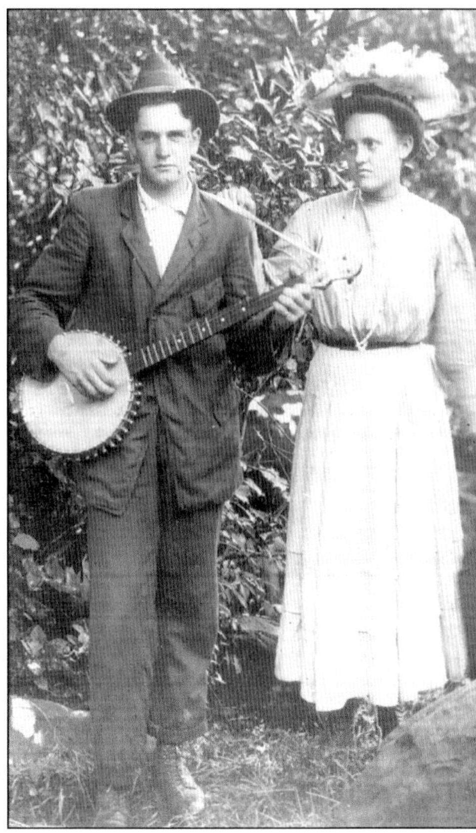

Music has always been a part of life for the folks living in Pigeon Forge. People such as Dock Whaley brought the traditions of mountain music with them when they left the Smokies. Whaley is pictured with an unidentified cousin. (Courtesy of Sue Whaley Gibson.)

Marion Whaley is pictured here in his homespun suit made by his mother, Nancy Ownby Whaley, wife of John "Dudley" Whaley. He lived on Dixie Avenue. (Courtesy of Sarah Ball.)

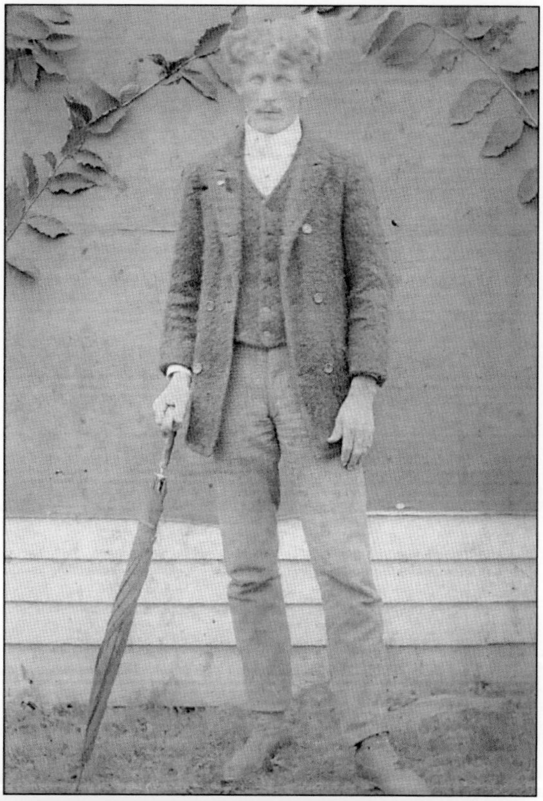

Sam and Sarah Whaley Ownby's family left the Great Smoky Mountains as the national park was being established. Many of their descendents live in Pigeon Forge today. Pictured in this 1915 photograph are, from left to right, (first row) Estel, Sam, Sarah, baby Velma, and Evolena; (second row) Marion, Mark and Ezalee Ownby Naugher, Dan and Nancy Ann Ownby Whaley, and Walter and Lillie Whaley Ownby. (Courtesy of Rena Ogle.)

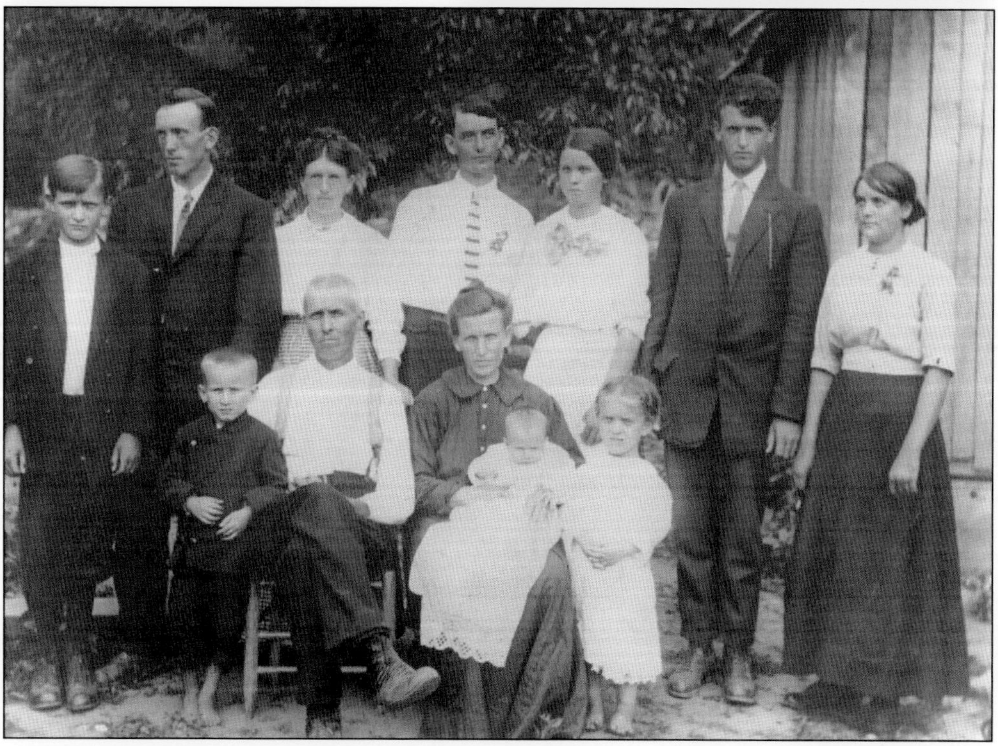

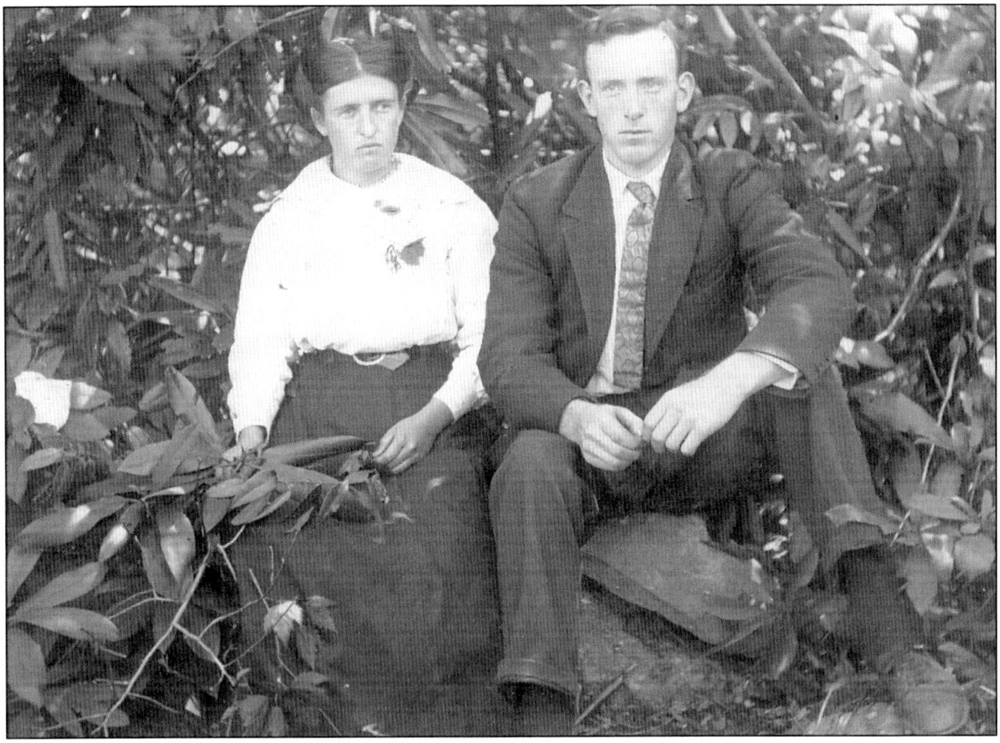

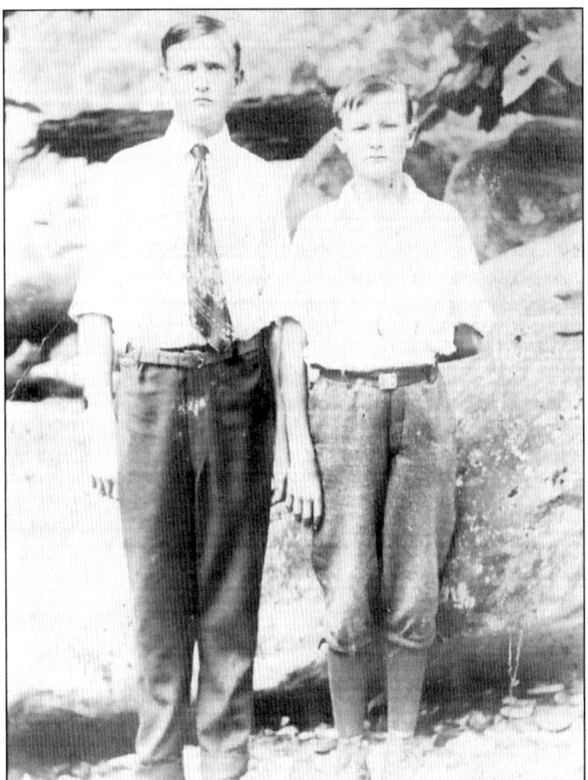

Mark and Ezalee Naugher are pictured in their courting days. Ezalee was the daughter of Sam and Sarah Ownby. The couple lived just off the Parkway near the north end of River Road. (Courtesy of Sarah Ball.)

Marion Ownby, of Greenbrier, stands with his cousin, Fred Whaley (right). Ownby married Jenny Martin, and the two lived in Pigeon Forge near the Old Mill area. Jenny's father, Davis Martin, owned the Old Mill in the 1930s. (Courtesy of Sarah Ball.)

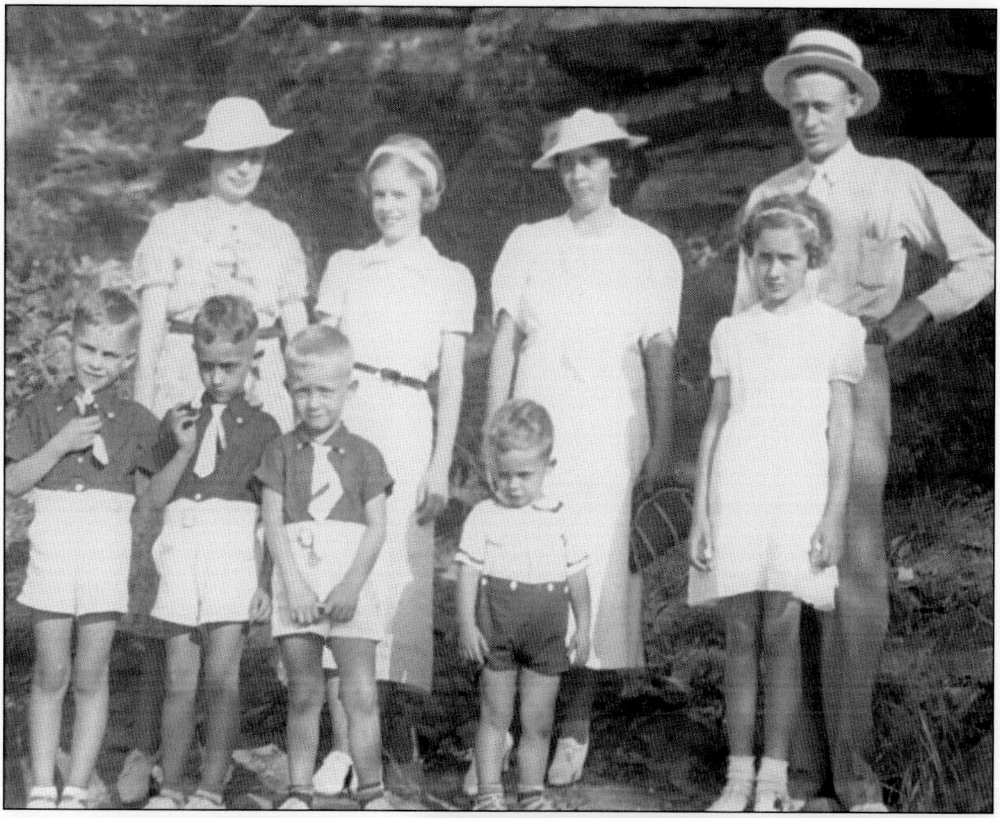

Pauline Law operated McMahan Place, a small inn located in Dott McMahan's old home built on the river in the 1950s. This building was on the original George Washington McMahan farm at the south end of Pigeon Forge. Members of her family are pictured, from left to right, as follows: (first row) Henry and Ralph Law, Jimmy and Reed Hutchins, and Pauline Law; (second row) Lucille Taylor Gobble, Mary Gobble Hutchins, Ada McMahan Law, and Clyde Gobble. (Dott L. McMahan collection; courtesy of Pauline Law Walters-Spencer.)

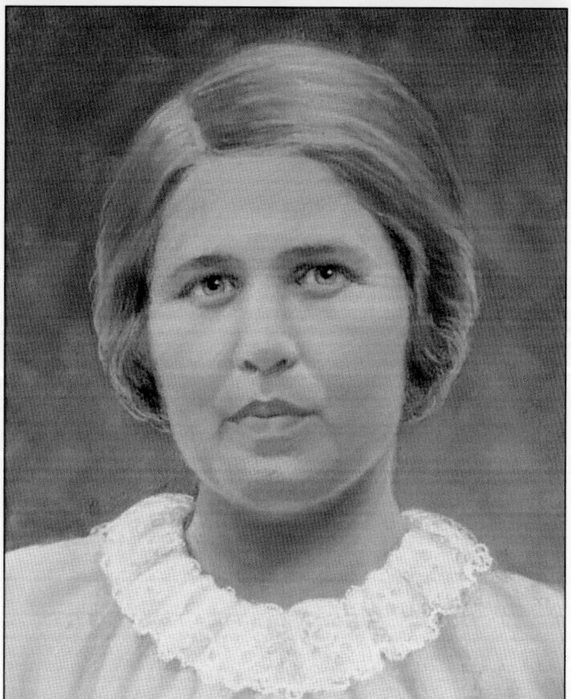

Hettie Odessa Townsend Wilson was the wife of Eli Alvin Wilson, who served on the Pigeon Forge Planning Commission in its early years. The couple lived at the corner of Dixie Avenue and Householder Street. (Courtesy of Wilda Lamon.)

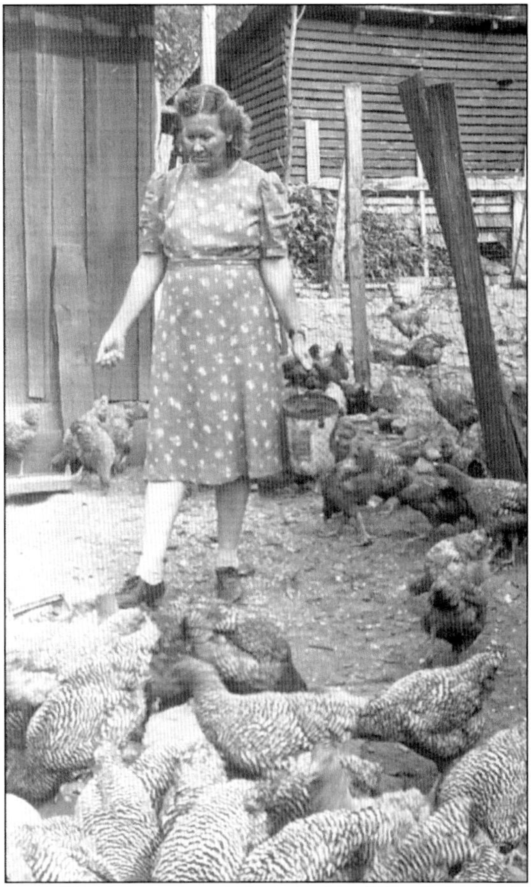

Feeding the chickens was an everyday chore for women in Pigeon Forge in the days when people still raised hens and gathered fresh eggs for breakfast. Laura Whaley Merritt's photograph was taken at this home in Elkmont. (Courtesy of Sue Whaley Gibson.)

Wayne Ogle was servicing cars just as the country was about to enter World War II. This photograph was dated July 11, 1941. Ogle operated this garage in a building he rented on present-day Old Mill Avenue. Pictured here are, from left to right, Harold Quarrels, Wayne Ogle, his brother Jess, and Darrell Pickel. (Courtesy of Rena Ogle.)

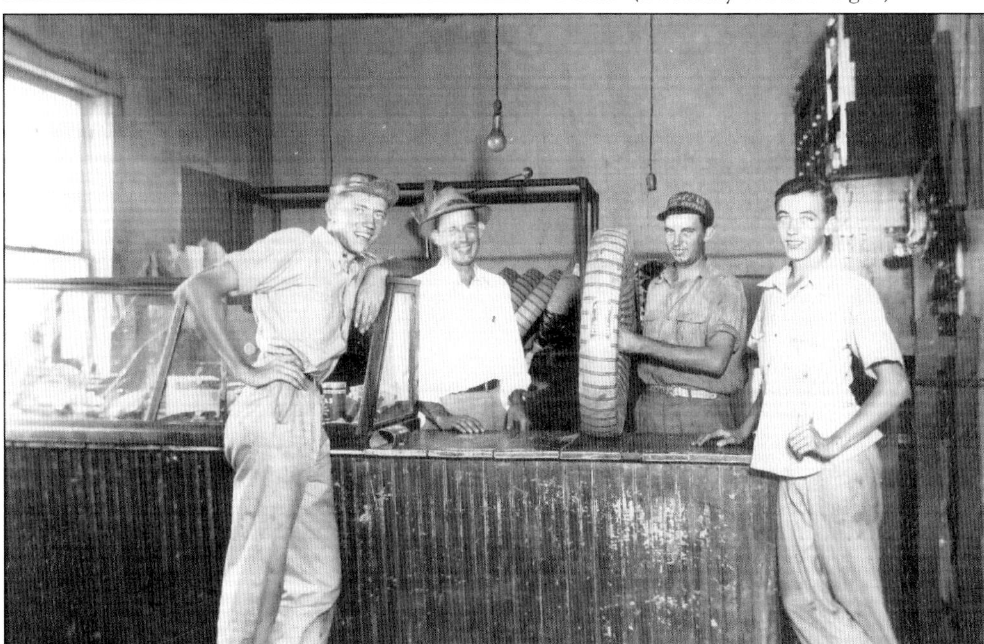

Two

The Great Smoky Mountains Change a Destiny

In 1934, Great Smoky Mountains National Park was established. One of the primary routes to the park was through the farming community of Pigeon Forge. A few landowners still owned the majority of the acreage along the main Pigeon Forge highway. Large fields of corn, beans, wheat, and hay were being cultivated.

In earlier times, a community threshing machine moved from farmer to farmer to thresh wheat. Community women waited for the sound of the cannery whistle calling them in to work when a new truckload of vegetables arrived for canning. A string of white farmhouses with wide porches and neatly trimmed yards lined River Road, and residents referred to the cluster of homes as String Town. A small power plant installed at the Old Mill provided electricity for a few homes and businesses until 1930, when the service came from the Tennessee Public Service Company.

Before World War II, young men in Pigeon Forge were taking advantage of Pres. Franklin D. Roosevelt's programs for rebuilding after the Great Depression. A National Youth Administration project was housed in the town, and young people from across the county came and learned woodcrafts. Some of Pigeon Forge's young men worked in Roosevelt's Civilian Conservation Corps building trails inside the newly formed national park. With the outbreak of World War II, most of the young men were shipped overseas to fight. When they returned, some resumed farming. Others found work at the Alcoa Aluminum Plant in Maryville or at TVA's Douglas Dam building project, and a few took jobs at the new factories opening near Sevierville.

Men who had left their families during the week to work in the lumber operations before the park's establishment would afterward have new opportunities. With the park's opening, vacationers would soon flock to their town.

The state government purchased what seemed like an unreasonably vast right-of-way for the new highway to the park in 1946 or 1947. This venture split big farms and caused the sparse number of business owners to reconsider their locations along the river in favor of facing the new asphalt ribbon of highway. The park's establishment would forever change Pigeon Forge.

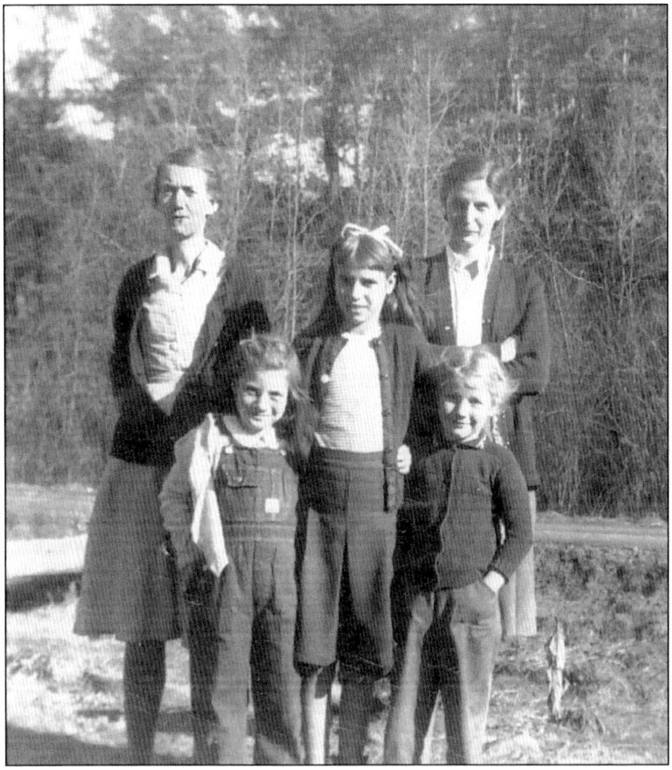

Viola Henry (back left) is pictured with family members. They are as follows: sister-in-law Grace Lemons Clabo and, from left to right, Wanda, Viola's daughter, and Edna and Bernice, Grace's daughters. Viola was married to Simeon Henry and lived on Lower Middle Creek. Clabo was married to Orville Clabo, and they lived on Upper Middle Creek. (Courtesy of Myrtle Henry.)

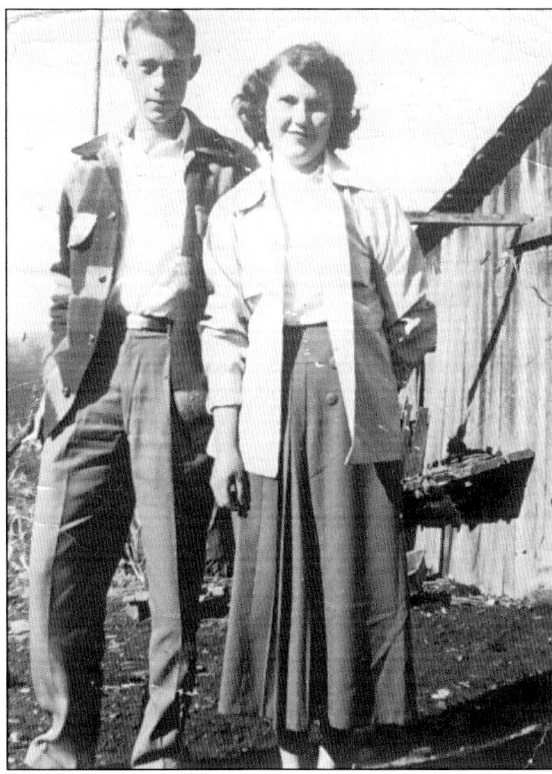

Carl Henry and Myrtle Ownby are pictured on Webb's Mountain out past Little Cove in February 1951. The couple married later that same year. They lived on Ore Bank Road until he went in service to Korea. The Henry family lived off Lower Middle Creek when their children were teenagers. (Courtesy of Myrtle Henry.)

Myrtle Ownby Henry is pictured with her brother, Gene, on Webb's Mountain near Little Cove. Myrtle and her husband, Carl, lived most of their married life in Pigeon Forge. Their children are Janice, Dwight, Debbie, Karen, and Brenda. Gene and Juanita Ownby, of Mill Creek, are the parents of Teddy, Dennis, Randy, and Regina. (Courtesy of Myrtle Henry.)

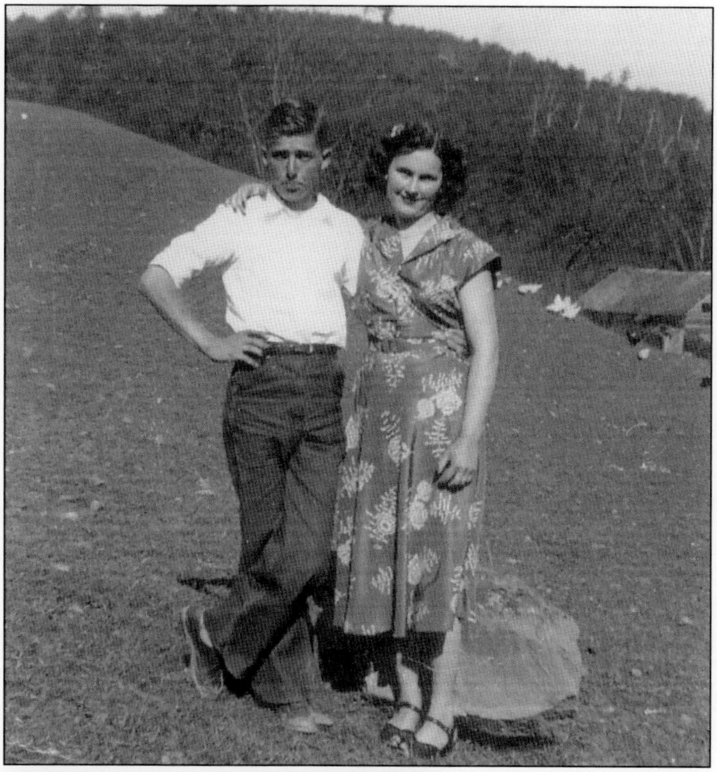

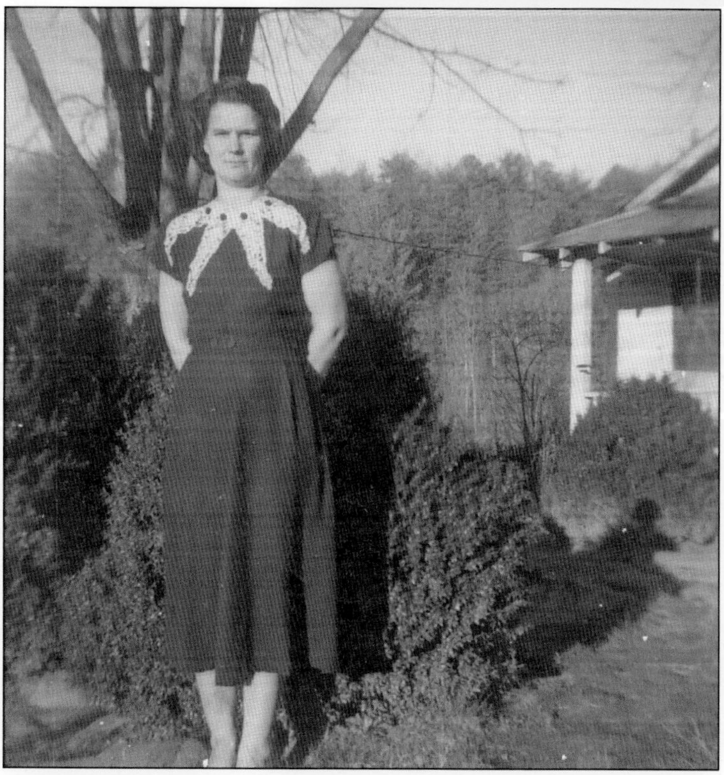

Emma Ogle Wright posed for this photograph in February 1957. Her dress depicts the 1950s style of the day. (Courtesy of Mary Lee Carver.)

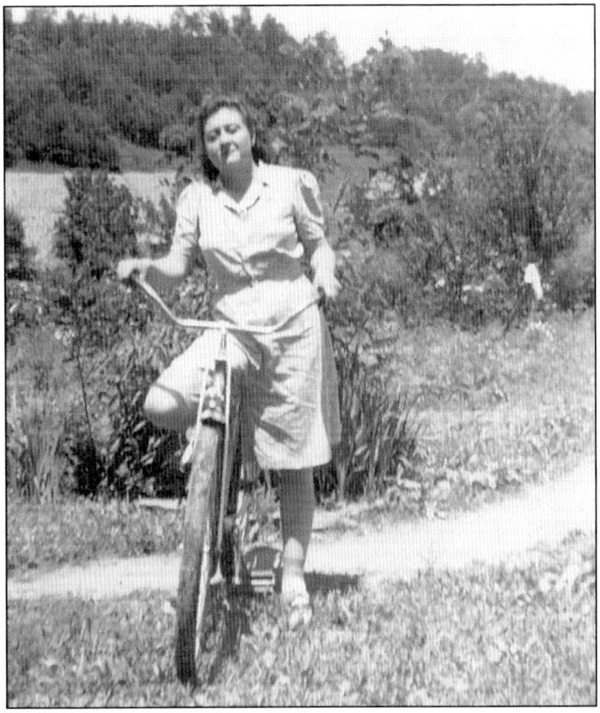

Grace Newman rides this larger-than-life bicycle along a country road. She visited many times with her sister, Frankie Oury, who lived in Pigeon Forge. (Courtesy of Mary Lee Carver.)

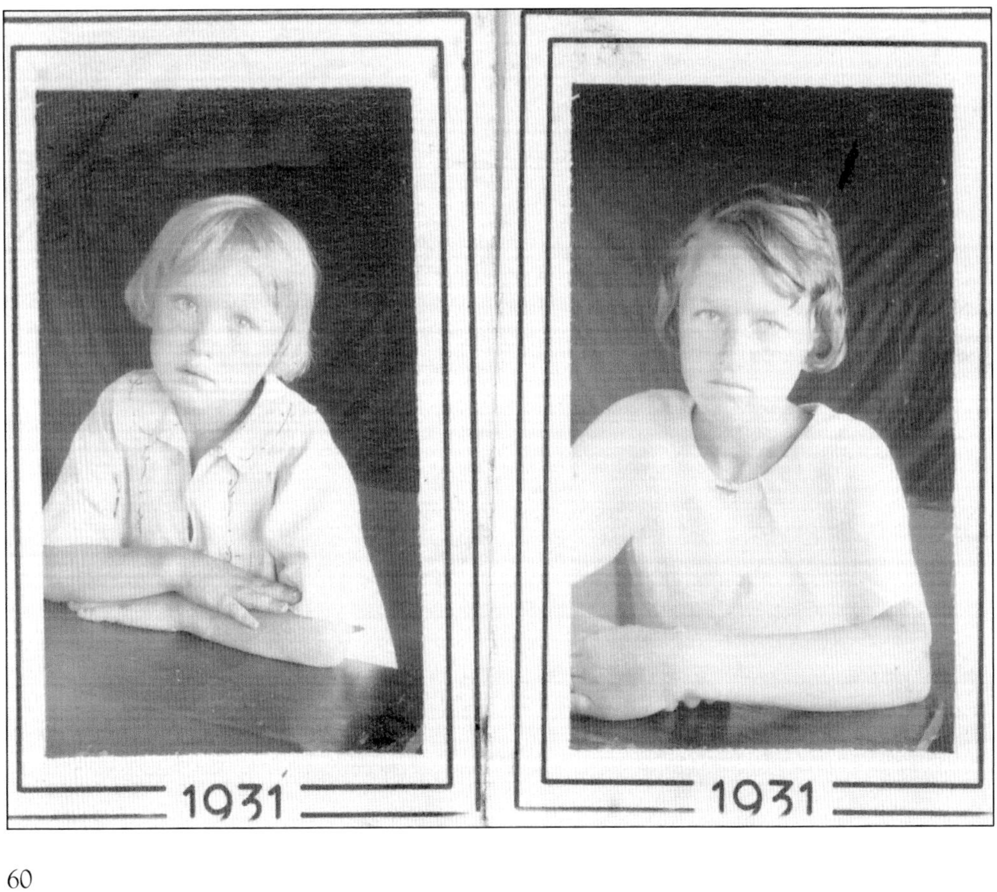

Calvin Whaley's daughters, Lillie (left) and Myrtle, are pictured here in 1931 school photographs. The family lived in Greenbrier in the Great Smoky Mountains and later in Pigeon Forge. (Courtesy of Sarah Ball.)

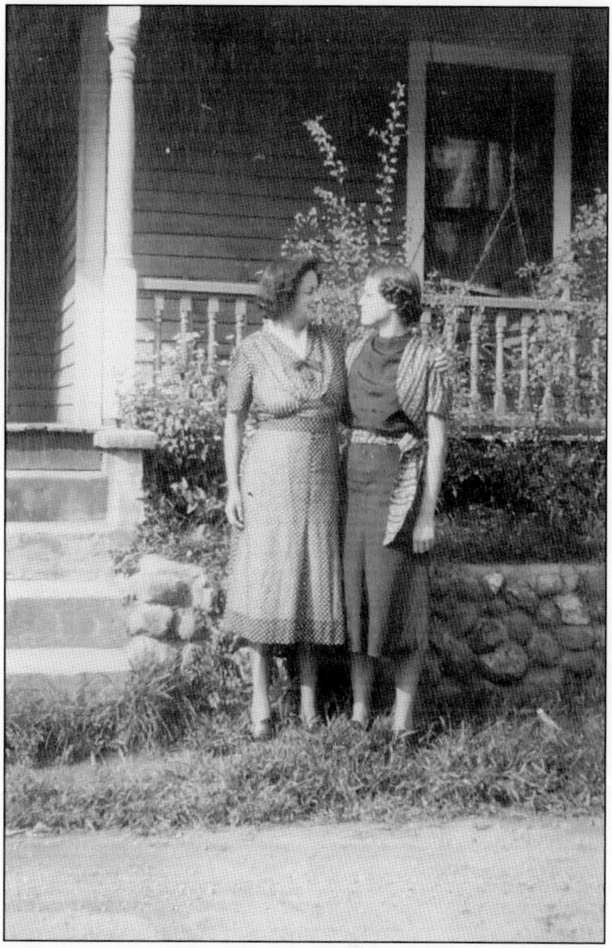

Laura Fain, wife of George, is pictured with her daughter, Helen Ruth (right), at their home on River Road. This home is one of the few remaining from a row of houses that stood along that road. It is now the historic BB&T bank building near the Old Mill. (Courtesy of Clara Watson Quarrels Killian.)

Pigeon Forge Pottery was housed in the renovated Butler family barn until it burned in 1957. This was one of the first Pigeon Forge businesses that attracted vacationers to the area. (Courtesy of Ruth Ferguson.)

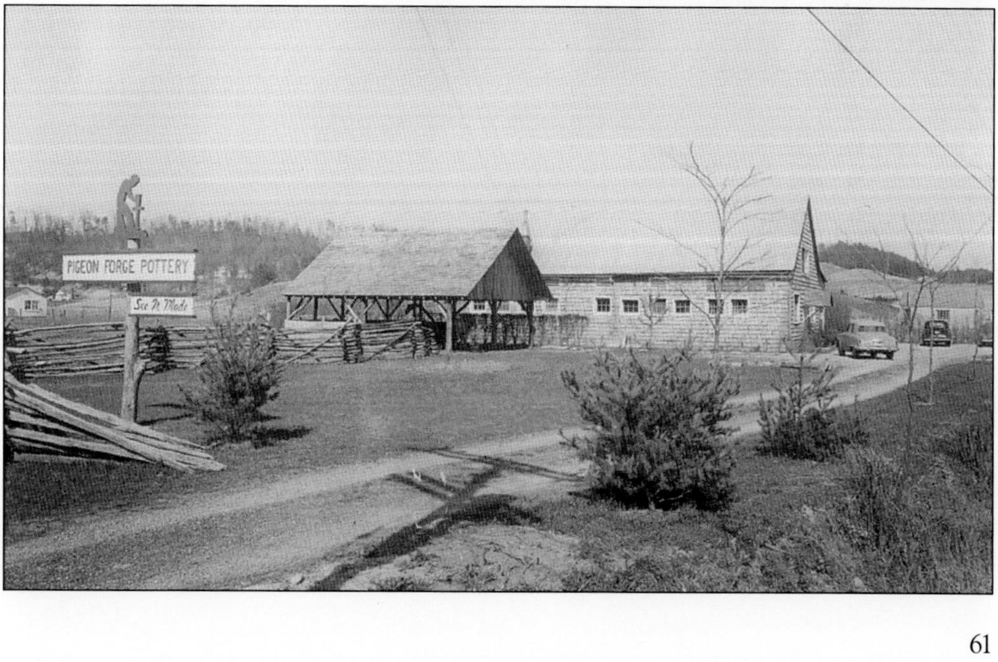

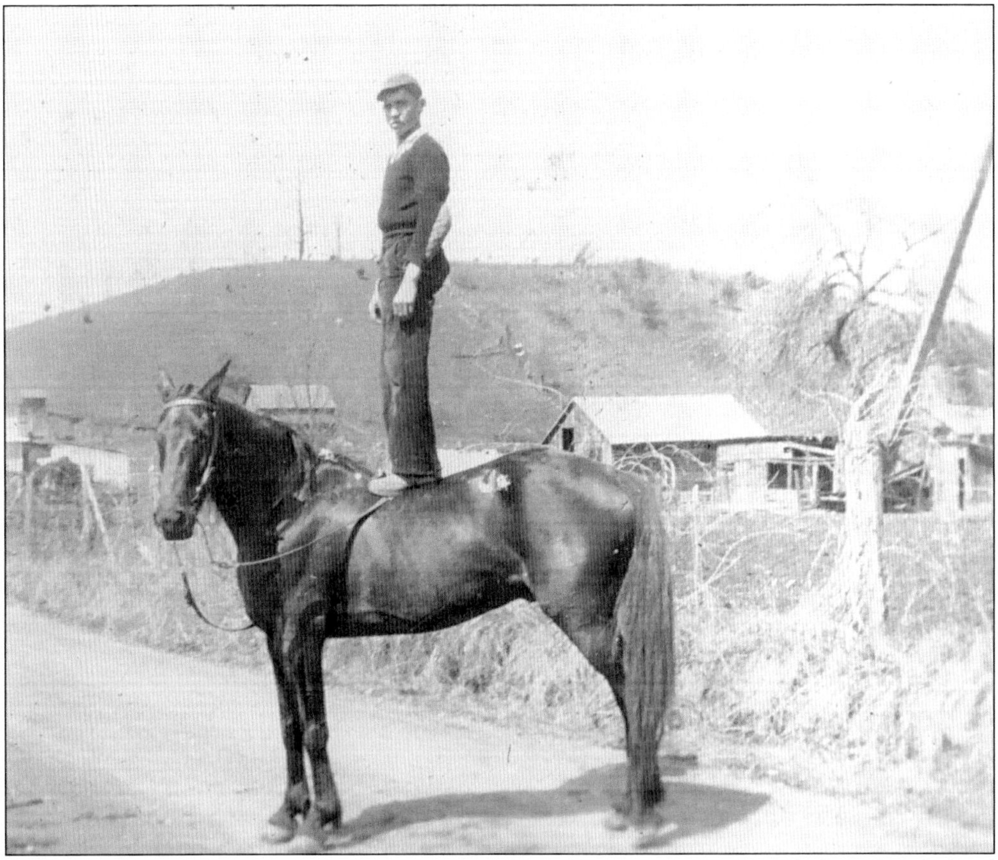

Ray Benson balances on his horse. He was the son of Walter Benson, who owned a large farm behind the Old Mill at the present site of Patriot Park. (Courtesy of Clara Quarrels Watson Killian.)

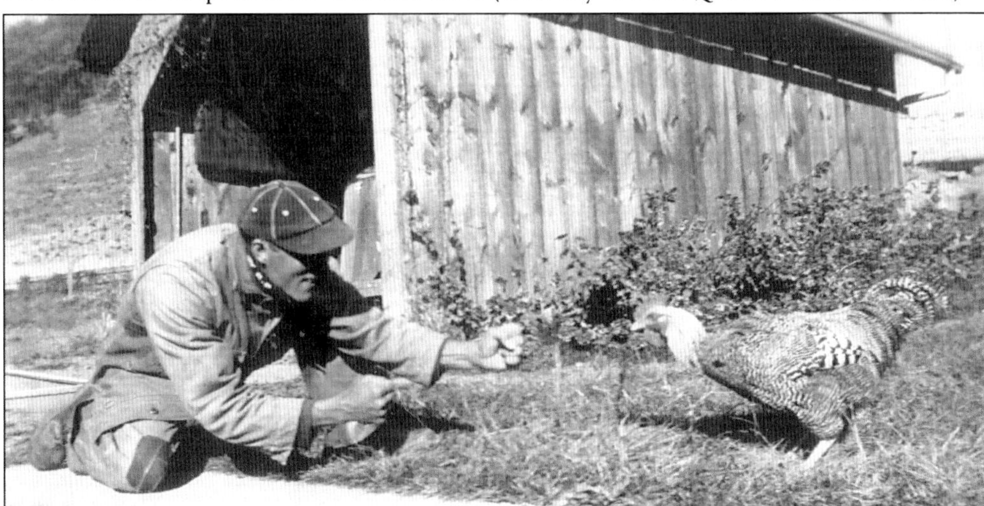

Osie Ownby lived at the foot of Pine Mountain, or "Piney Mountain" as he called it. He was an entertainer who loved to play the banjo or most any instrument he placed in his hands. Here he clowns with a rooster. (Courtesy of Mary Ownby.)

Osie Ownby is pictured with his fishing buddies Harold (left) and Houston (center) Myers in the spring of 1938. Ownby was married to Adis Myers; his half brother was Brother Oswald of Grand Ole Opry fame. (Courtesy of Mary Ownby.)

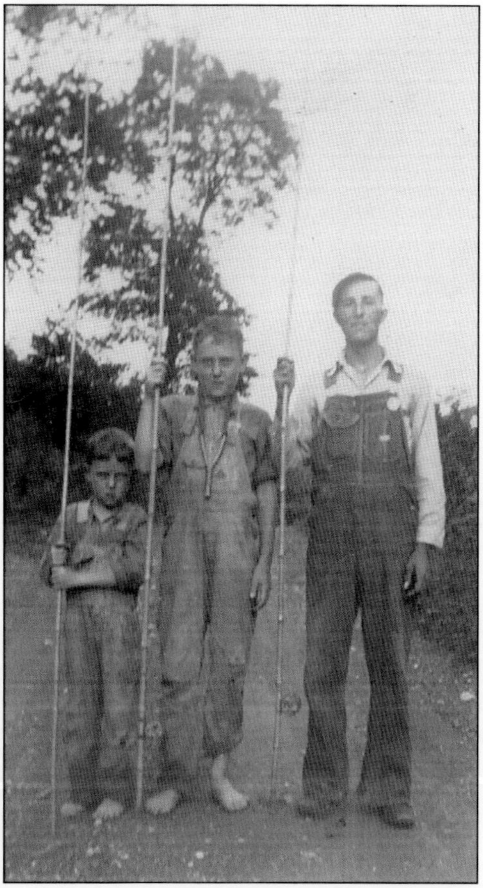

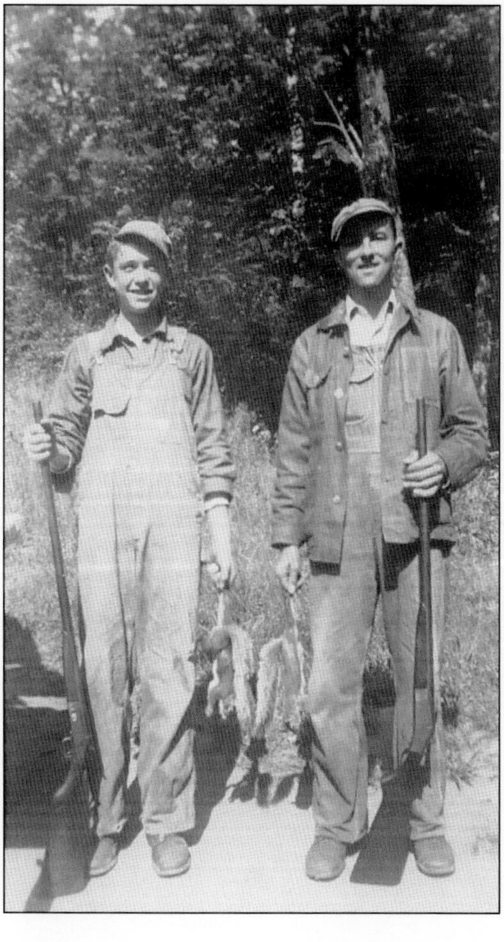

Osie Ownby (right) and J. P. Myers return after squirrel hunting on Bluff Mountain in 1938. Sitting under a large hickory tree listening for the squirrels was a fine way to pass the time for men of earlier days. (Courtesy of Mary Ownby.)

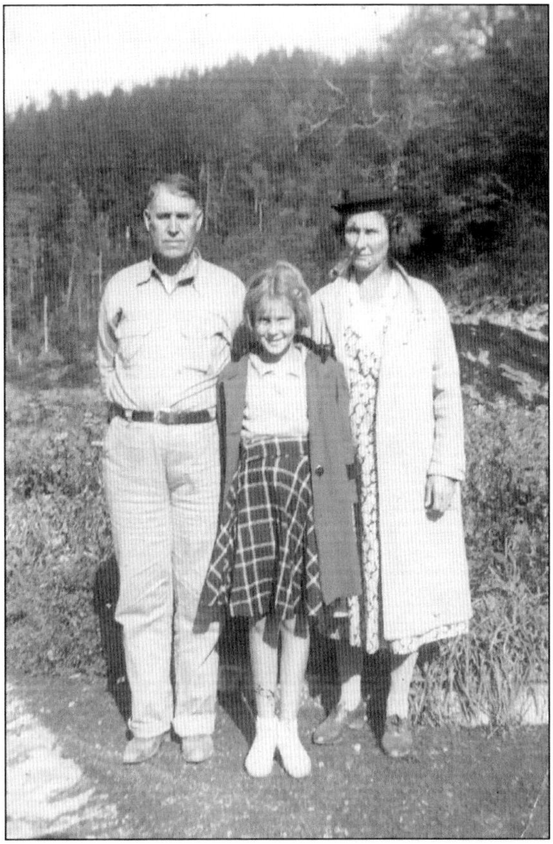

Henrietta Franklin stands with her parents, Wiley and Carrie Wear Franklin, in the late 1930s. The family lived on Mill Creek near Sugar Camp Mountain, which was earlier named for the sugar maples there. There were three or four trees at the base of the mountain that were tapped in earlier days by a few Cherokee men who camped up on the mountain before returning across the Smokies. (Courtesy of Henrietta Franklin Sharp.)

William "Bill" Runnels Franklin was buried in the Pigeon Forge Methodist Cemetery, also known as the Pigeon Forge Community Cemetery, after his death on May 24, 1947. Family members gather for the last goodbye. Pictured are his sons and daughters, from left to right, William, Perman, Wiley, Ben, Nola, Lillie, and Julia. (Courtesy of Henrietta Franklin Sharp.)

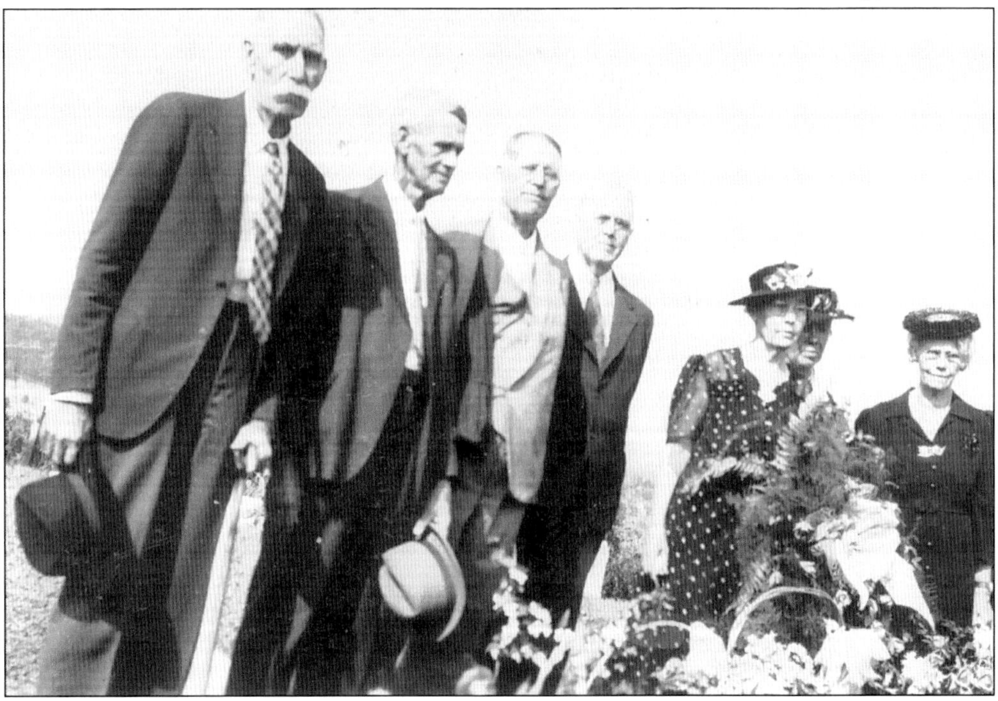

English McCarter poses for this photograph while on furlough from his service in World War II. He lived in the Banner community in his childhood. Later he was the mayor of Pigeon Forge and held the longest-running term as commissioner. (Courtesy of English McCarter.)

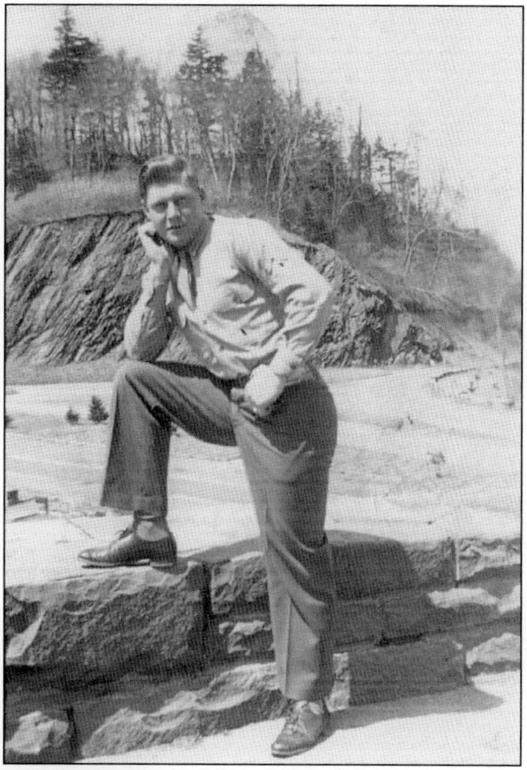

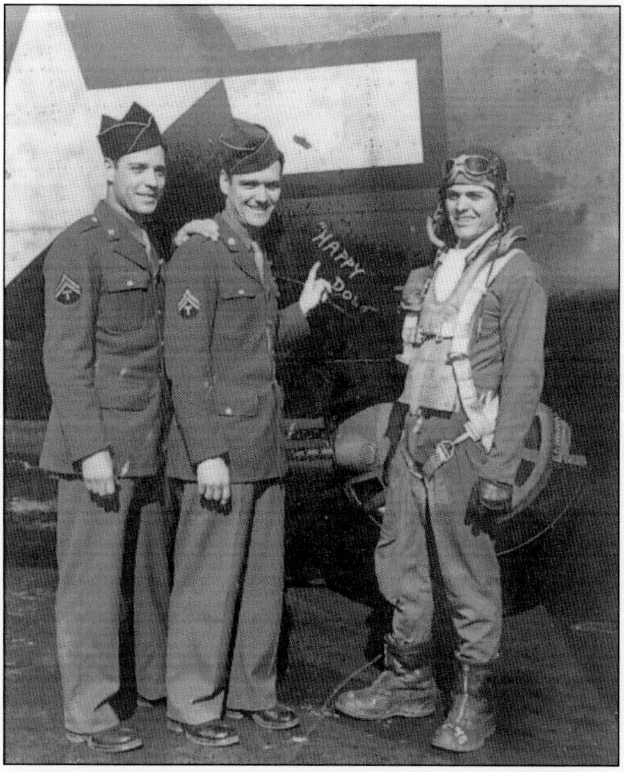

John (left) and George (center) Worsham visited their brother Doug just after he completed a bombing mission from England. George and Doug both lived in Pigeon Forge most of their lives after returning from World War II. (George Worsham collection; courtesy of Pigeon Forge Public Library.)

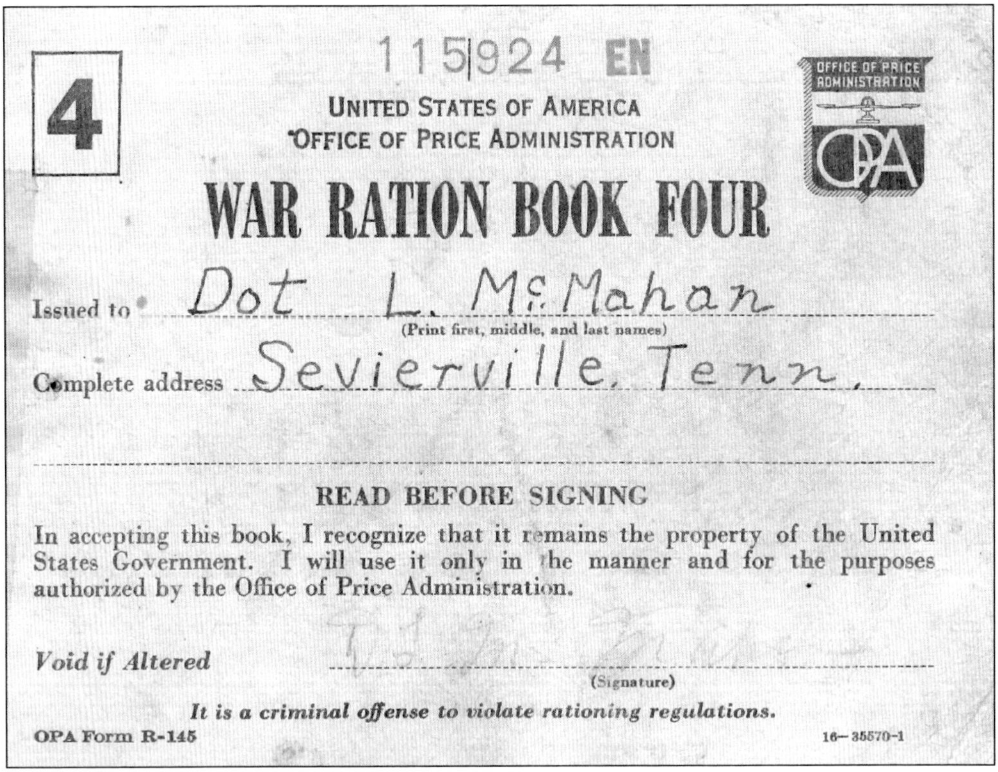

4

115924 EN

UNITED STATES OF AMERICA
OFFICE OF PRICE ADMINISTRATION

OFFICE OF PRICE ADMINISTRATION OPA

WAR RATION BOOK FOUR

Issued to Dot L. McMahan
(Print first, middle, and last names)

Complete address Sevierville, Tenn.

READ BEFORE SIGNING

In accepting this book, I recognize that it remains the property of the United States Government. I will use it only in the manner and for the purposes authorized by the Office of Price Administration.

Void if Altered (Signature)

It is a criminal offense to violate rationing regulations.

OPA Form R-145 16—35570-1

War ration books limited the purchase of items such as sugar and coffee during World War II. This ration book belonged to Dott L. McMahan.

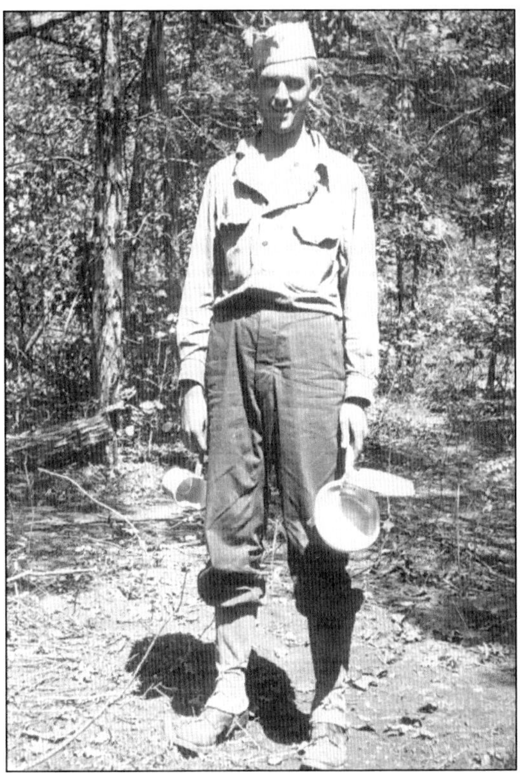

Frank Trotter was a soldier in World War II. The son of Mitchell and Hettie Hatcher Trotter, he lived on Ore Bank Road before Teaster Lane was constructed. (Courtesy of Clara Quarrels Killian.)

John Trotter stands with his son, John Dale, in this photograph taken around 1948. John was the son of Mitchell and Hettie Hatcher Trotter. (Courtesy of Clara Quarrels Watson Killian.)

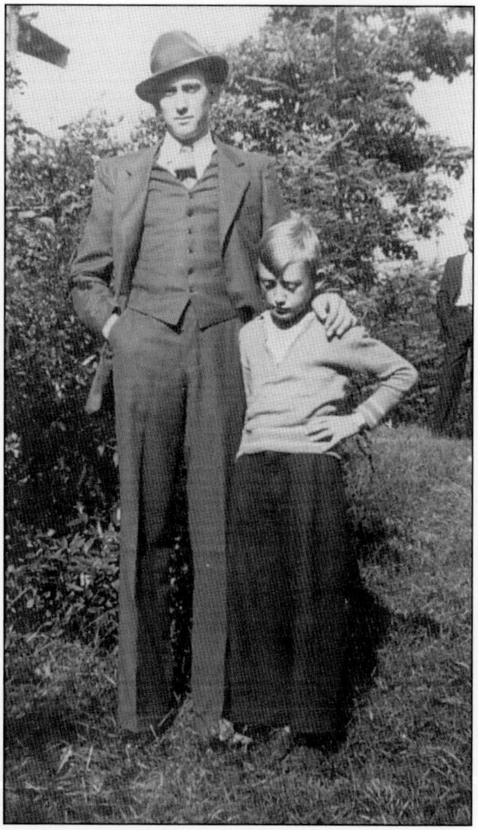

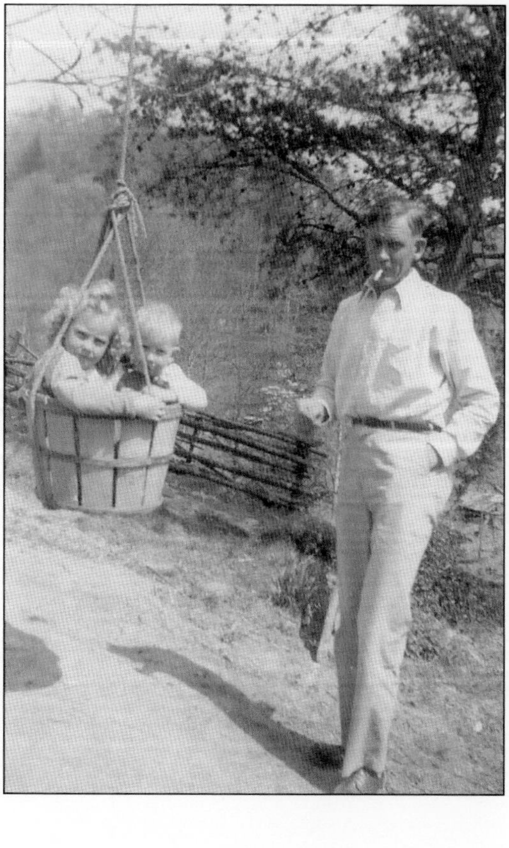

Herman Trotter, son of Mitchell and Hettie Hatcher Trotter, is pictured with two of his children—Martha Raye and Pete—in this Easter photograph taken April 17, 1949. (Courtesy of Clara Quarrels Watson Killian.)

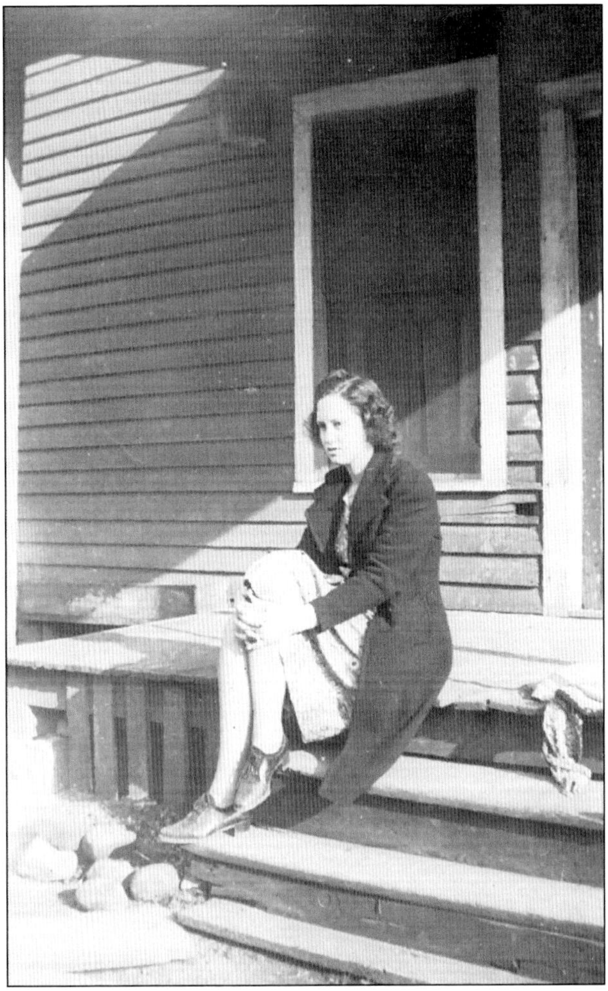

Marjorie Trotter Dixon's photograph was taken in the 1940s. She lived with her parents, Mitchell and Hettie Hatcher Trotter, in Pigeon Forge in her youth. (Courtesy of Clara Quarrels Killian.)

These young Pigeon Forge boys are pictured in the 1930s. They are, from left to right, Fred Spurling, Hugh Emert Robertson, Frank Trotter, David Butler Jr., Victor Marshall Jr., and Phillip Seaton. (Courtesy of James Householder.)

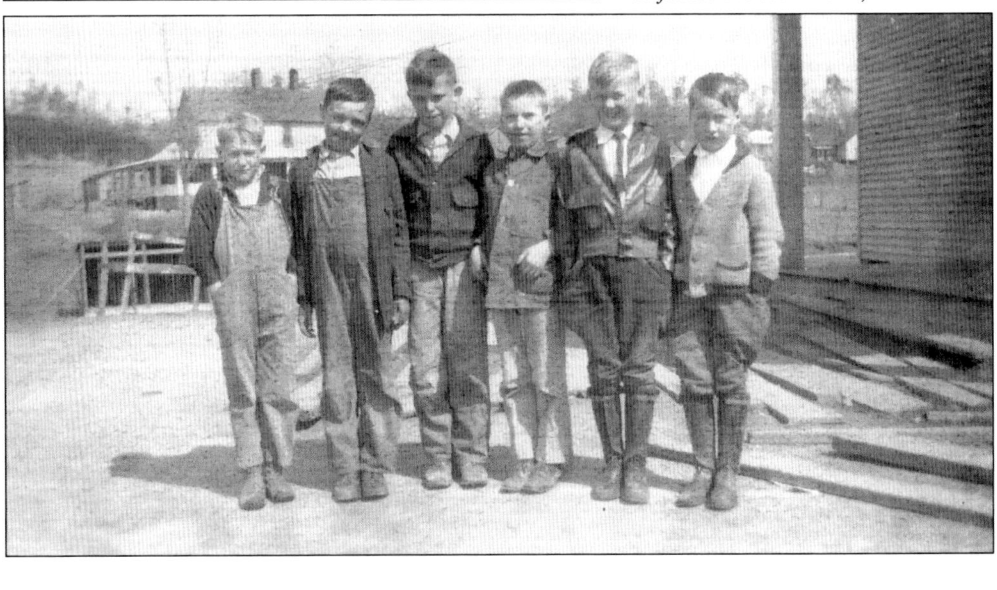

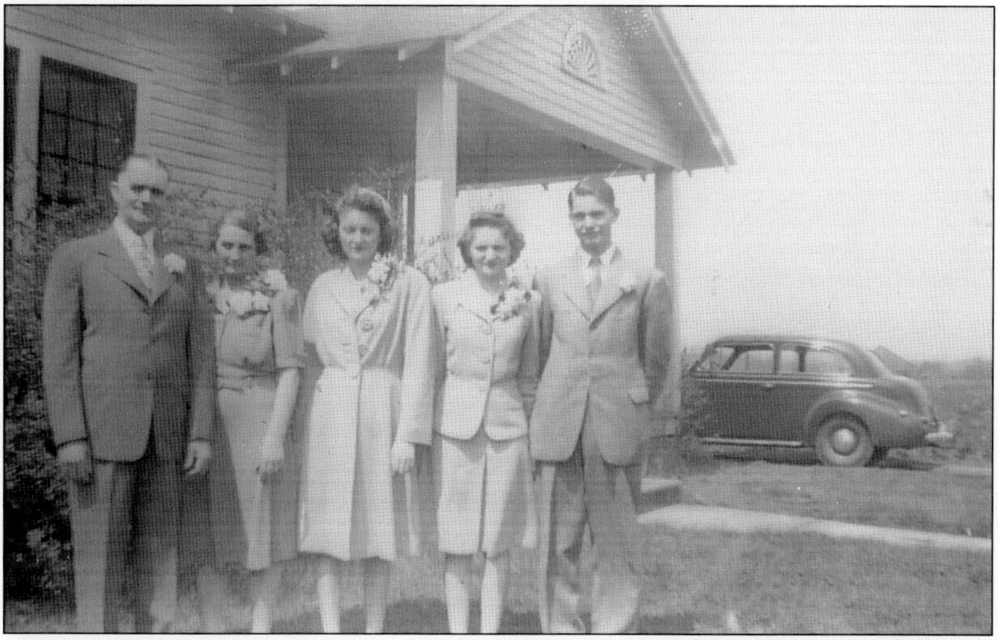

The Householder family is pictured on an Easter Sunday in 1944. They are, from left to right, Dave, Mattie, Belle, Katherine, Marceil, and James. (Courtesy of James Householder.)

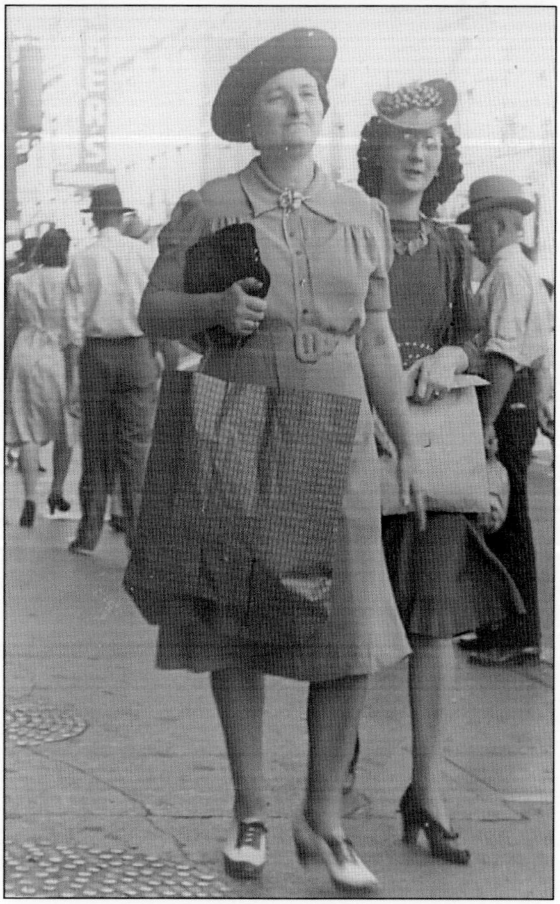

Myrtle Householder and her daughter, Pauline, are shown shopping in Knoxville. Photographers in the larger cities at the time took photographs along the streets and sold them. (Courtesy of James Householder.)

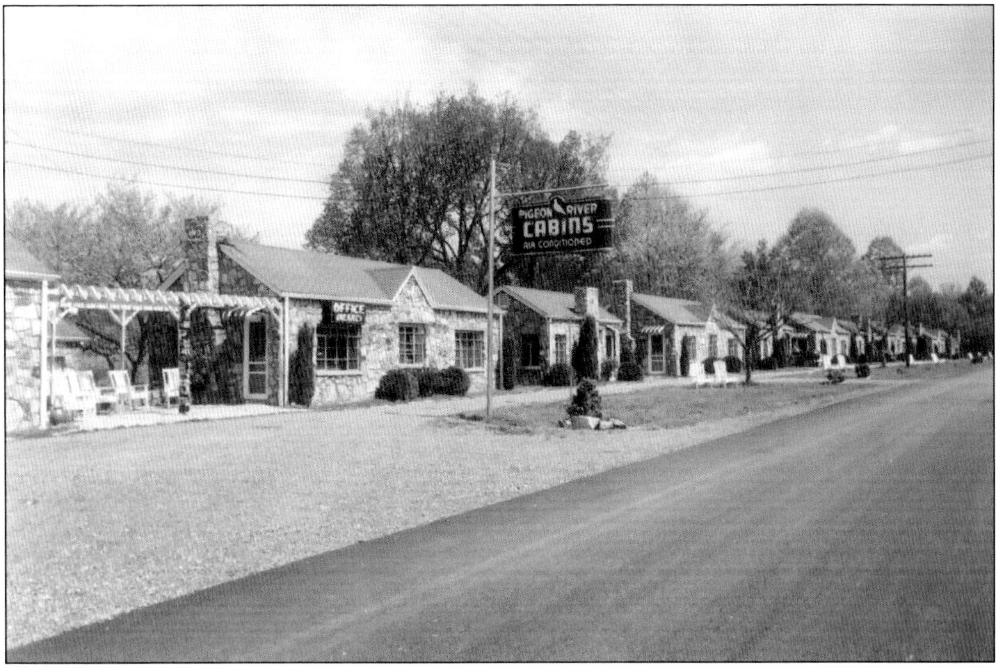

Pigeon River Court, originally owned by Dr. R. A. Broady, was among the first tourism businesses in Pigeon Forge. It was on the south end of the town near the river. At one time, George Worsham and James Maples owned and operated it and rented rooms for only a few dollars a night. (Photograph by Thompson Photo Products, Knoxville.)

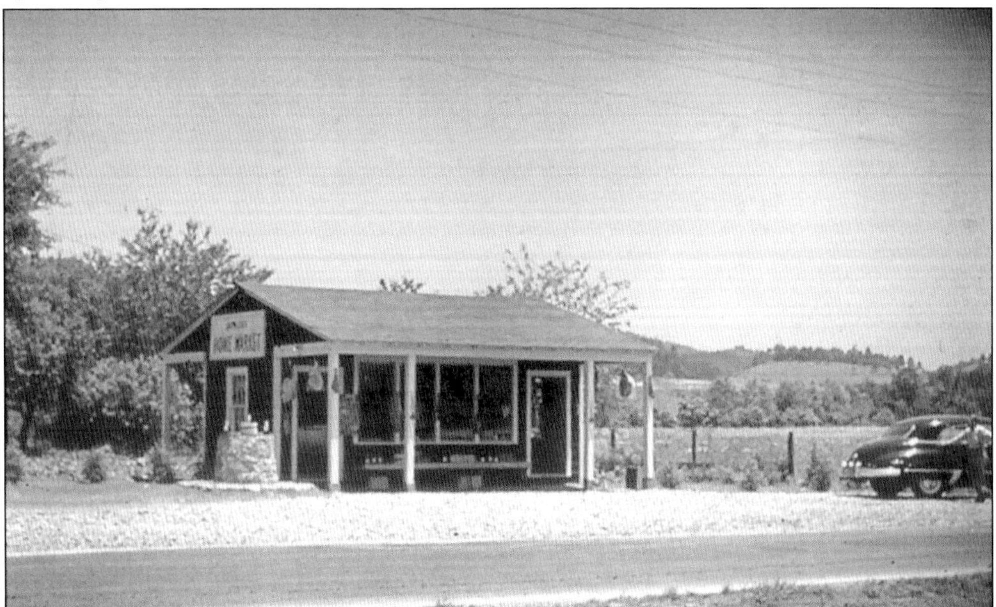

Butler's Home Market operated along the Parkway, selling country hams, honey, hand-woven rugs, and baskets in the middle of the 1900s. This roadside stand later became Forge Hammer Grill and was also a favorite family-style restaurant named Apple Tree Inn for many years. (Courtesy of James and Julia Householder.)

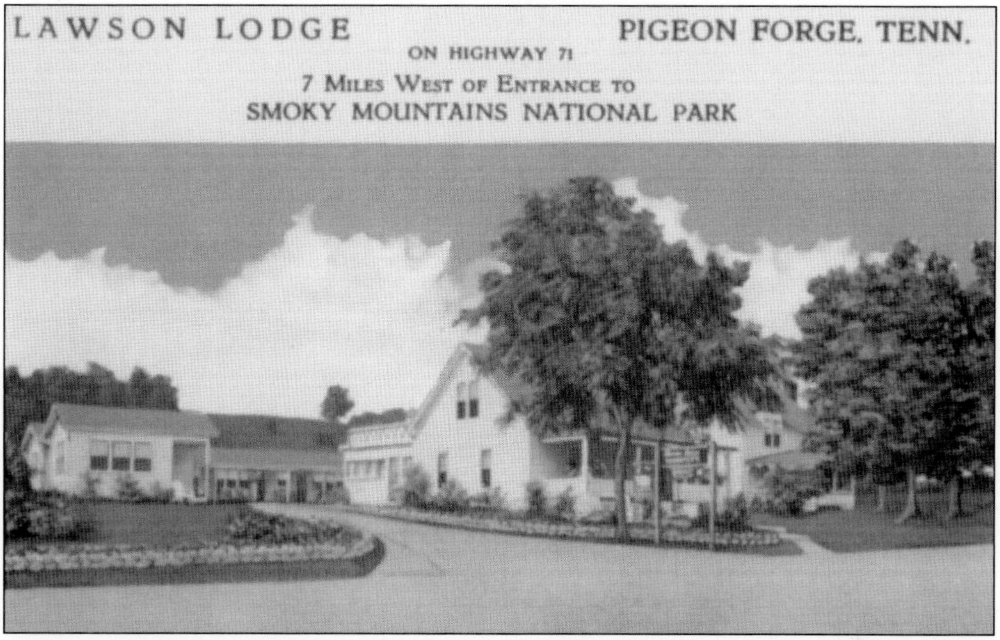

Mel Lawson's Lawson Lodge was a small, family-run lodging operation near the Methodist church. In the 1950s, Tom and Sally Morrisey purchased it and renamed it the Forge Motel. As the town grew, the business was razed, and Tennessee Mountain Lodge is in its place today. (Courtesy of Janice M. Crowe.)

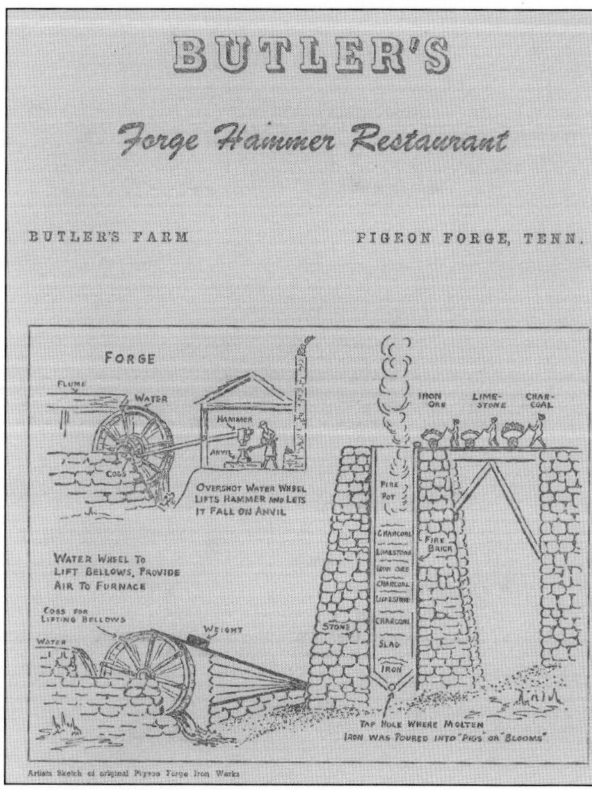

Butler's Forge Hammer Grill menu presented a sketch of the early ironworks operation in the town. It showed how the iron ore was placed into the furnace and smelted and how the waterwheel powered the bellows for the forges. Henry Butler's restaurant was located on his father Ashley Butler's family farm along the new highway in the 1950s. Kyle and Garnett Cole later operated the restaurant, known as the Apple Tree Inn. It had a live apple tree growing through the patio roof. (Courtesy of Jerry Loveday.)

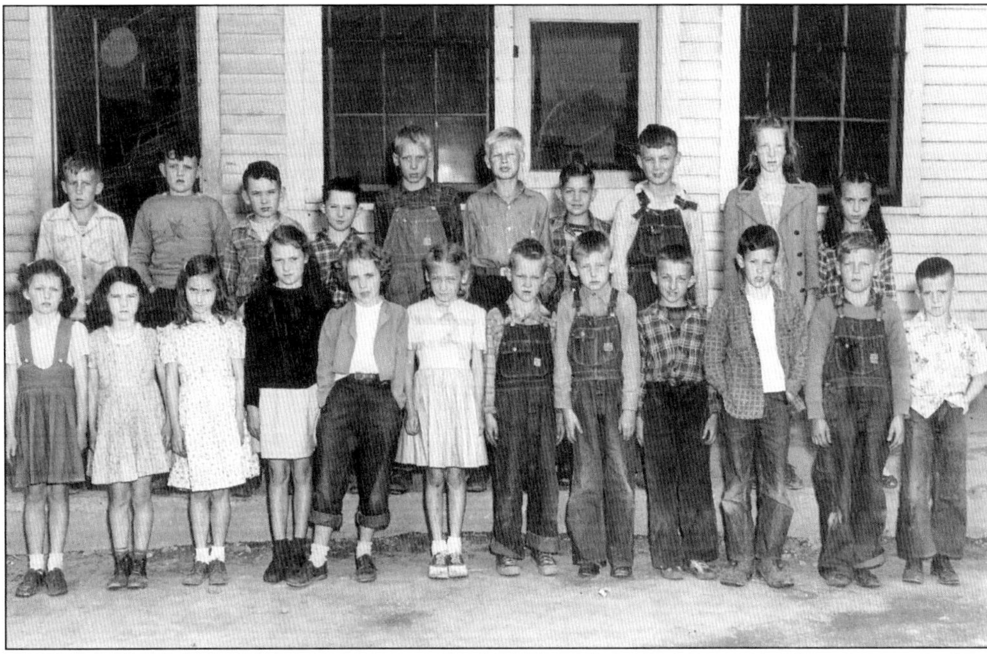

These students were attending Pigeon Forge Grammar School in 1948 when it was a white weatherboard building on the hill near the Old Mill area. The students are, from left to right, (first row) Wanda Trevena, Shirley Canton, Carolyn Barnes, Christine McCarter, Avalee Ward, Mary Lou Cardwell, Junior Reagan, James Stogner, David Householder, David Montgomery, Bob Woodruff, and Billy Ray Whaley; (second row) Max Trotter, Ted Campbell, James David Ogle, Jerry Ogle, R. Ogle, Perry (Cotton) Adams, James Delozier, Glenn Maples, Ruby Henry, and Carolyn Whaley. (Courtesy of Rena Ogle.)

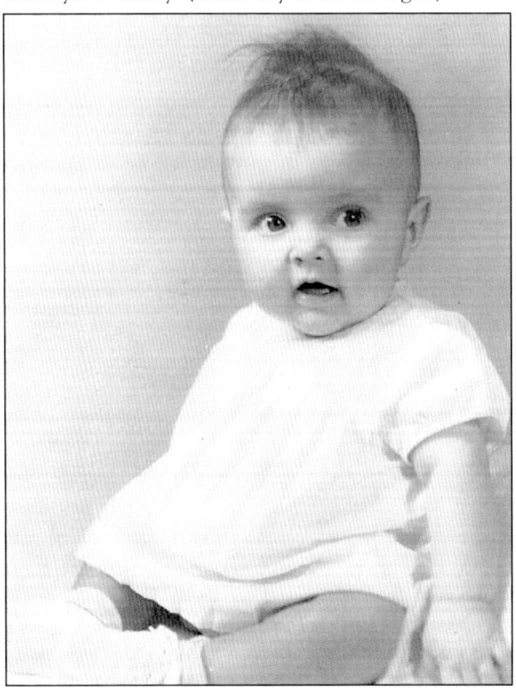

Gwendell Lamons lived on Dixie Avenue in Pigeon Forge in her youth. She is the daughter of Wiley and Kate Proffitt Lamons. Gwendell's mother died when she was a little girl, and she spent much time with her grandparents and learned from their years of wisdom the ways of a generation removed. (Courtesy of Gwendell Lamons Cody.)

Ronny Rader stands by his home just off Ogle Drive sometime around 1944. His parents were Al and Louise Ogle Rader and his brother was Ricky. Ron's mother operated a store by the Old Mill area, and his grandfather, Dr. John Ogle, was a longtime physician in the area. (Courtesy of Ron Rader.)

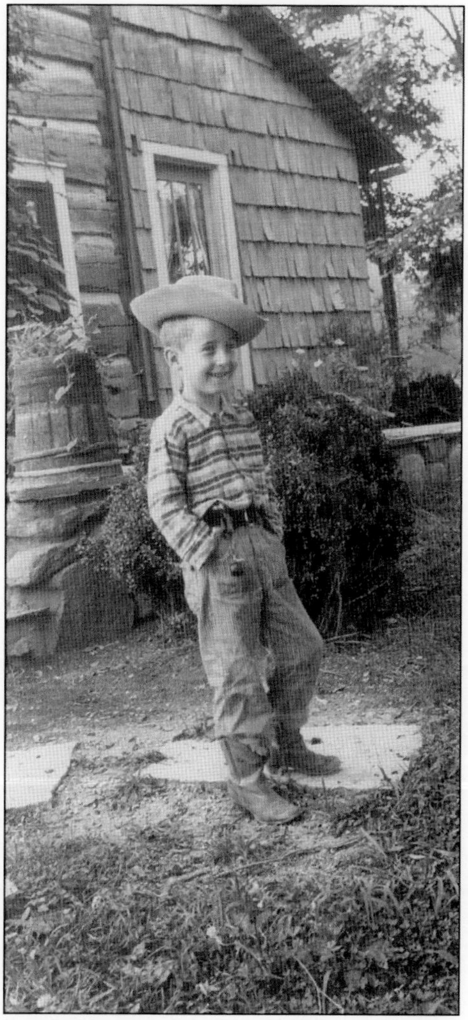

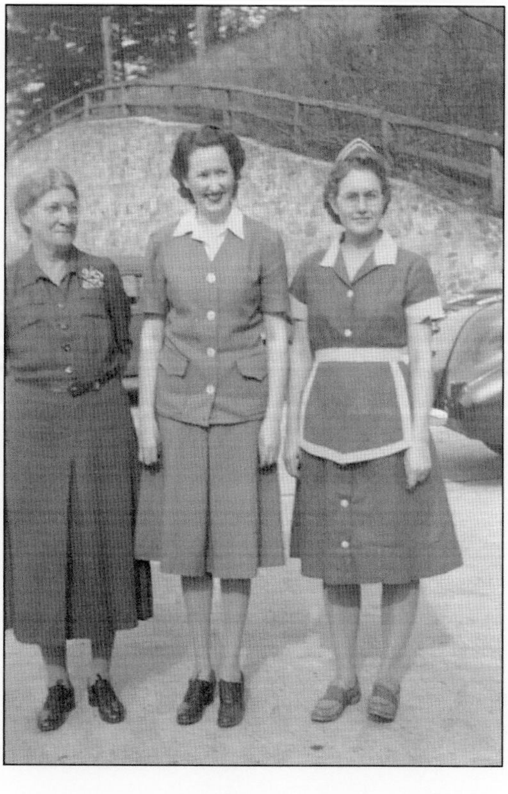

Evelyn McCarter was a waitress at the Hotel Greystone in Gatlinburg in her early years. She is married to English McCarter, former mayor of Pigeon Forge. She is pictured here, at right, with two unidentified women. (Courtesy of English McCarter.)

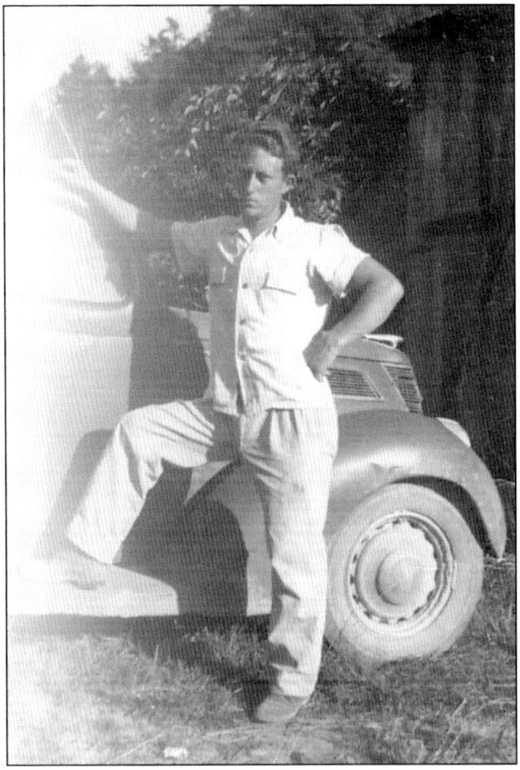

Alvin Ogle poses with this 1930s automobile. He was born in Baskin's Creek and moved to Walden's Creek, where he and his wife, Sue Wilson Ogle, live. Ogle served in World War II. (Courtesy of Alvin Ogle.)

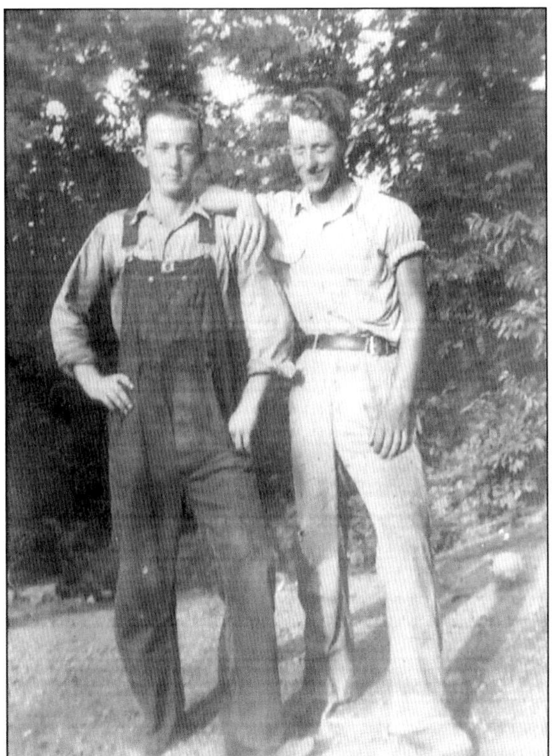

Alvin Ogle, right, stands with his brother, Elmer. They are the sons of Dewey and Mollie Ogle, who lived on Walden's Creek. Others in the family are sisters Mattie and Nelma Rose. Alvin and Nelma Rose are the only two of the Ogle family still living. (Courtesy of Alvin Ogle.)

Hugh Emert Robertson, right, is pictured with Phil Seaton outside this Esso service station owned by Hugh's father, Sam Robertson. Family members believe the woman in the background is Jessie Sims. The garage sat between Louise Rader's shop, the Pigeon Forge Center, and the Parkway. It was later operated by Gus Ward and Glenn Beal in a new building they constructed a few hundred feet north of this site. (Courtesy of Pigeon Forge Public Library.)

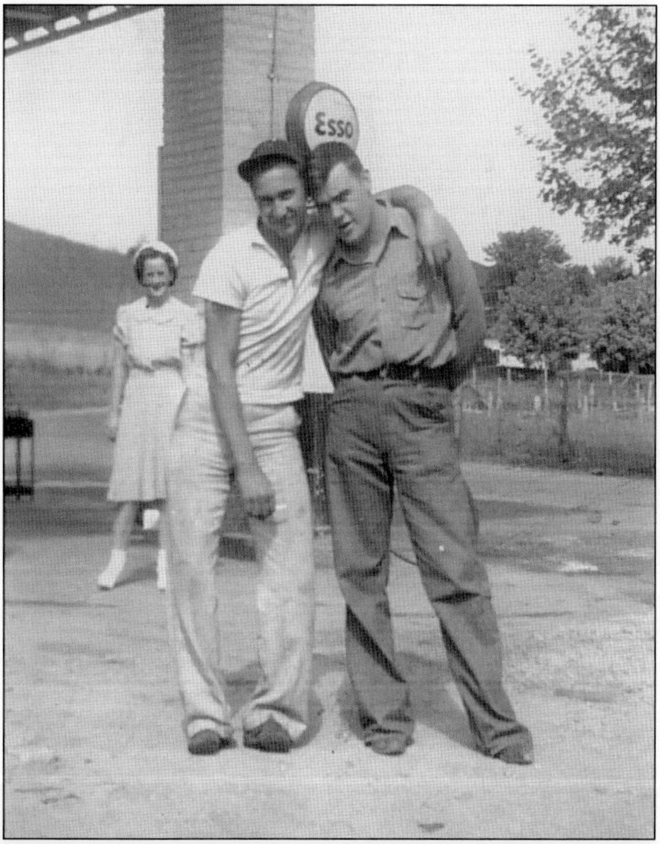

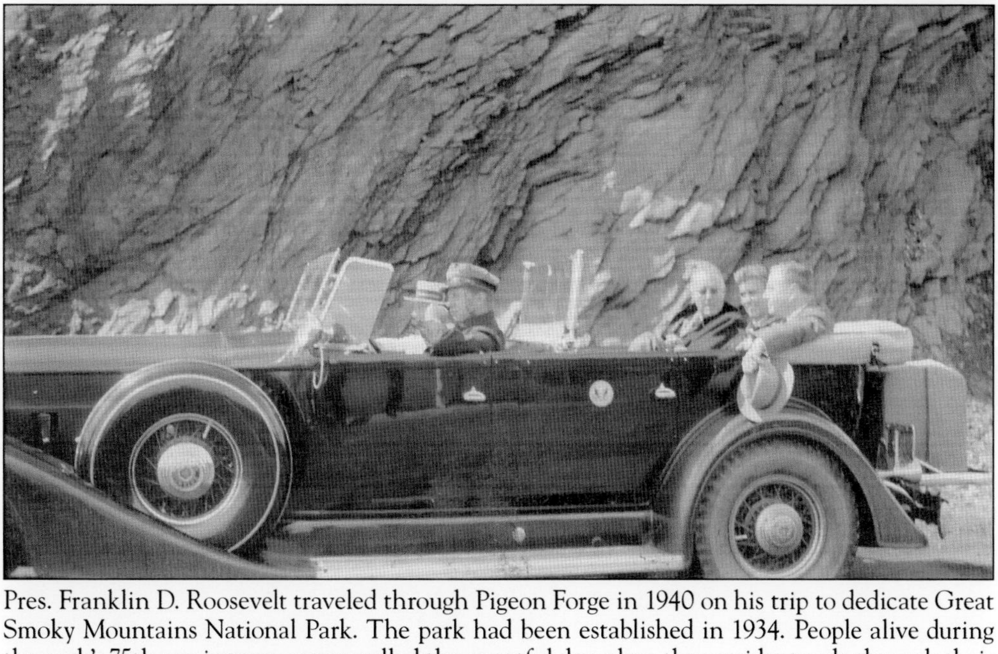

Pres. Franklin D. Roosevelt traveled through Pigeon Forge in 1940 on his trip to dedicate Great Smoky Mountains National Park. The park had been established in 1934. People alive during the park's 75th anniversary year recalled the eventful day when the president rode through their town. (Courtesy of Henrietta Franklin Sharp.)

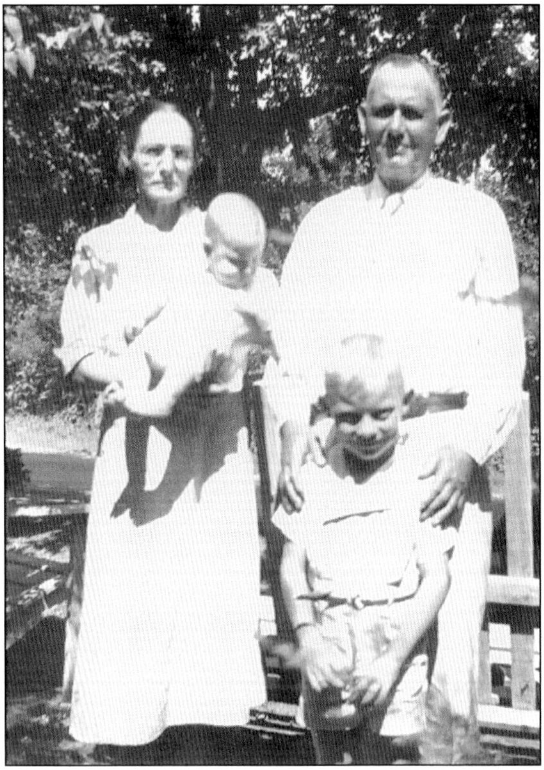

John T. and Emma Householder Wynn are pictured in this 1940s photograph with granddaughter Emma Sue Delozier and grandson Billy Wynn Allen. (Courtesy of Bill and Jody Allen.)

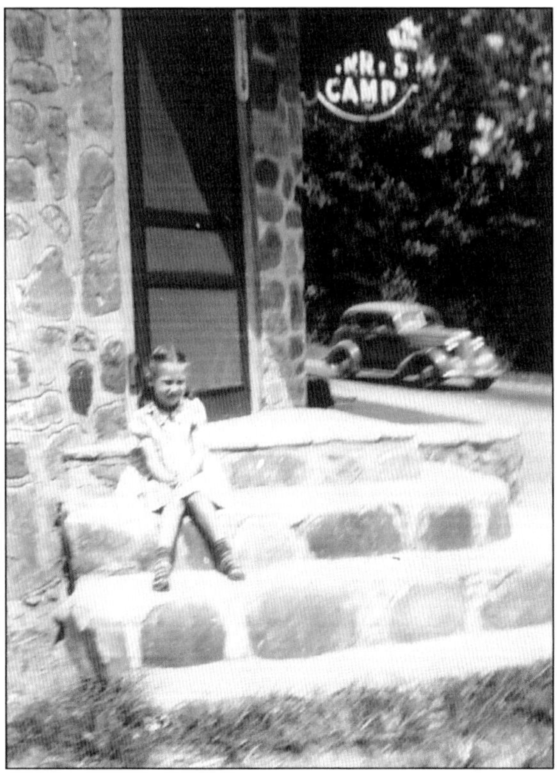

Clara Quarrels sits on the steps of Perry's Camp, which was located on the road between Pigeon Forge and Gatlinburg. This 1939 photograph was taken when there was one small, precarious road between the two communities. The girl's father was a friend of the camp owner. A few years after this picture was taken, the owner and one other woman were brutally murdered at this site. (Courtesy of Clara Quarrels Watson Killian.)

Young Bobby Quarrels lived in the two-story white farmhouse pictured below with his parents, Bill and Ruth Quarrels; his sister, Clara; and his half brother, Harold. Neighbors along this row of nice homes included the Emory, Fain, Davis, Stott, Delozier, and Householder families. (Courtesy of Clara Quarrels Watson Killian.)

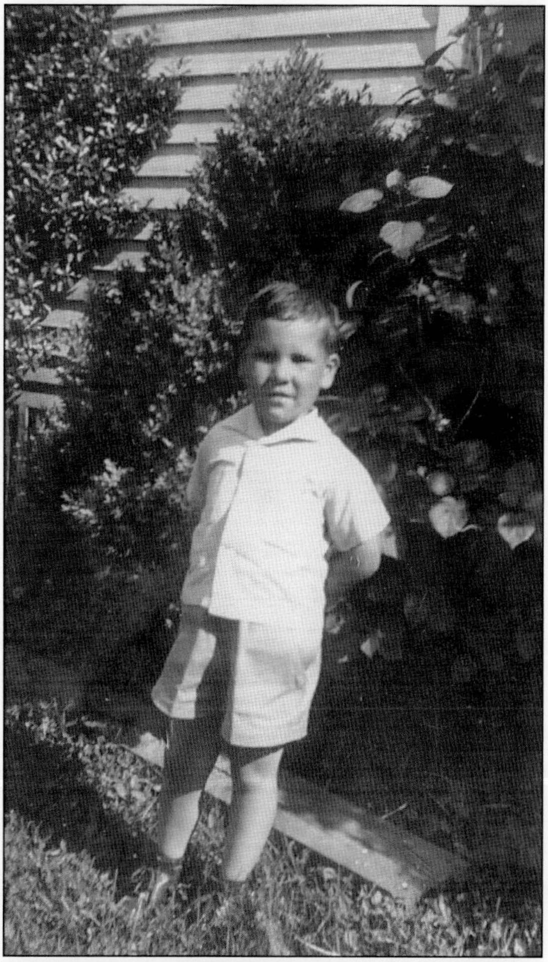

Bill and Ruth Quarrels are pictured with their daughter, Clara, and Bill's son, Harold, at their home on River Road near the historic Old Mill. When Clara was young, she loved to sleep on the screened second-story balcony and listen to the night sounds. (Courtesy of Clara Quarrels Killian.)

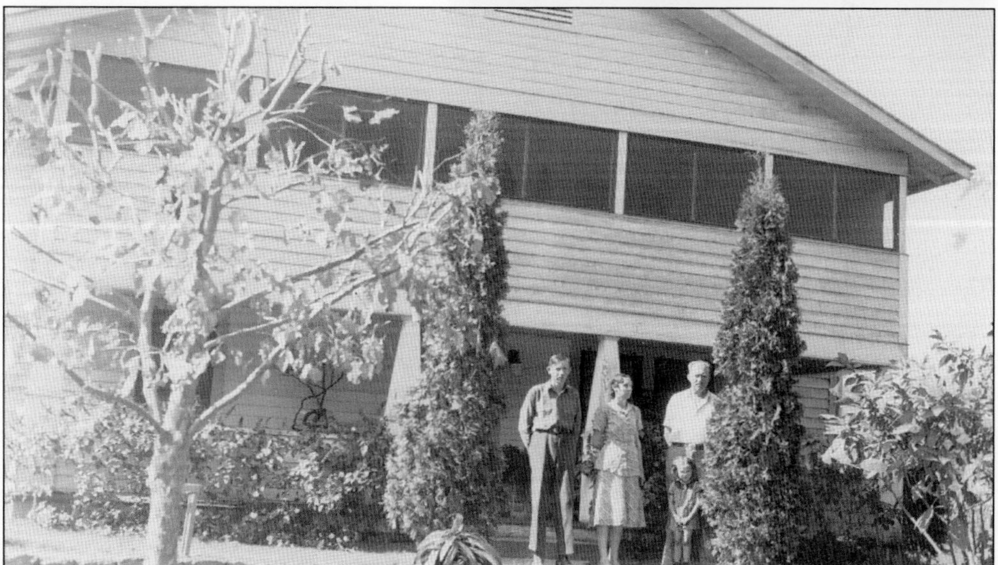

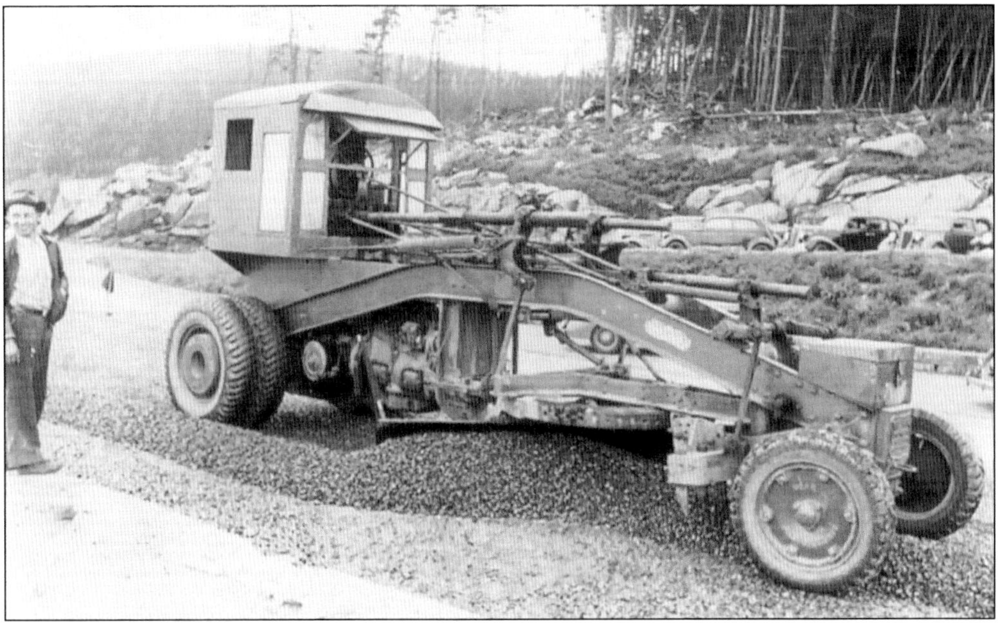

Ernest Ogle drove this grader for Great Smoky Mountains National Park for 20 years. The son of Dave and Mollie Ogle, he lived in Pigeon Forge when he and Lucinda Oakley (daughter of Wiley and Rebecca Oakley) were first married. (Lucinda Oakley Ogle collection.)

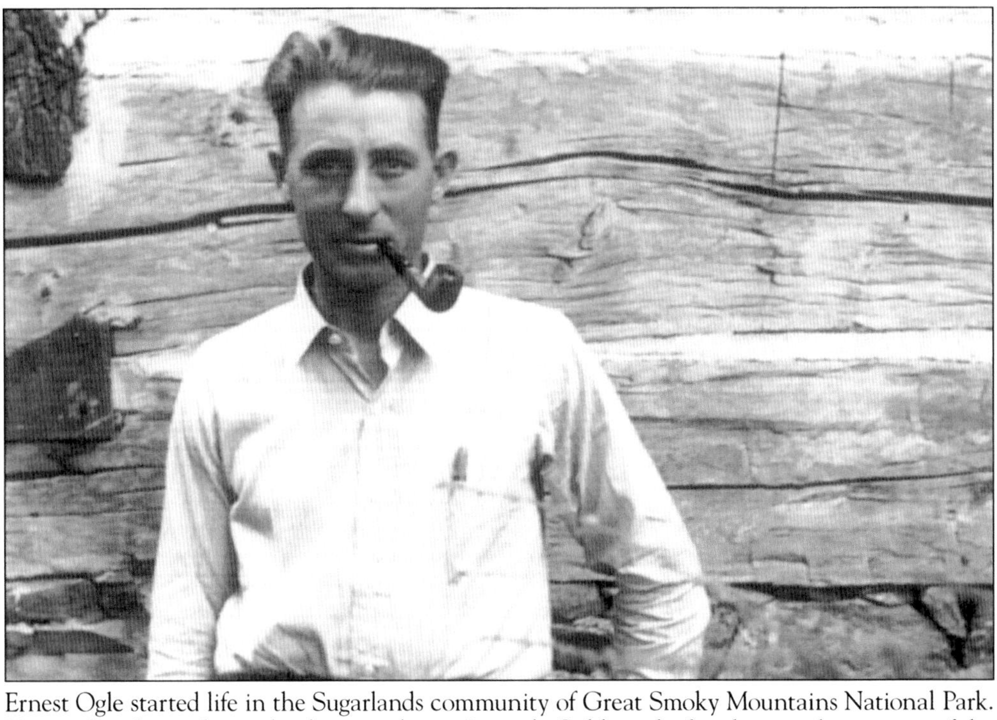

Ernest Ogle started life in the Sugarlands community of Great Smoky Mountains National Park. He sent love letters by mail to his sweetheart, Lucinda Oakley, who lived in another section of the park before they married. While living in Pigeon Forge, the couple traveled to the 1939 New York World's Fair with their two daughters, Frances and Billie, and presented the mountain way of life in a cabin on-site. They were there for one month. (Courtesy of Pigeon Forge Public Library.)

Billy Wynn Allen was two years old when this photograph was taken in 1936. From his childhood, he remembers the slow easy pace of small-town Pigeon Forge and playing in the historic Old Mill. (Courtesy of Bill and Jody Allen.)

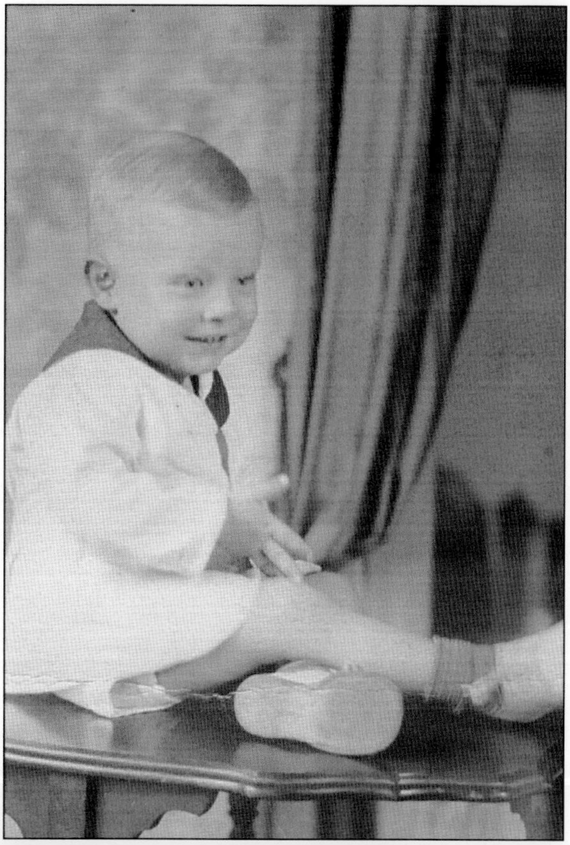

Pictured in this 1940s photograph are the children of Jess and Beedie Cole. From left to right are Judy, Charles, and Jody. The family lived just off Walden's Creek Road. (Courtesy of Bill and Jody Allen.)

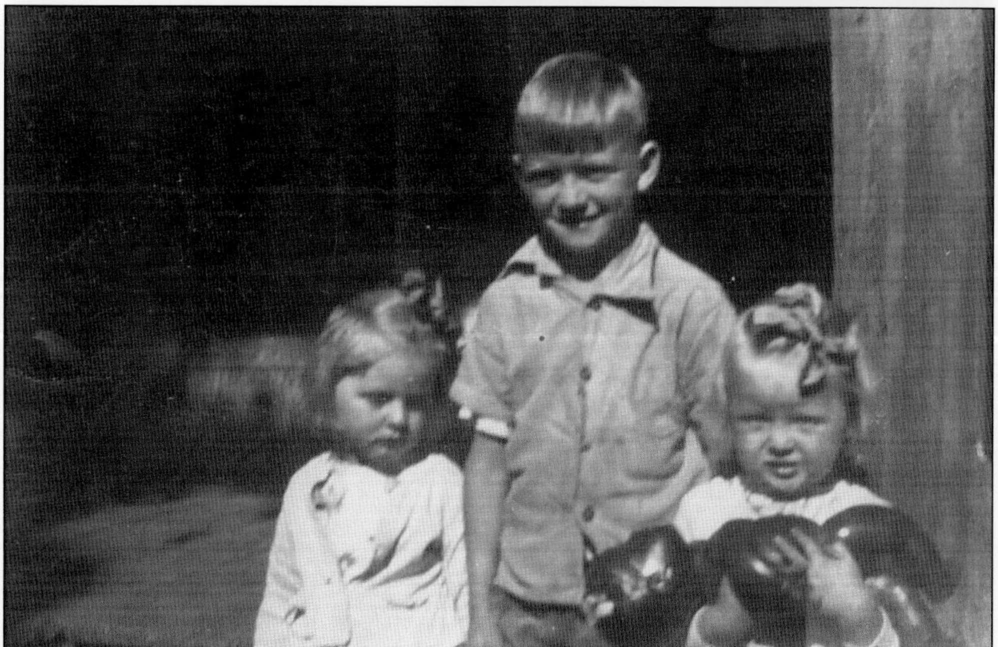

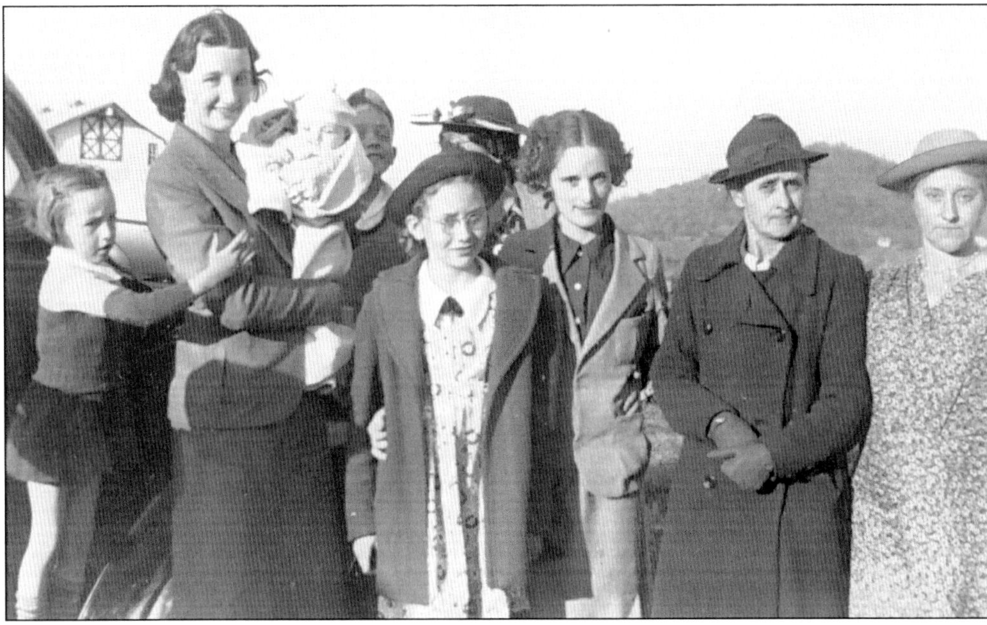

Lydia Robertson Householder, standing with her baby David, is pictured with family and friends. Standing at left is her daughter Jo Ann and hidden behind Lydia is her son Marion. Pictured to the right of Lydia are, from left to right, Ada McMahan, Mildred Householder, Carrie Gobble Householder, and Kettie Emert Gobble. Hidden behind Ada may be Elizabeth Gobble. (Courtesy of the Dott L. McMahan collection.)

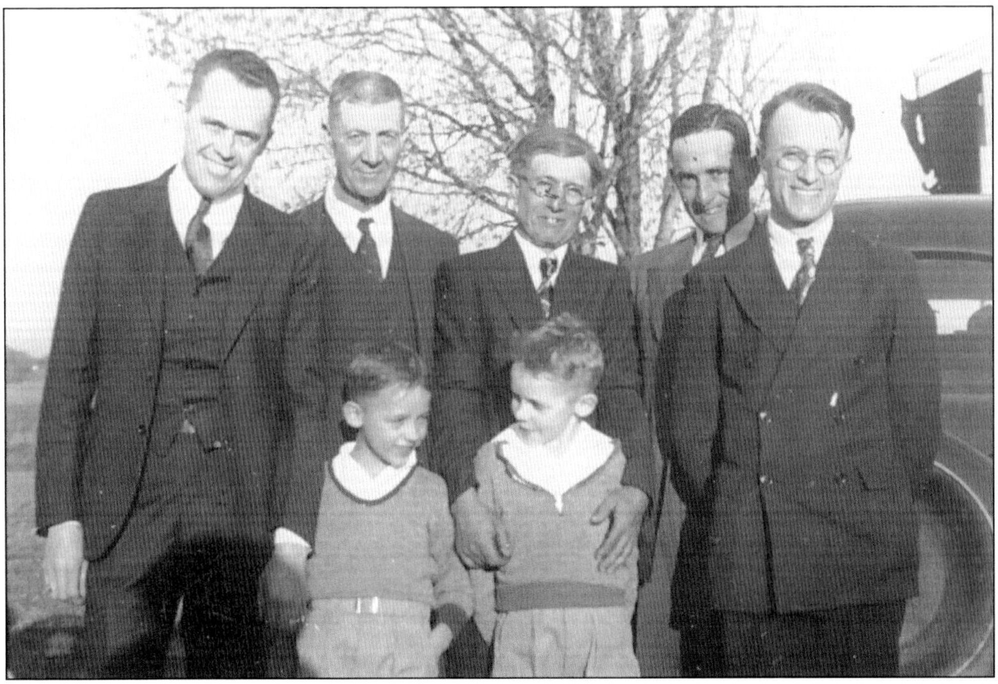

Householder and Gobble family members are pictured from left to right as follows: (first row) Ralph and Henry Law; (second row) Paul Law, George McMahan, Charley Gobble, Henry Householder, and Emert Gobble. (Courtesy of the Dott L. McMahan collection.)

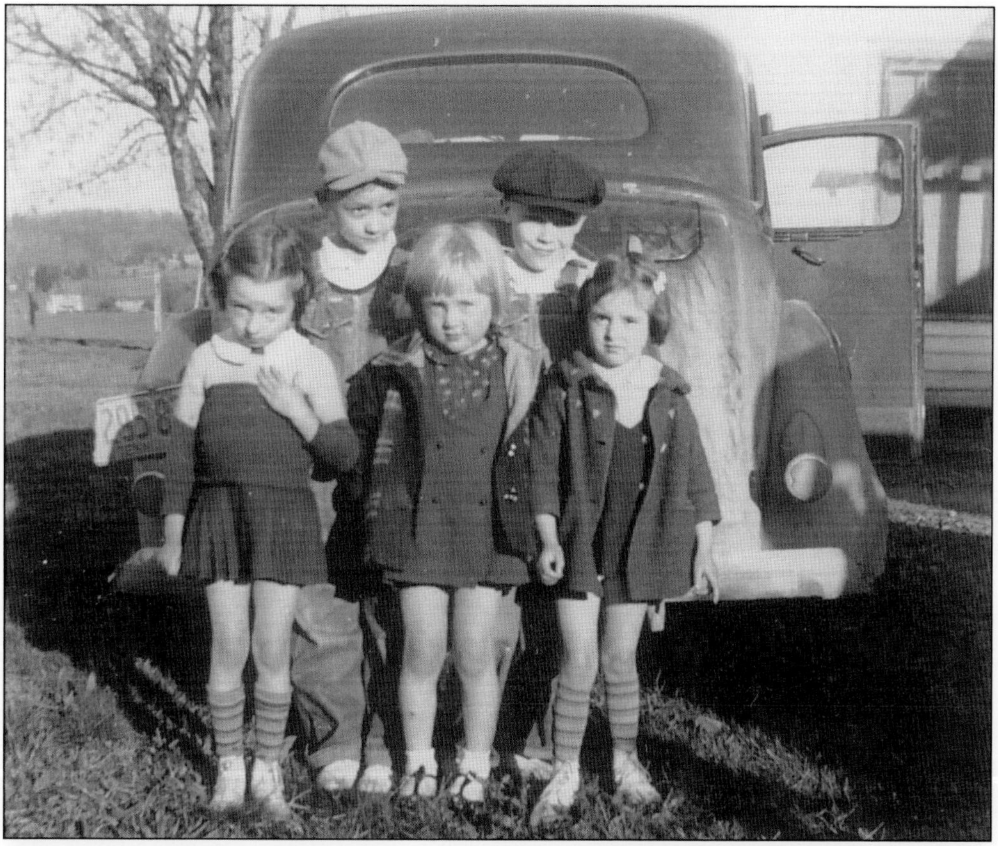

These youngsters look as if they have stepped from a Shirley Temple film. Pictured are, from left to right, (first row) Jo Ann and Louise Householder and Margaret Ogle; (second row) Ralph and Henry Law. Jo Ann was the daughter of Henry Householder, and Louise's father was Mayford Householder, who died when Louise was a baby. Margaret's parents were Rellie and Mildred Householder Ogle. The Law boys were sons of Paul and Ada McMahan Law. (Courtesy of the Dott L. McMahan collection.)

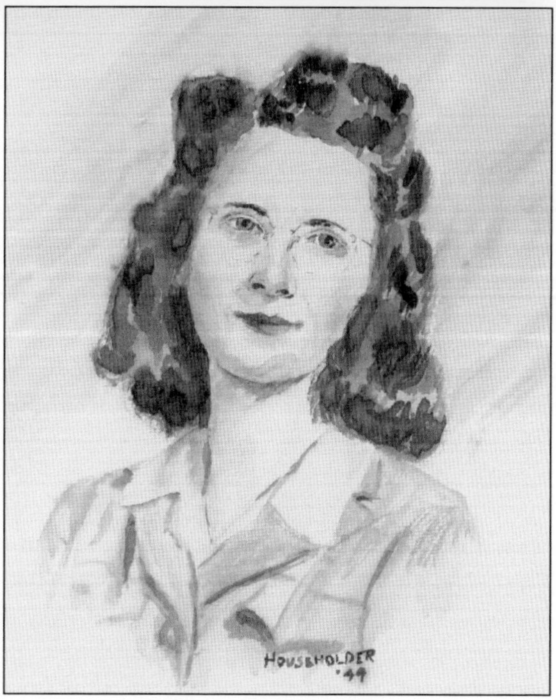

This artist's sketch is a self-portrait of Pauline Householder made in 1944. The schoolteacher, with her paintbrush in hand, spent many hours painting the Old Mill, river scenes, and wildflowers. She helped to record and present the history of Pigeon Forge. (Courtesy of Jerry Loveday.)

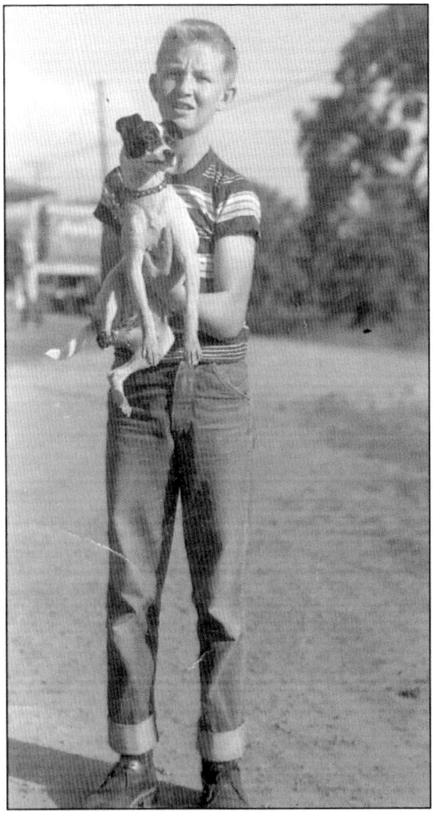

Herman Adams poses for this mid-1950s photograph with his dog Cricket. Herman seemed to often be the target for his brother's camera as Herbert experimented with picture taking. (Courtesy of Herman Adams.)

Herbert Adams (left) stands with his brother Herman Adams on a day when the Old Mill dam's floodgates were opened around 1953. This was done periodically for repairs. The two boys lived within walking distance of the Old Mill. (Courtesy of Herman Adams.)

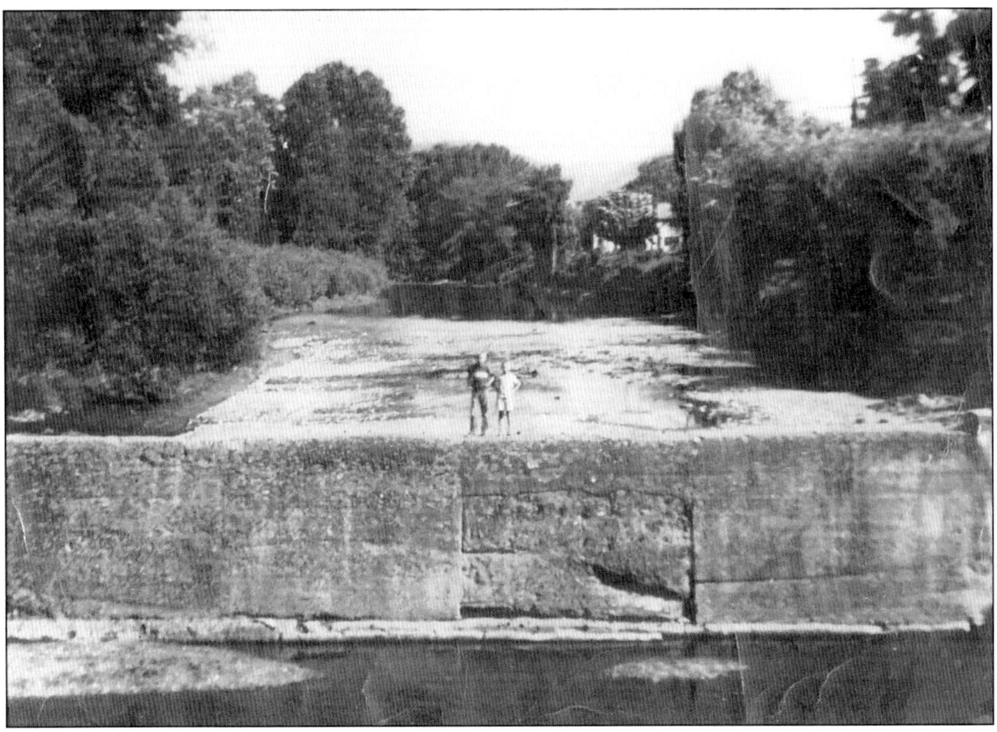

Three

Roadside Cottages and Smoked Hams Beckon Tourists

Once Great Smoky Mountains National Park was established, Pigeon Forge residents likely gave it little thought until the 1950s. By then, more vacationing families had discovered the national park, and residents saw it as an opportunity to invest in tourism. The Great Smoky Mountains National Park's greatest presence was felt when the road machinery carved out a new divided highway through town as a major park access. After the Second World War, life became simple again. Pigeon Forge had its few cafés, garages, and the little post office that relocated from one general store to another depending on the politics. Young people rode bicycles everywhere; they fished in the Little Pigeon River. There was ice-skating on the millpond or roller-skating in the old school building. On sunny days, young men and women drove their wide 1955 Chevrolets into the mountains for picnics. Until the mid-1950s, youngsters attended grammar school at the white weatherboard building above the Old Mill near the site once used for a cannery. The population of this unincorporated area was around 650.

According to a "Pigeon Forge Anvil" article by Betty Edmondson, houses were being built on the east side of the river in Butler Addition, on the west side in Conner Heights, and in the area known as the Flannigan Addition. All across the county, new subdivisions were popping up in the postwar building expansion as families moved from the farms. Many of these families became the pioneers of Pigeon Forge's fledgling tourism industry. Vacation accommodations operating were Dr. Robert A. Broady's Pigeon River Courts, Vic Marshall's Marshall Courts, the Forge Motel owned by Mel Lawson, and the Flower Garden owned by Ben Robertson. Restaurants included the Pigeon Valley or the Green Pigeon, Butler's Forge Hammer Grill, Steele's Drive-In, and Tebo Watson's Pigeon Forge Restaurant. The Miller Brothers of circus fame operated Fort Weare, a zoo with animal acts that was known later as Jungle Cargo. In late 1961 came Rebel Railroad just outside Pigeon Forge. This was the attraction that later became Goldrush Junction, then Silver Dollar City, and finally Dollywood.

The tourism business community expanded, offering lower-priced lodging and home-cooked family-style meals to entice travelers before they reached more well-established Gatlinburg. In years to come, these men and women of vision, along with the town's strong leadership, would shape Pigeon Forge into a premier resort destination at the foot of the Great Smoky Mountains.

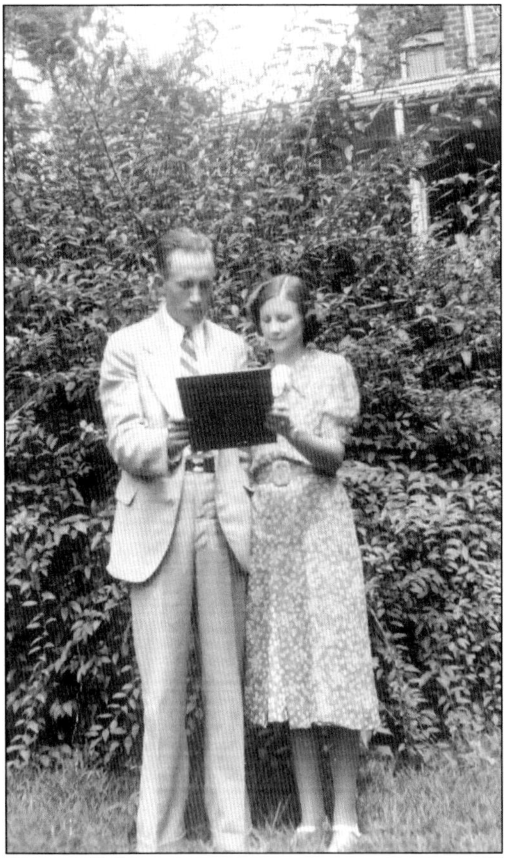

Estel Ownby proudly examines his wife Ruth's degree from Carson-Newman College in the late 1930s or early 1940s. The couple had one daughter, Sarah; all three were active in First Baptist Church of Pigeon Forge. (Courtesy of Sarah Ball.)

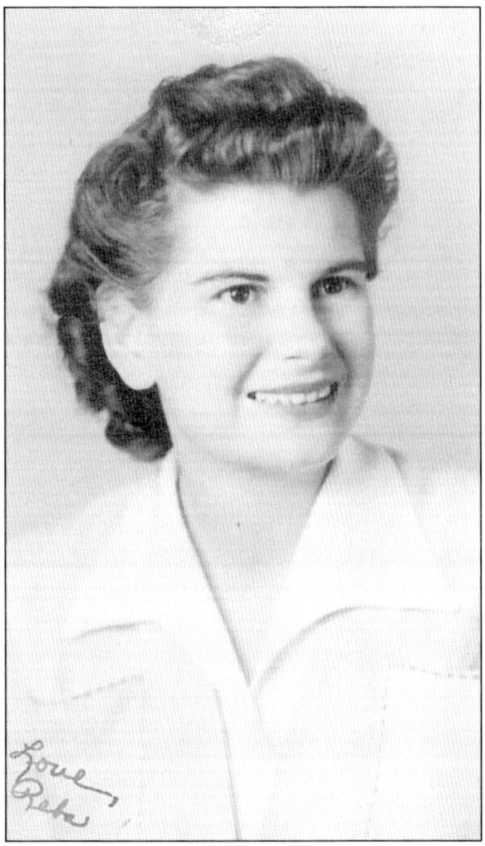

Reba Caughron Hood taught three or four generations of first graders at Pigeon Forge Grammar School. Her warm smile eased first-day jitters for many little boys and girls in the area. (Courtesy of Sarah Ball.)

Friends gather for a Christmas celebration in 1962. Pictured are, from left to right, Ruby and Vic Allen, Oliver and Mary Trotter, and Mark and Nina Delozier. These couples have family roots tracing back to some of Pigeon Forge's earliest settlers. (Courtesy of Bill and Jody Allen.)

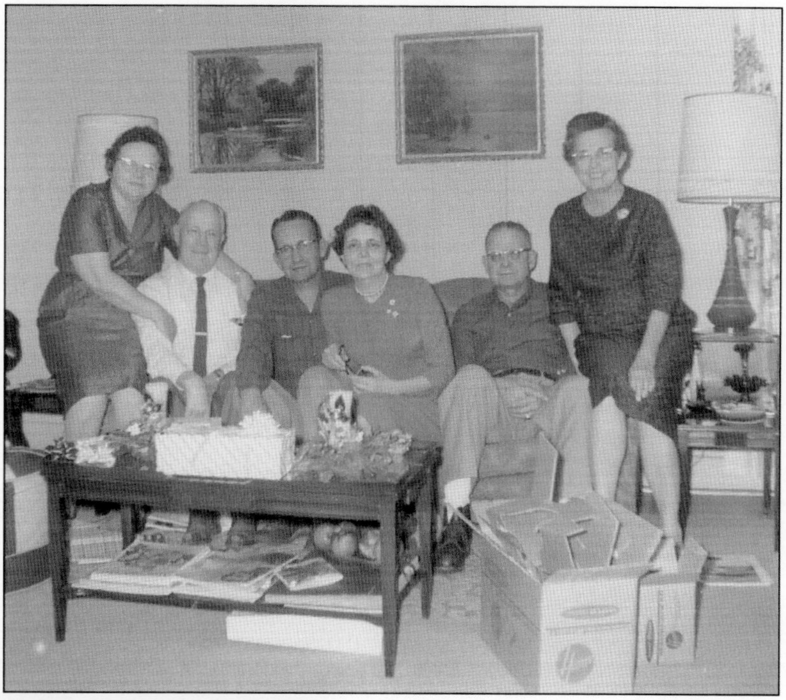

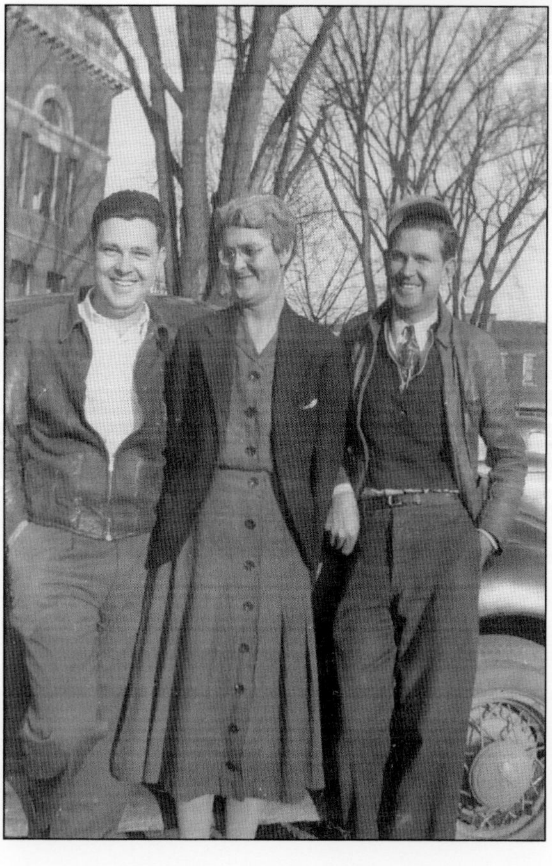

Becky Fleming Davenport Watson stands with her two boys, Xan (left) and Herman by the Sevier County Courthouse. Xan was one of Pigeon Forge's first three city commissioners, and he served as register of deeds for the county. Herman retired from the Alcoa Aluminum Plant. (Courtesy of Bill Davenport.)

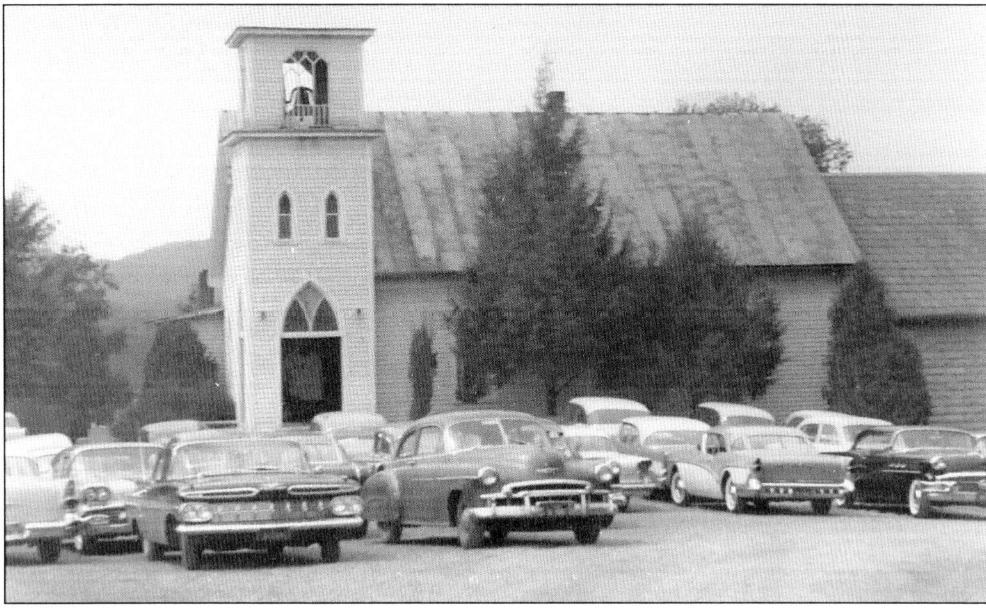

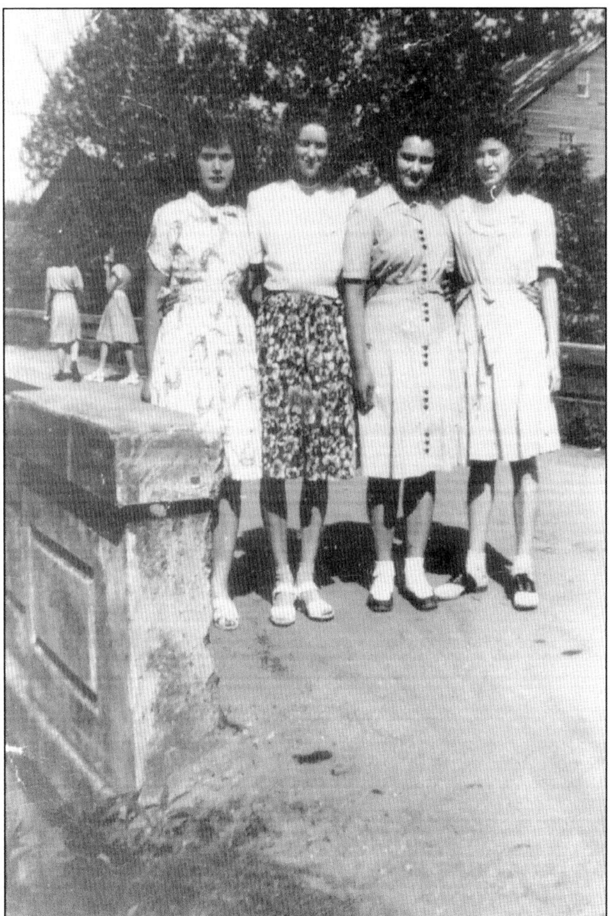

The First Baptist Church of Pigeon Forge was organized in the early 1900s. It was located on the hill by the Baptist cemetery near present-day Dollywood Lane. Sometime before the new church was constructed, a windstorm destroyed its bell tower. (Courtesy of Pigeon Forge Public Library.)

After church on Sundays, friends walked home together and ate Sunday dinner at the home of one or the other. Pictured here are two Wilson sisters visiting with the Maples girls. From left to right are Irene Wilson, Blanche Maples, Ruby Wilson, and Kate Maples. (Courtesy of the Ruth Wilson family.)

It was a red-letter day for the First Baptist Church of Pigeon Forge when they broke ground for a new building on the Parkway in the spring of 1959. Some of those attending are pictured here, from left to right, Gertrude Householder Roberts, a charter member; Linda Sue McCarter, the youngest member of the congregation; James Lauderback, pastor; and Sam Ownby, oldest attending member. (Photograph by Bashor's Photos, Sevierville; courtesy of Sarah Ball.)

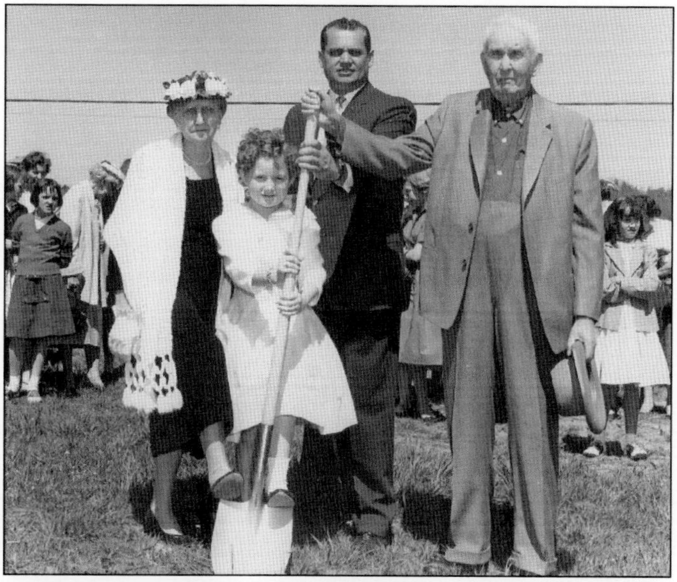

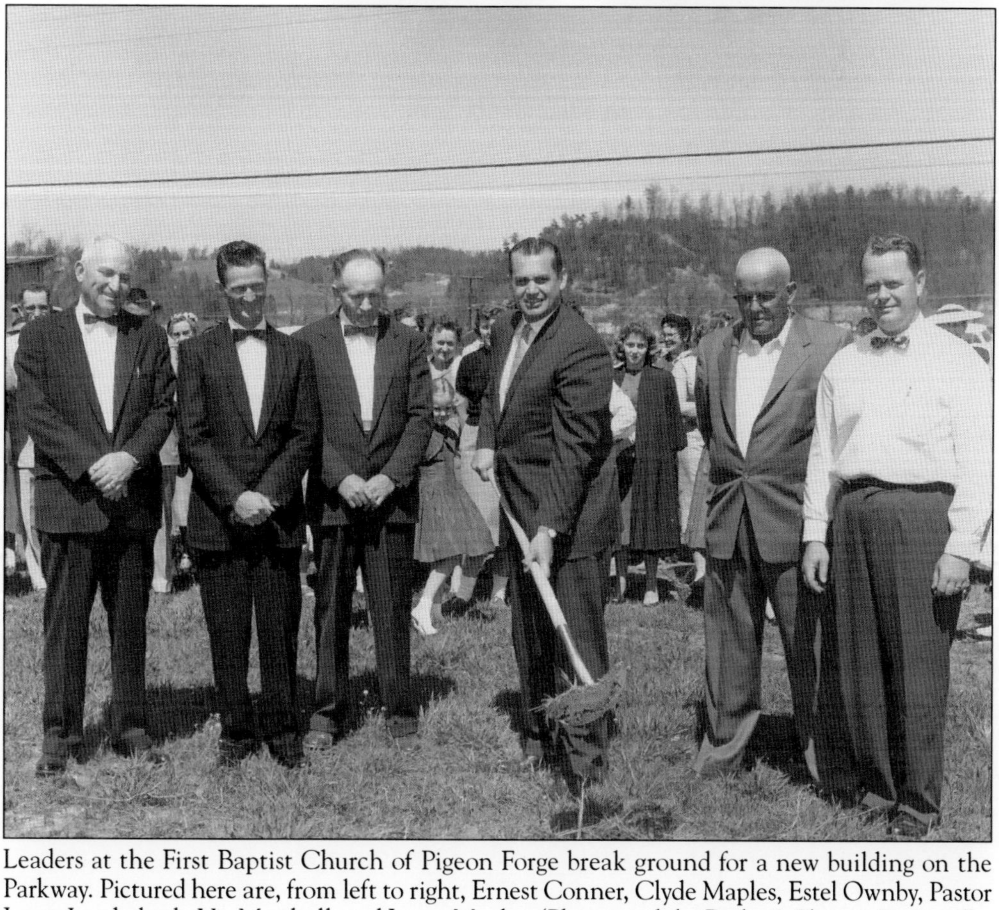

Leaders at the First Baptist Church of Pigeon Forge break ground for a new building on the Parkway. Pictured here are, from left to right, Ernest Conner, Clyde Maples, Estel Ownby, Pastor James Lauderback, Vic Marshall, and James Maples. (Photograph by Bashor's Photos, Sevierville; courtesy of Sarah Ball.)

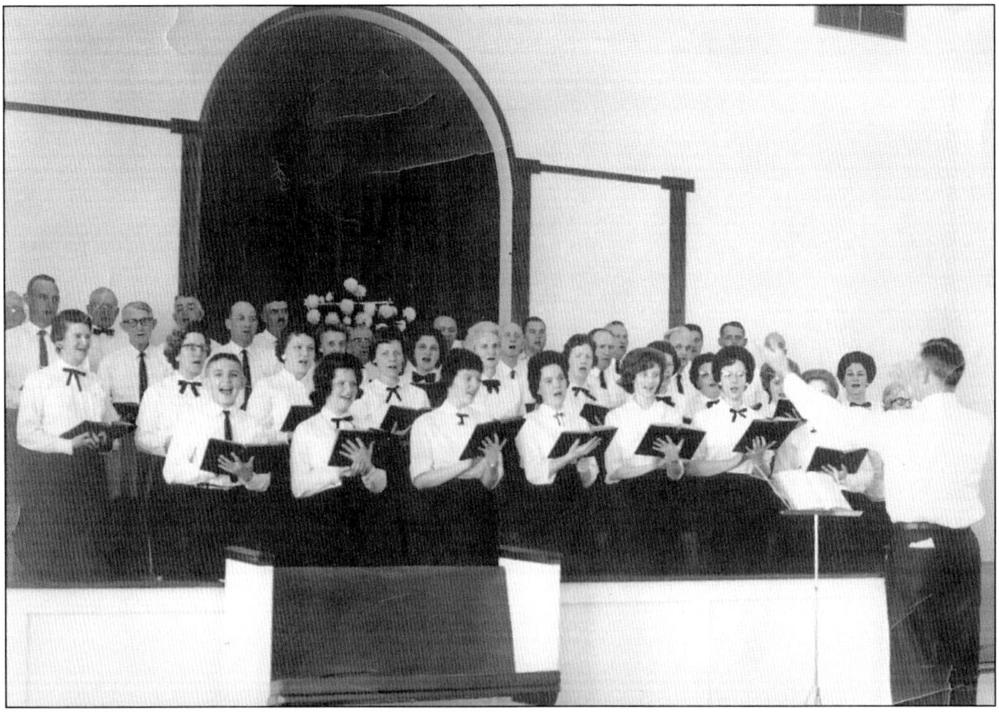

The First Baptist Church of Pigeon Forge's choir sings songs of praise in their new sanctuary. (Photograph by Bashor's Photos, Sevierville; courtesy of Sarah Ball.)

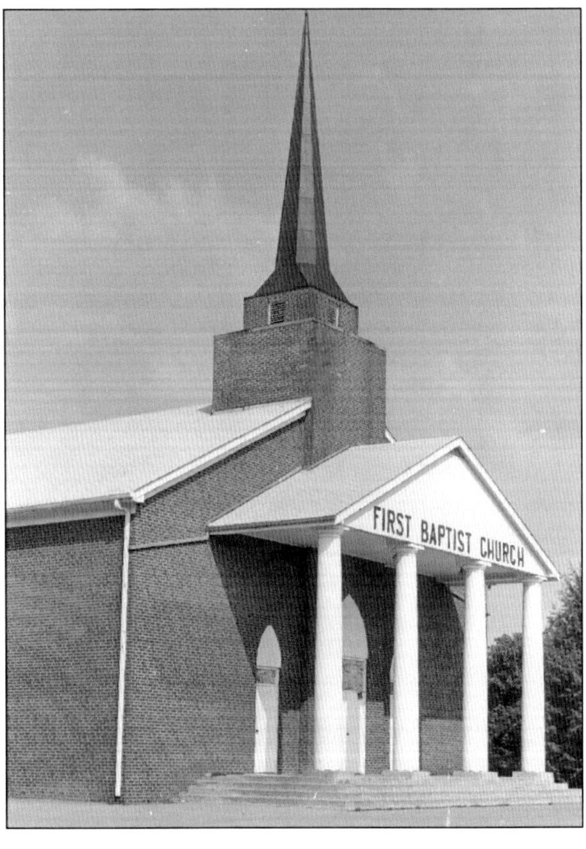

The First Baptist Church of Pigeon Forge is pictured in the 1960s, soon after the building was constructed. The Baptists organized their first church in 1914. In October of that year, there were 62 members. (Courtesy of the *Mountain Press*.)

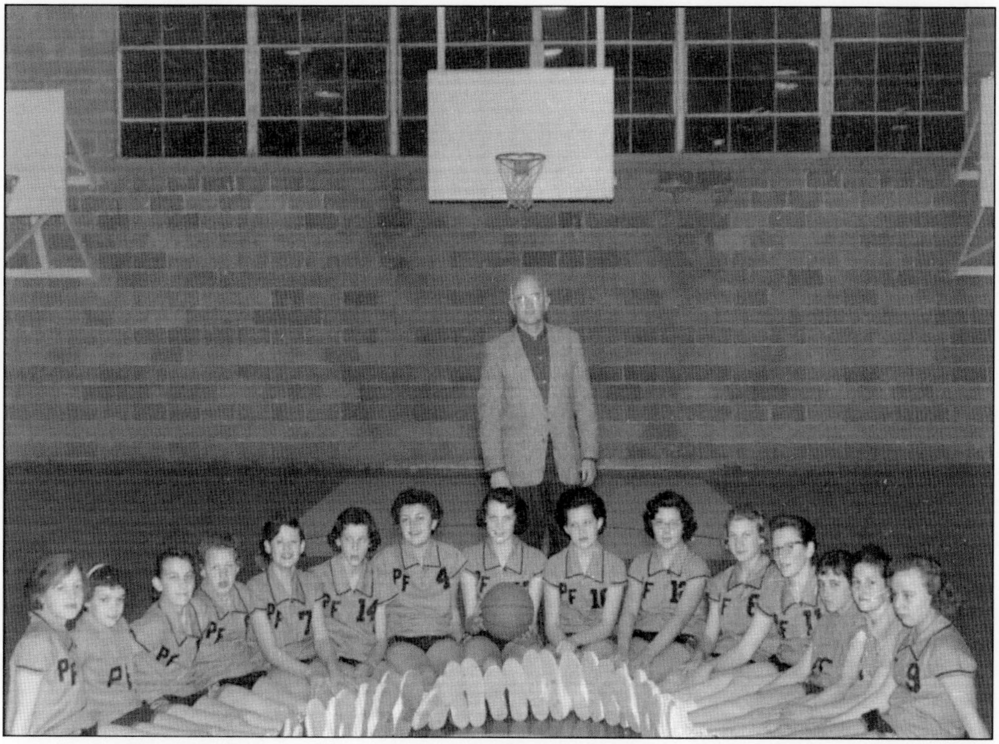

The Pigeon Forge Elementary School girl's basketball team is pictured with coach Frank Marshall in the gymnasium of the school. From left to right are Judy Cardwell, forward; Kay Trotter, forward; Jeanette Reagan, forward; Nancy Whaley, forward; Lela Parton, guard; Barbara King, guard; Gwendell Lamons, guard; Karen Campbell, forward; Donna Moncy, guard; Mary Ann Fleming, guard; Betty Maples, forward; Faye Trotter, guard; Ann Ward, forward; Betty King, guard; and Joan Whaley, guard. (Courtesy of Donna Allen.)

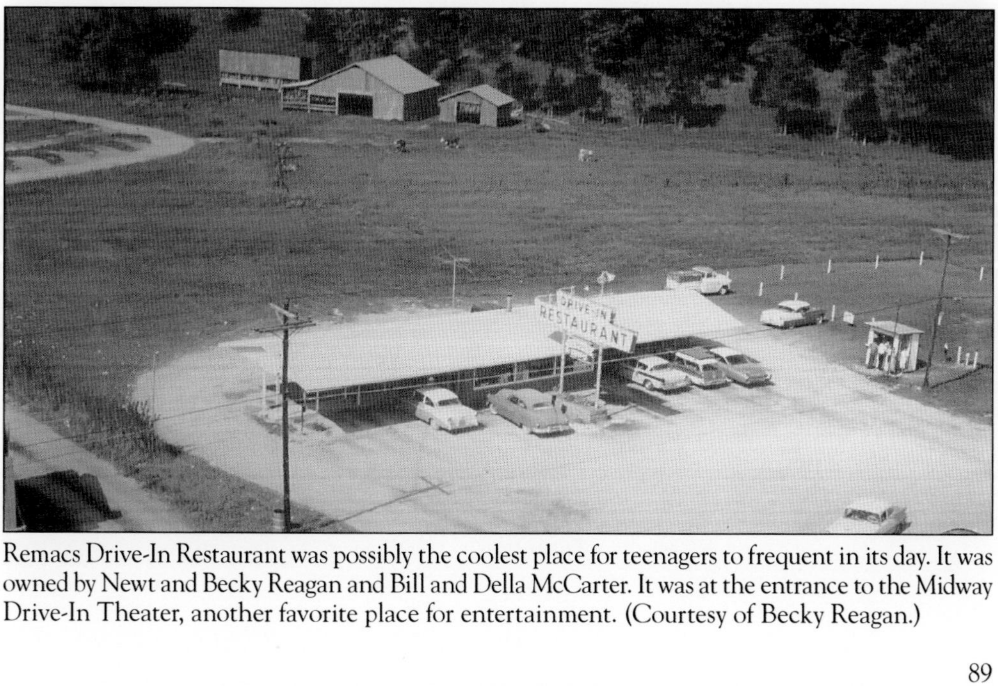

Remacs Drive-In Restaurant was possibly the coolest place for teenagers to frequent in its day. It was owned by Newt and Becky Reagan and Bill and Della McCarter. It was at the entrance to the Midway Drive-In Theater, another favorite place for entertainment. (Courtesy of Becky Reagan.)

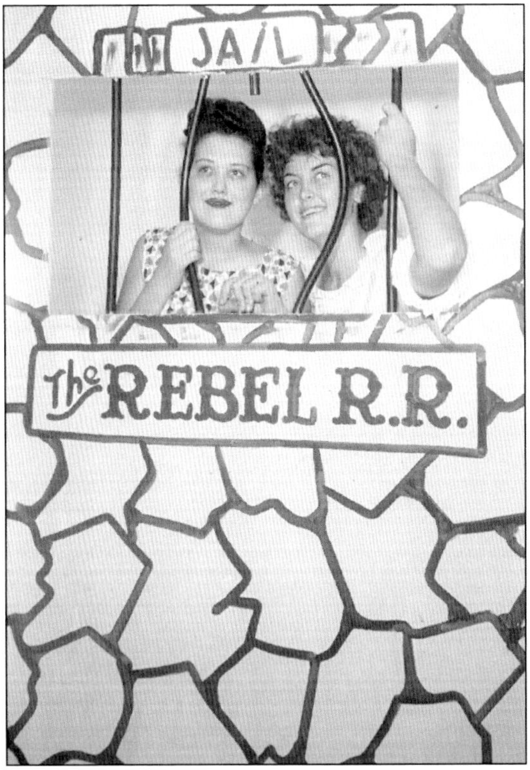

Donna Moncy (left) and Gwendell Lamons were young during the carefree days of the 1950s and 1960s. They are pictured at one of Rebel Railroad's jail photograph props. (Courtesy of Donna Moncy Allen.)

Coil Moncy sits in his fine automobile with the big sidewalls in front of Arlie Roberts's service station across the Parkway from Wayne's Motel (later the Vacation Lodge). (Courtesy of Donna Moncy Allen.)

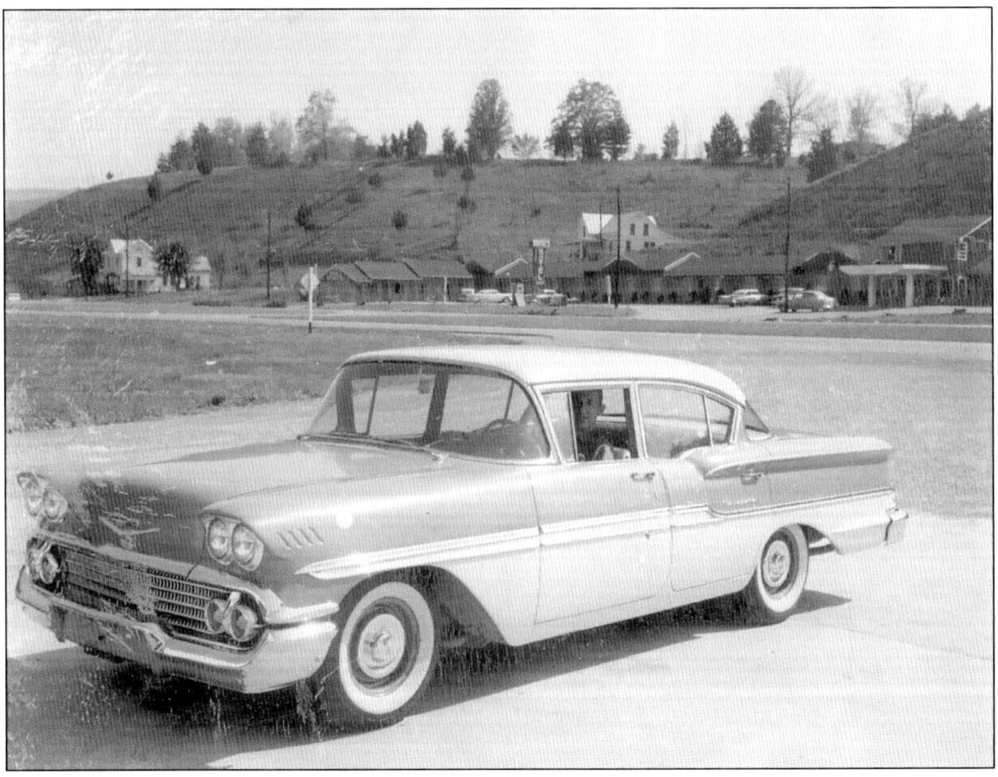

Janice Huff Walker, daughter of Roy and Genevieve Franklin Huff, lived in the Walden's Creek community as a child. Her grandparents were Wiley and Carrie Wear Franklin. (Courtesy of Henrietta Franklin Sharp.)

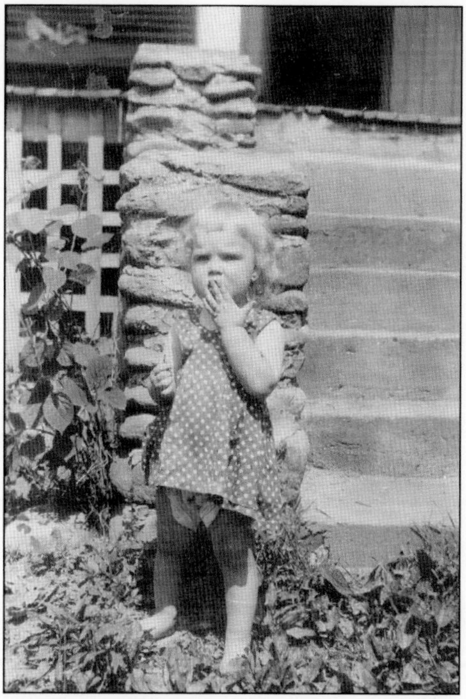

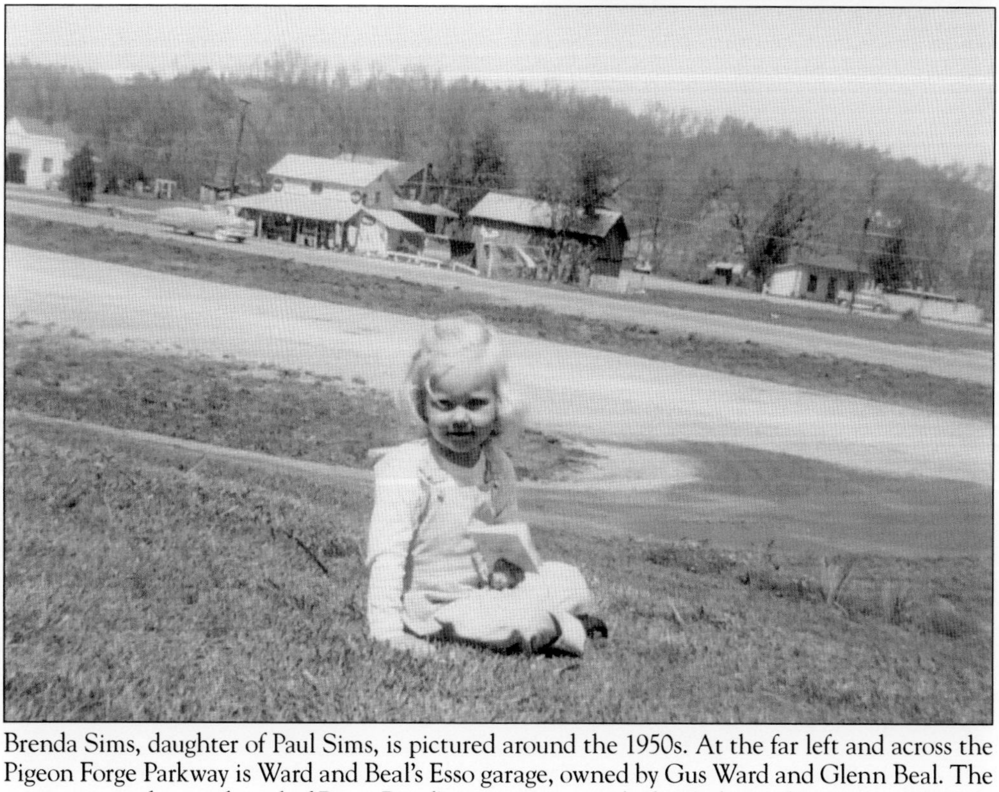

Brenda Sims, daughter of Paul Sims, is pictured around the 1950s. At the far left and across the Pigeon Forge Parkway is Ward and Beal's Esso garage, owned by Gus Ward and Glenn Beal. The garage sat at the north end of River Road's intersection with the Parkway. (Courtesy of Brenda Sims Rudder.)

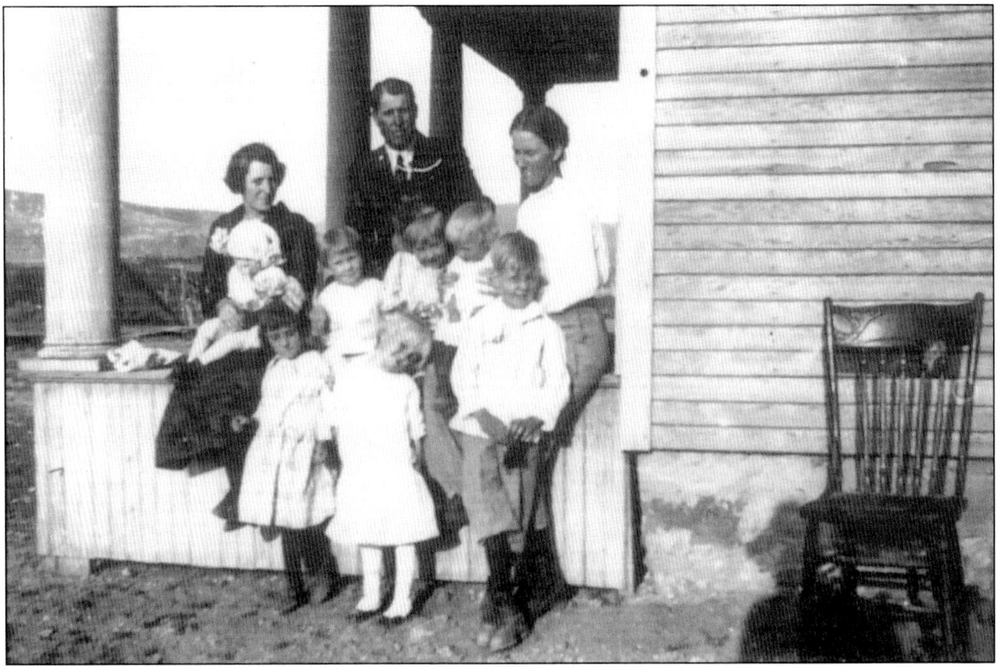

The Wiley and Carrie Franklin family of the Mill Creek community is pictured here, from left to right, (first row, standing by the porch) Perna, Genevieve, and Clark Franklin; (second row, seated on porch) Anna Wear Powell with infant Billy Dean Powell, Iva Franklin, Martha Franklin, Carrie Wear Franklin with infant Emma Franklin; (at back) Wiley Franklin. (Courtesy of Henrietta Franklin Sharp.)

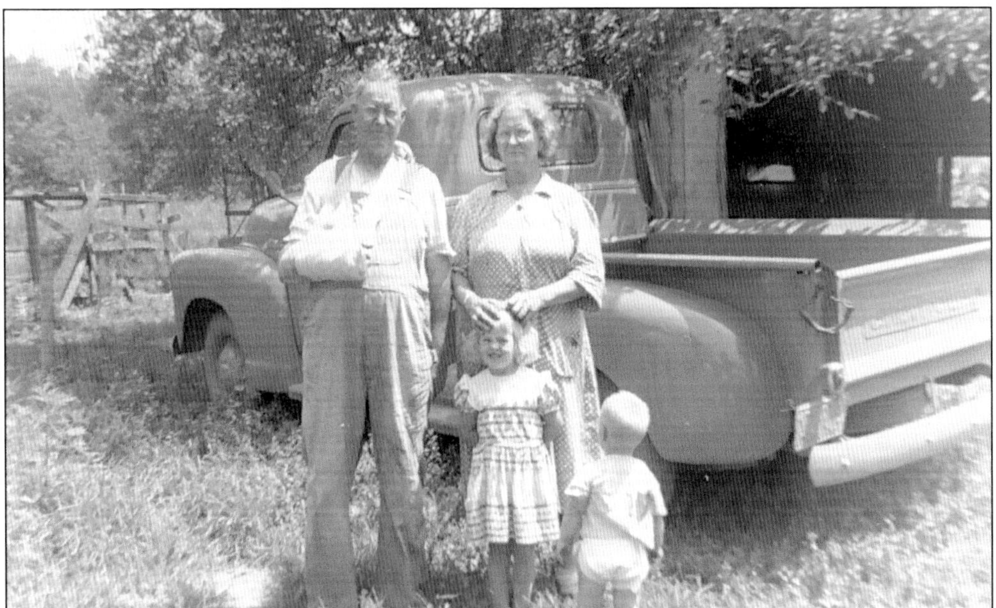

Wiley and Carrie Franklin stand with grandchildren Peggy and Larry Sharp. The two youngsters are the children of George W. and Henrietta Franklin Sharp. (Courtesy of Henrietta Franklin Sharp.)

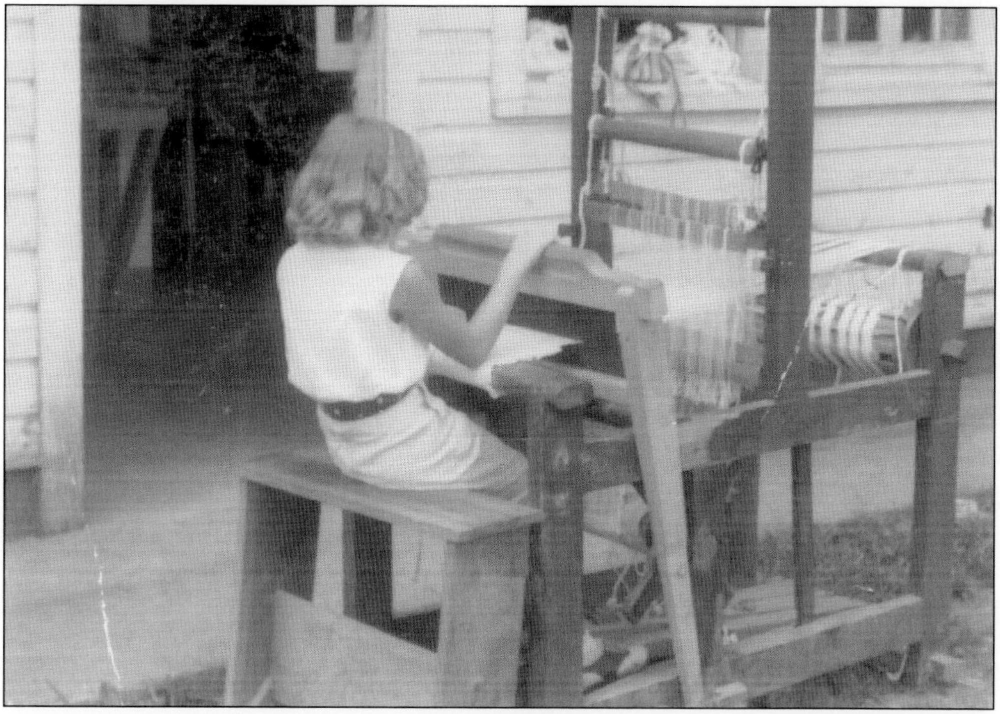

Doris Jean Parton weaves outside her mother Jean Parton's weave shop in Pigeon Forge. Some women earned extra income by weaving bags (purses), table scarves, napkins, and other helpful items in their homes and in shops such as Parton's. This shop sat near the northern intersection of River Road and the Parkway. (Courtesy of Christine Shults.)

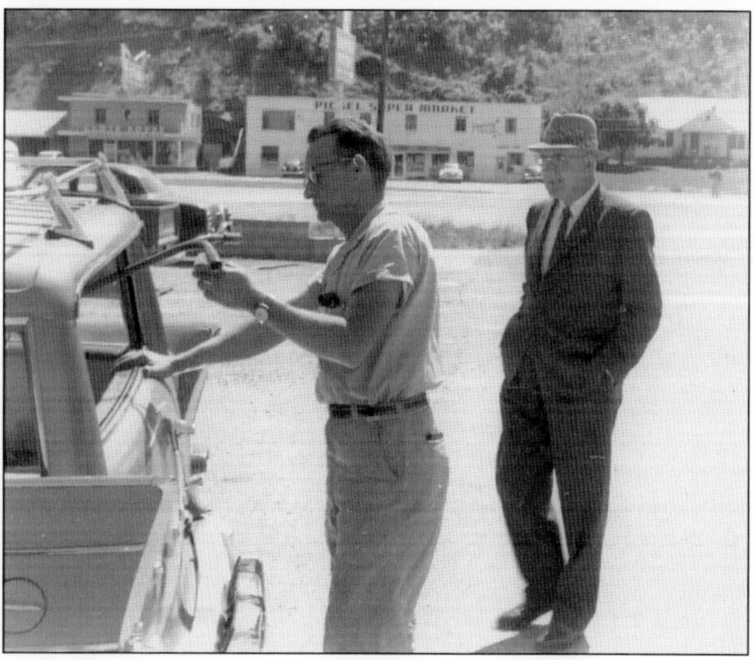

Pictured across the street from Pickel's Supermarket and the Cherokee Textile Mills' Cloth Store are Oliver Trotter (left), of Trotter Plumbing and Electric, and Orlie Trentham. As the local power company expanded in the late 1940s and 1950s, Trotter wired many of the homes in Pigeon Forge that had never previously had electricity. (Courtesy of Bill and Jody Allen.)

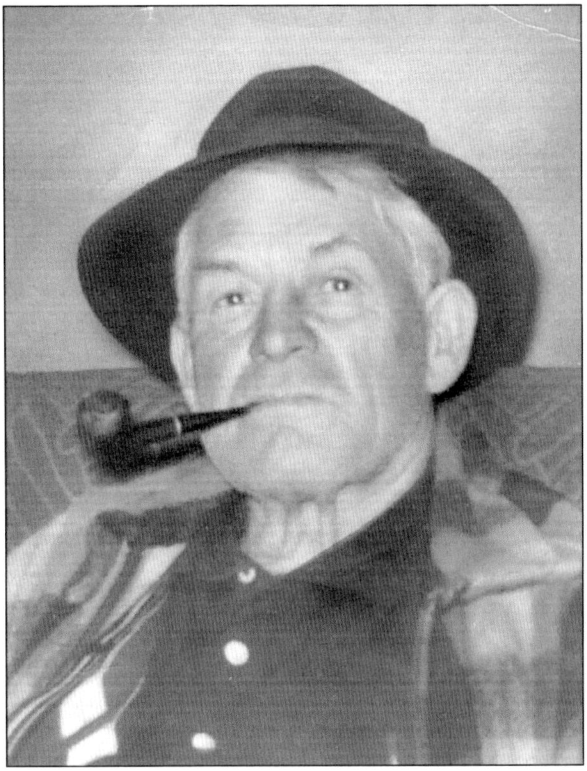

Pink Huskey lived on present-day Two View Road in Pigeon Forge. He was married to Polly Bradley, and the two had seven children—Ina, Parlon, Burl, Paulas, David, Billy, and Hoover. Hoover died in a rainstorm as a young man. He was found in a creek; the family never knew the cause of his death. (Courtesy of Randy Huskey.)

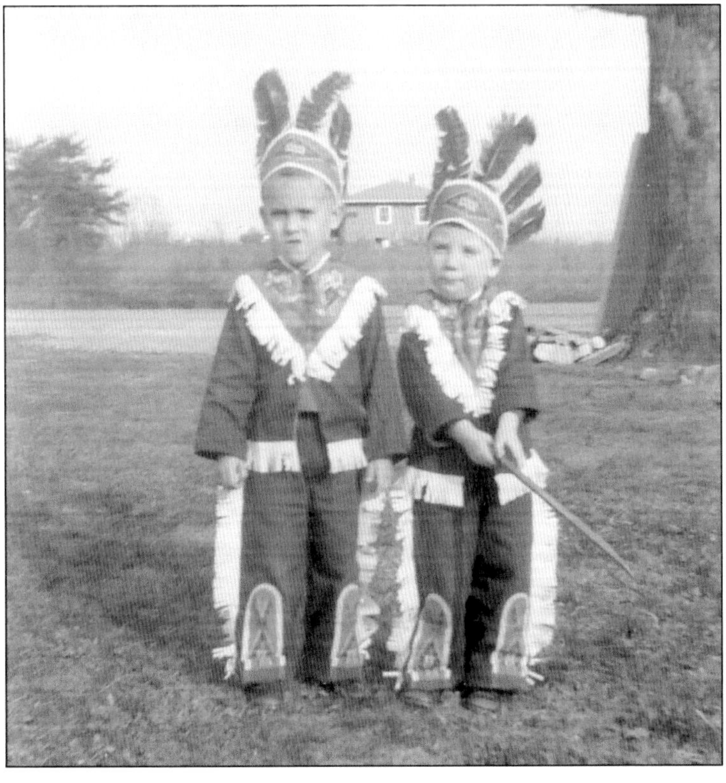

Steve (left) and his brother, William Watson, pose for a January 1956 photograph, Indian chiefs all the way. They are the sons of John Watson and Clara Quarrels Watson Killian. The family lived in the Flannigan Addition. (Courtesy of Clara Quarrels Watson Killian.)

On December 12, 1959, Shirley Shults marries Christine Wilson at the church of her youth, Oldham's Creek Baptist. Pictured also are the bride's sister Linda Wilson (left) and the groom's sister Jewel Shults. The Shults couple lived in the Conner Heights community in their early married years. A few short months after Shirley and Christine celebrated their 50th wedding anniversary, Shirley passed away suddenly, in 2010. (Courtesy of Christine Shults.)

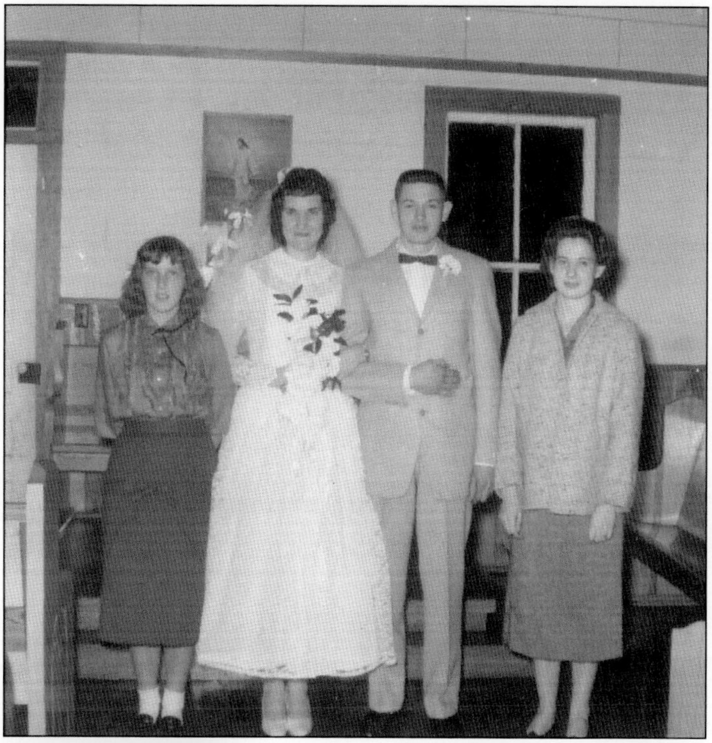

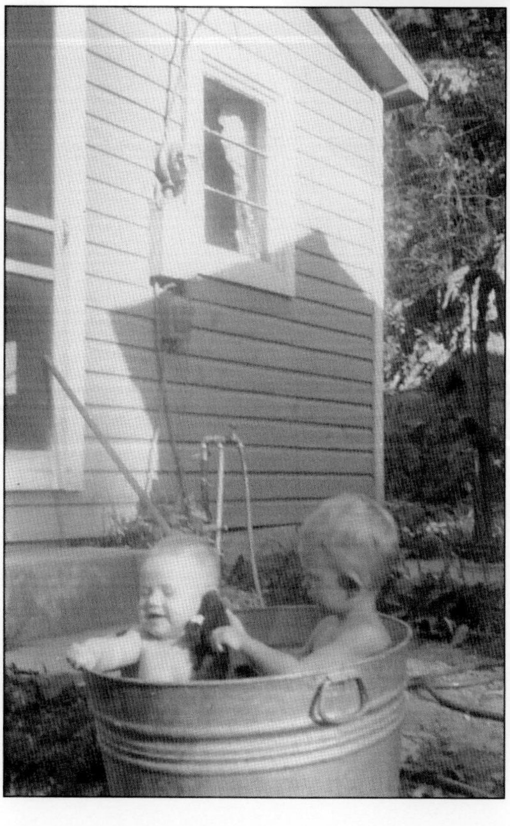

Rodney and Alvin Shults of the Conner Heights community take advantage of the summer sun for this outside bath. The Shults boys are the sons of Shirley and Christine Wilson Shults. Others in the family are Randy and twins Artie and Shirley Shults Botkin. (Courtesy of Christine Shults.)

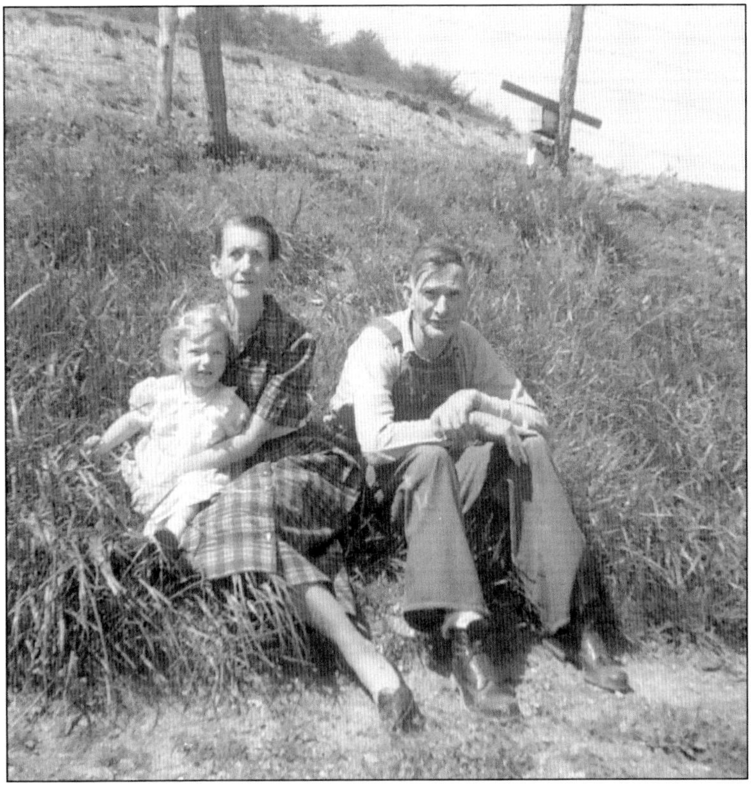

Simeon and Viola Henry rest for a moment with granddaughter Loretta Smith in the 1960s. The Henry family lived on Lower Middle Creek. (Courtesy of Myrtle Henry.)

Ice-cold winters make picture perfect scenes at the Old Mill in Pigeon Forge. Residents tell of skating and playing hockey on the frozen millpond in earlier times. (Courtesy of the Old Mill.)

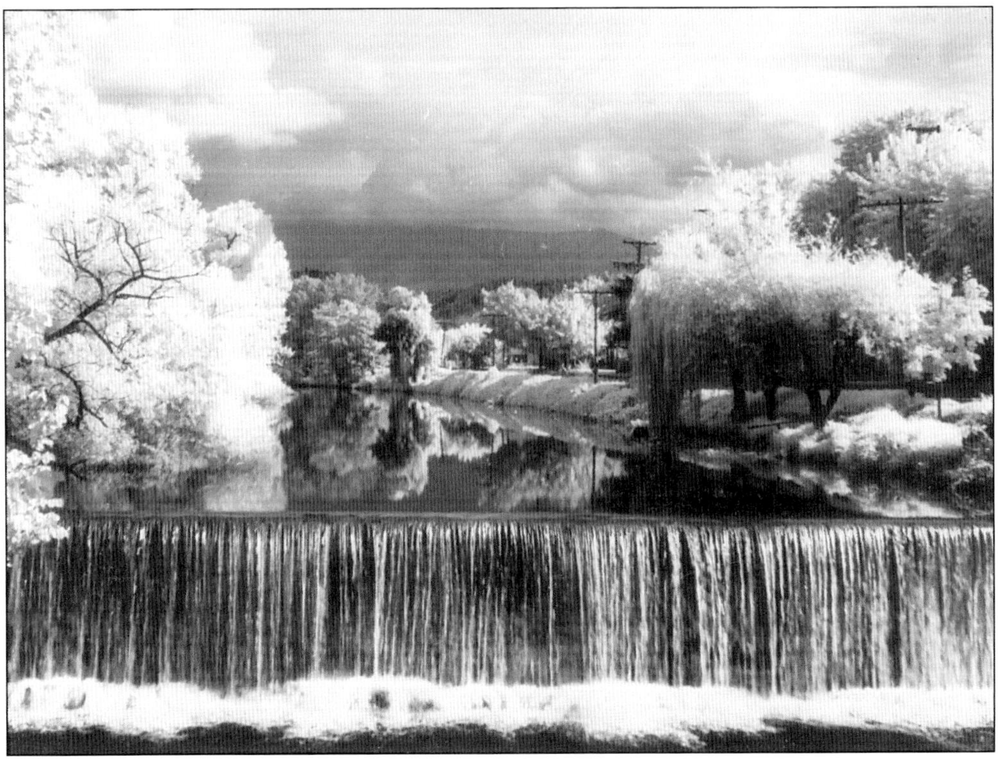

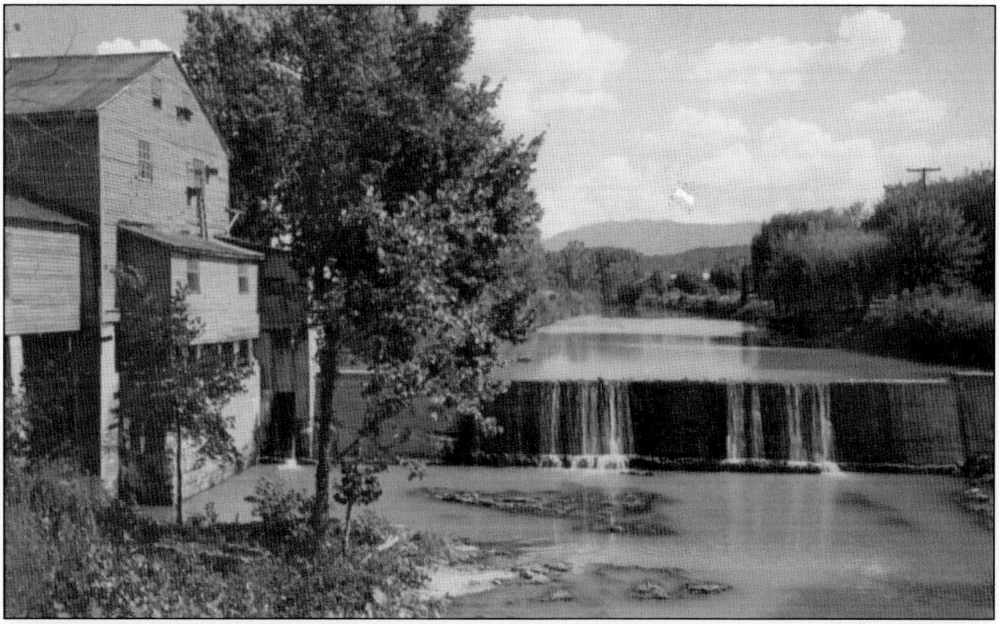

Pigeon Forge's Old Mill is pictured here without the large breast wheel seen in so many photographs. Historians believe there was an earlier wheel, but it is unclear if it was destroyed in a flood or removed because of wear. Former owner Kathy Stout Simmons said her father brought in the present wheel in the 1950s from a Virginia mill that had burned. (Courtesy of Jerry Loveday.)

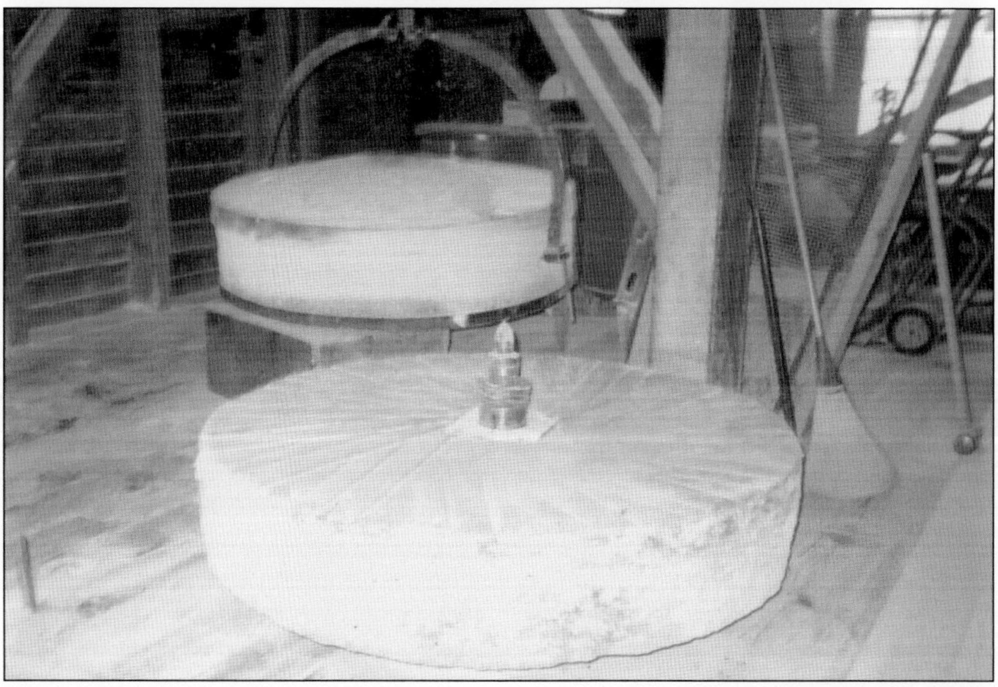

These great millstones, known as buhrstones, were imported from France. They are the second set ever used in the history of the Old Mill. A previous set is on display on-site. The Little Pigeon River powers underwater turbine or tub mills to grind the corn, and the visible breast wheel powers the grain elevator. (Courtesy of the Old Mill.)

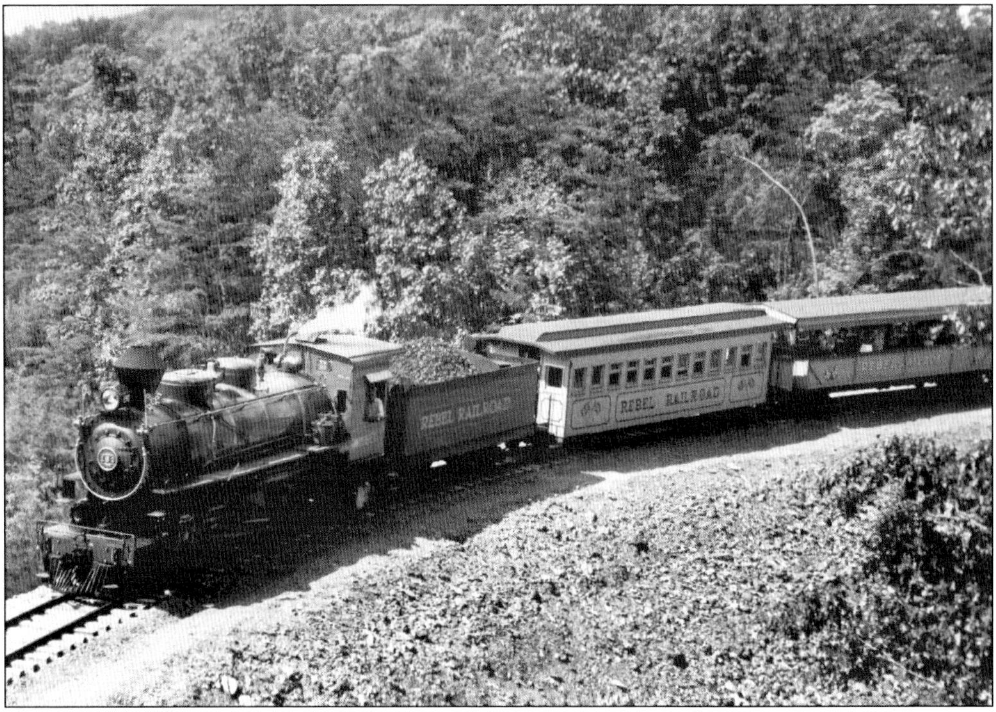

Rebel Railroad's train, pulled by locomotive "Klondike Kate," was an exciting new ride in the early 1960s; "robbers" held up the train as part of the ride's drama. This amusement later became Goldrush Junction, Silver Dollar City, and finally the Herschend family and Dolly Parton's Dollywood. (Courtesy of Dollywood.)

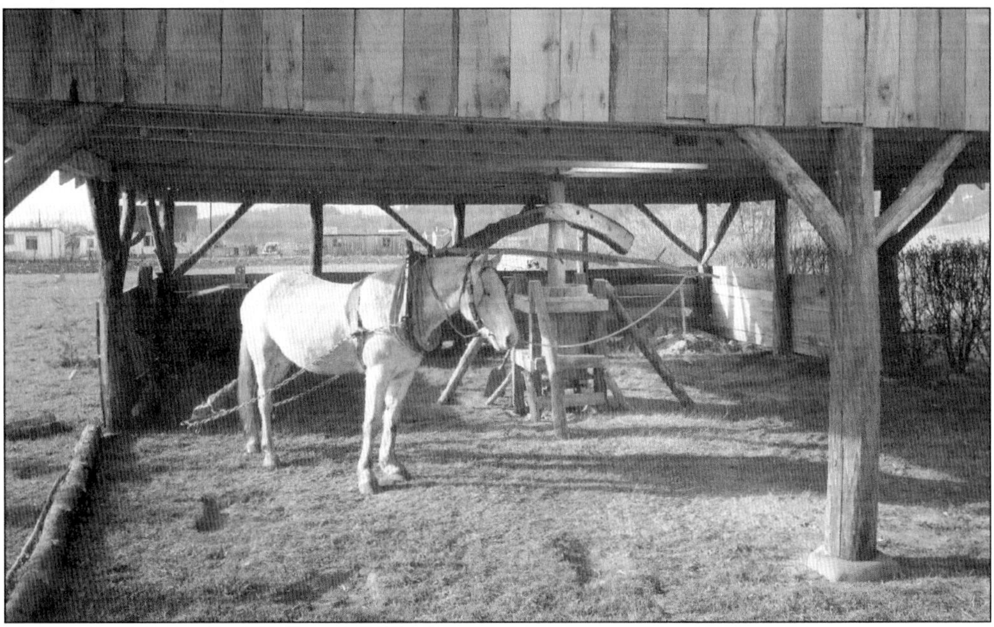

Cyclone Jim was a horse used in powering a clay-grinding mill at Pigeon Forge Pottery. More than one "Cyclone Jim" was used. Each became a special attraction for those visiting the pottery. This photograph was taken around 1955. (Photograph by Thompson Photo Products, Knoxville.)

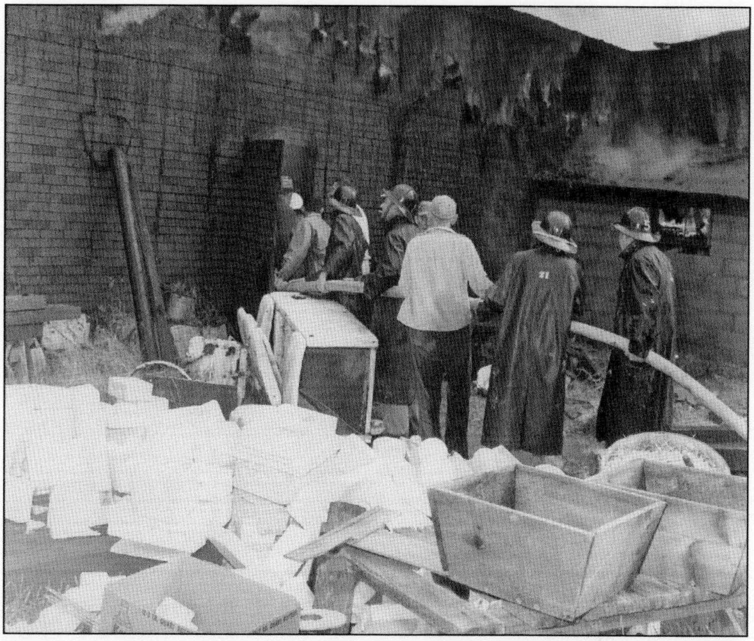

Firefighters tried in vain to save Pigeon Forge Pottery, which burned in November 1957. The pottery was a renovated barn on the Ashley Butler farm. In the early years, the Ferguson family, who owned the pottery, lived in an apartment over their business. (Photograph by Bashor's Photos, Sevierville; courtesy of Ruth Ferguson.)

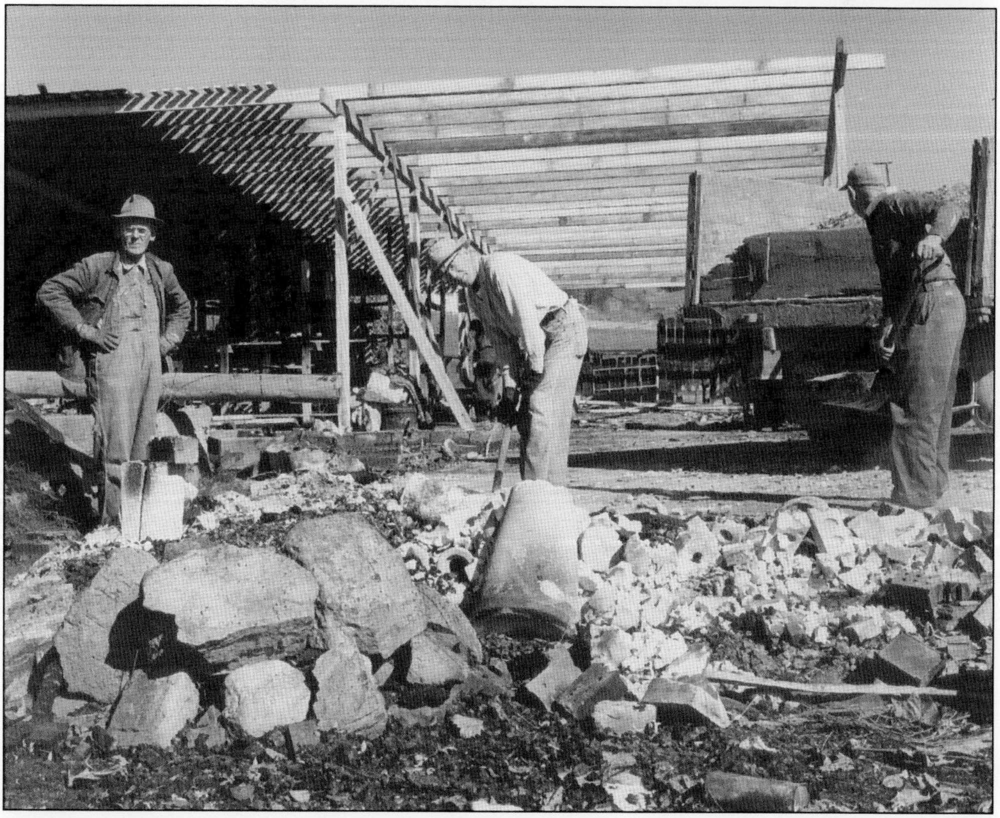

Workers rebuild after Pigeon Forge Pottery was destroyed by fire. Tents were brought by the Miller family, who owned Fort Weare Game Park, to protect the undamaged molds and materials. (Photograph by Bashor's photos, Sevierville; courtesy of Ruth Ferguson.)

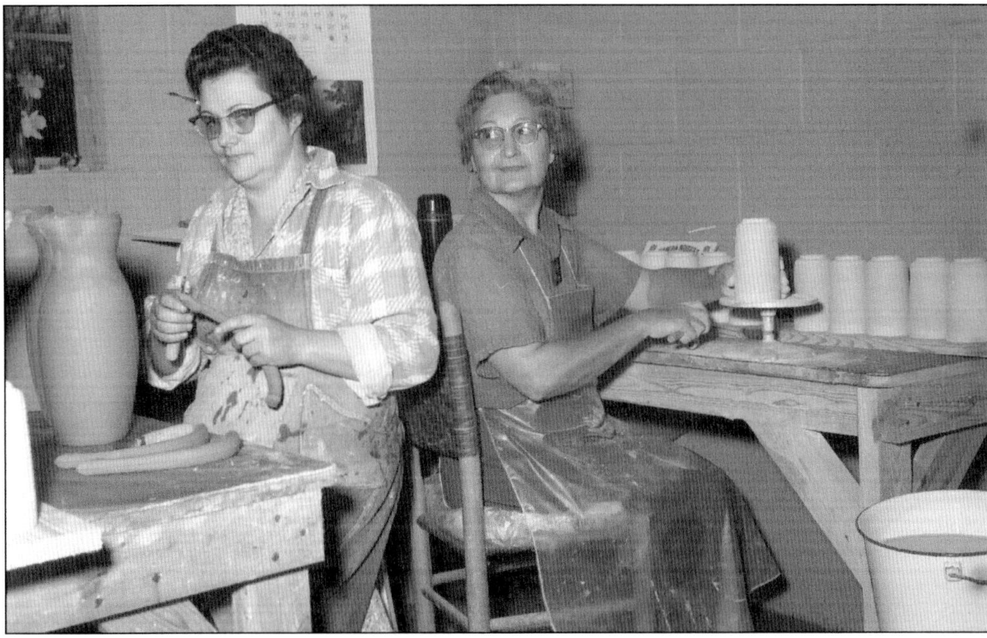

Veryl Campbell (left) was employed with Pigeon Forge Pottery for 50 years; her coworker, Aura Fox, worked there for 35 years. (Photograph by Bashor's Photos, Sevierville; courtesy of Ruth Ferguson.)

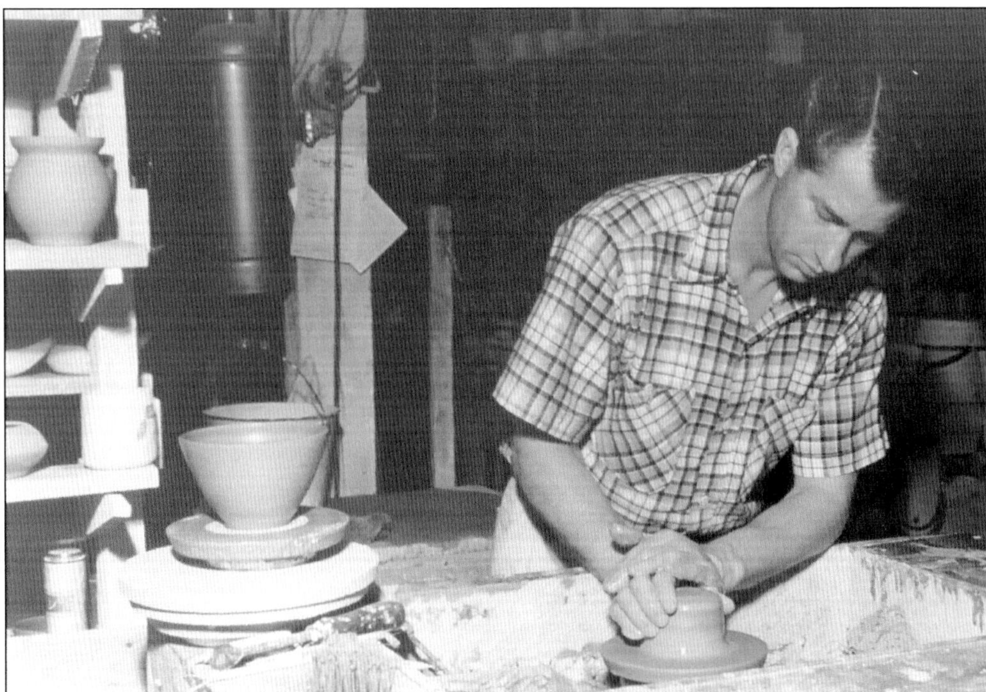

Douglas Ferguson carefully molds this piece of local clay to become a work of art. He expanded his work to include murals and sculptures, some currently on display at Mars Hill College, where he studied. This photograph was taken in the 1950s. (Courtesy of Ruth Ferguson.)

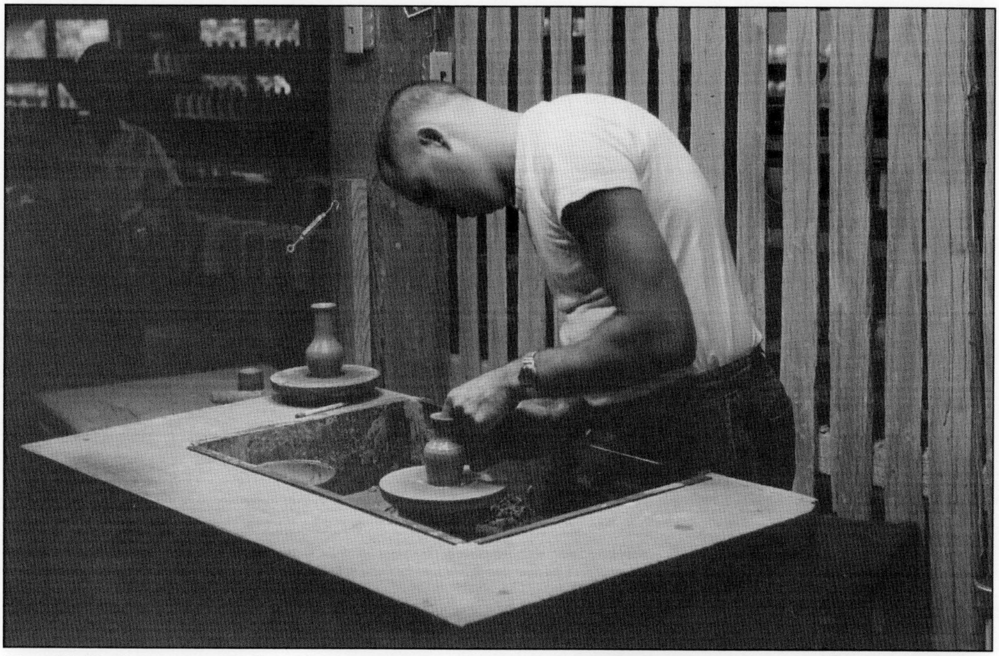

Harold Shults is pictured turning on the potter's wheel at Pigeon Forge Pottery sometime in the 1950s or 1960s. He was the son of Bedford and Relda Shults of the Walden's Creek community. (Photograph by Edward H. Thompson Photos, Miami, Florida; courtesy of Ruth Ferguson.)

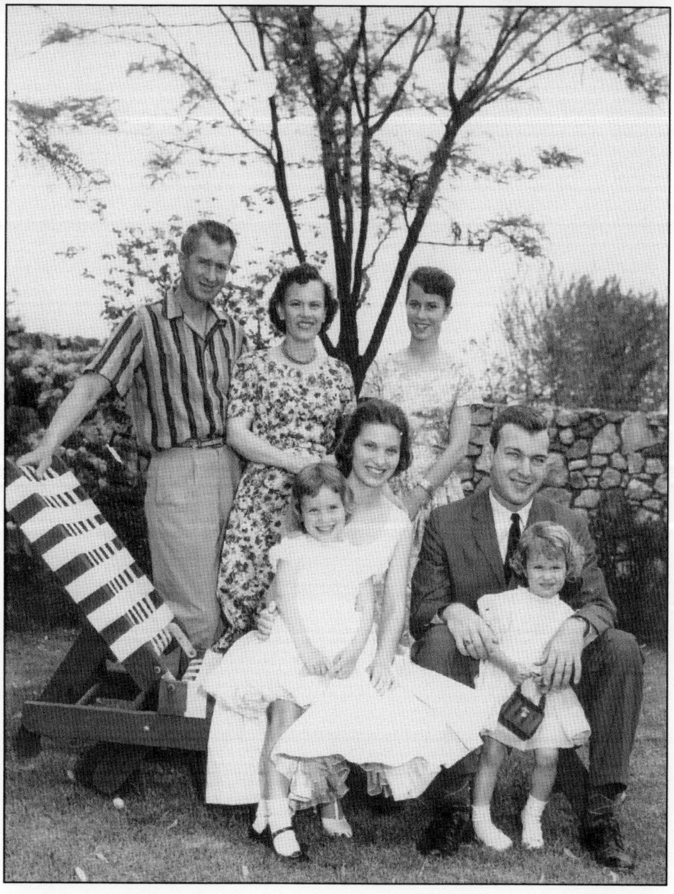

This spring photograph of the Ferguson family shows, from left to right, (first row) daughter Ardith; Sarah,; Sarah's husband, Dale Owens; and daughter Jane; (second row) Douglas, Ruth, and their daughter Esther. This photograph was taken around 1959. (Courtesy of Ruth Ferguson.)

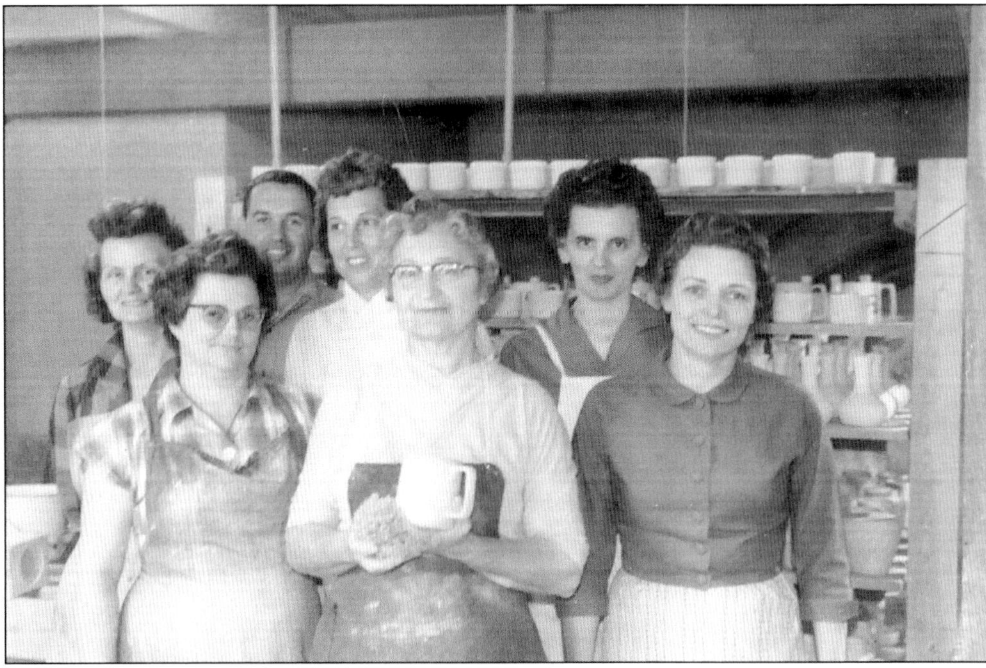

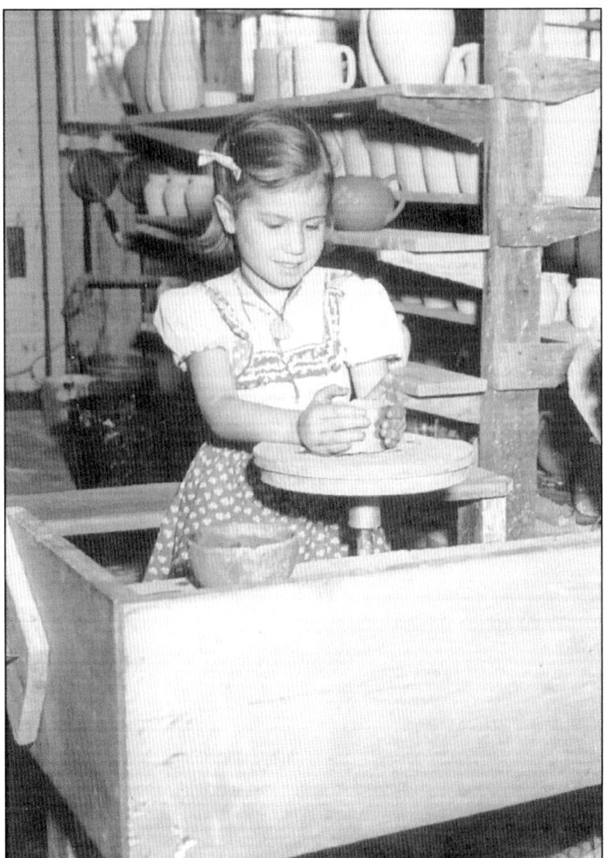

Pigeon Forge Pottery employees take a break from work. This small cottage industry offered an opportunity for area residents to learn the art of pottery making and provided employment for approximately 20 people. Pictured here are, from left to right, (first row) Veryl Campbell, Aura Fox, and Luna Myers; (second row) Pearl Campbell, Ruth Quarrels, and Aileen Blalock; (third row) Harold Shults. (Courtesy of Clara Quarrels Killian.)

Ardith Ferguson learned the arts at a very young age. Here she turns on the wheel at Pigeon Forge Pottery near the Old Mill. Her parents are Doug and Ruth Ferguson, who owned and operated the pottery for about a half a century. (Courtesy of Ruth Ferguson.)

Pictured in this 1950s photograph are, from left to right, (first row) twins Judy and Jody Cole; (second row) Lib (Elizabeth) and Charles Cole. The Coles' parents are Jess and Beedie Cole of the current Maplecrest area of Pigeon Forge. (Courtesy of Bill and Jody Allen.)

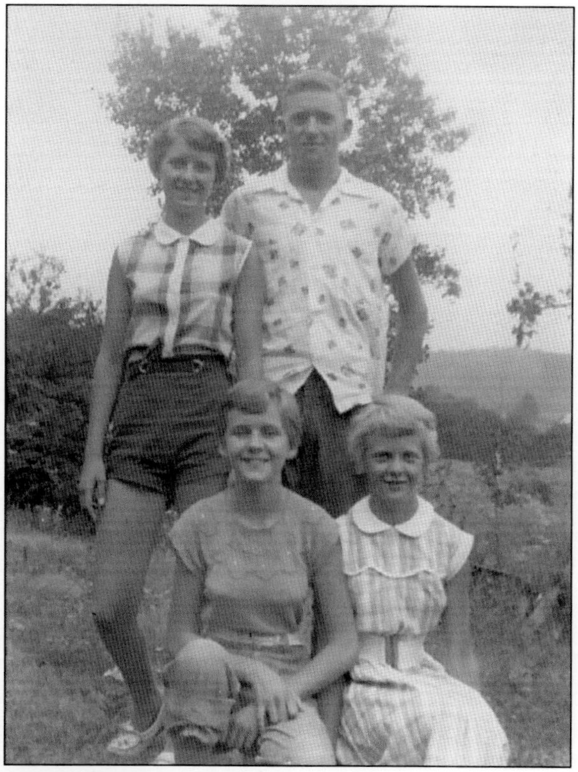

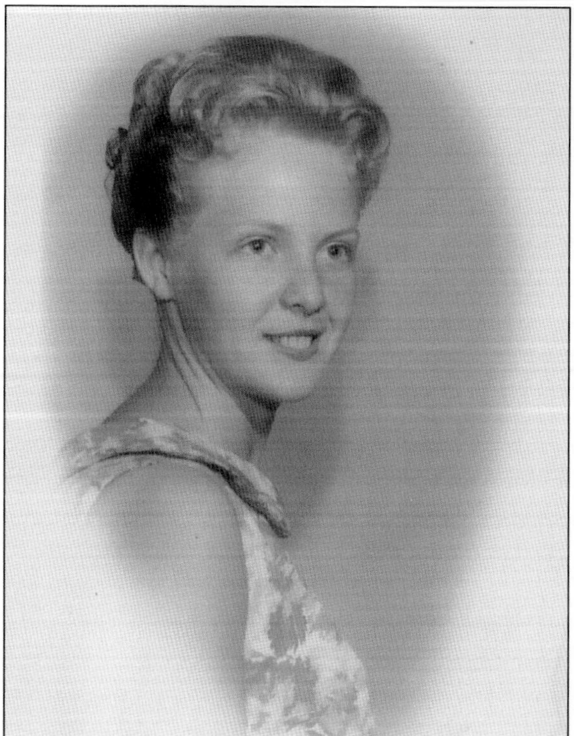

Jody Cole is pictured here in 1957. Her family moved from the Sugarlands area of the Great Smoky Mountains to Pigeon Forge. Jody and her husband, Bill Allen, live today in downtown Pigeon Forge. When they married in 1961, the couple rented a home on Marshall Street for $50 per month. (Courtesy of Bill and Jody Allen.)

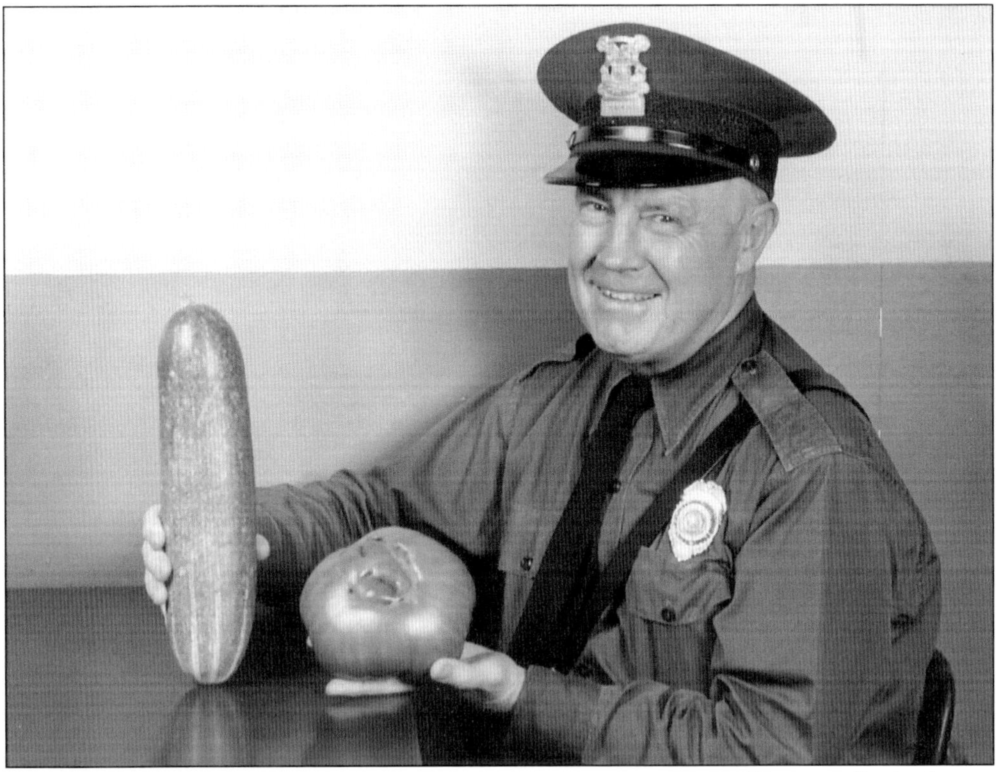

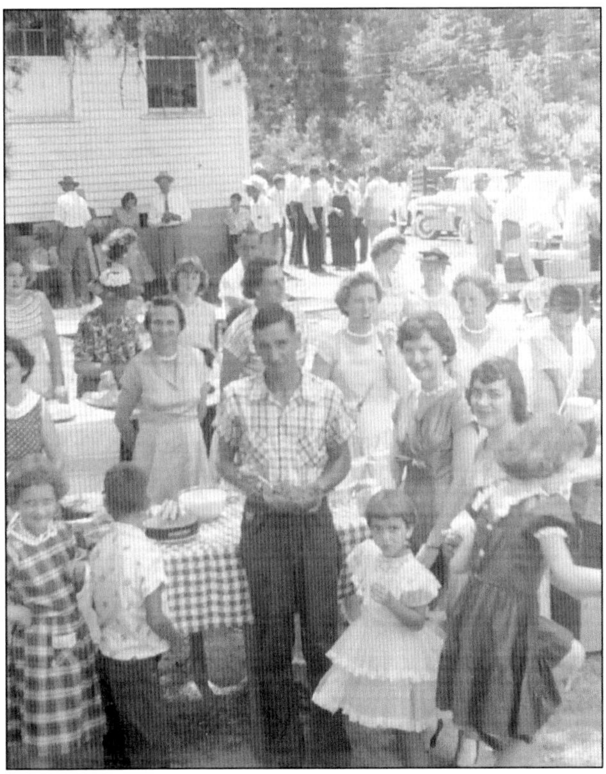

Victor V. Allen proudly displays vegetables from his garden. His home was on River Road near the Old Mill, and he was employed in security for the Alcoa aluminum plant for many years. (Courtesy of Bill and Jody Allen.)

This photograph is typical of the many family reunions held in the Pigeon Forge area. Here the Myers family gathers at Little Cove Baptist Church. (Courtesy of Charlotte Myers McClure.)

Charlotte Myers McClure is pictured wearing a special necklace sent to her when she was a child by her father while he was in World War II. (Courtesy of Charlotte Myers McClure.)

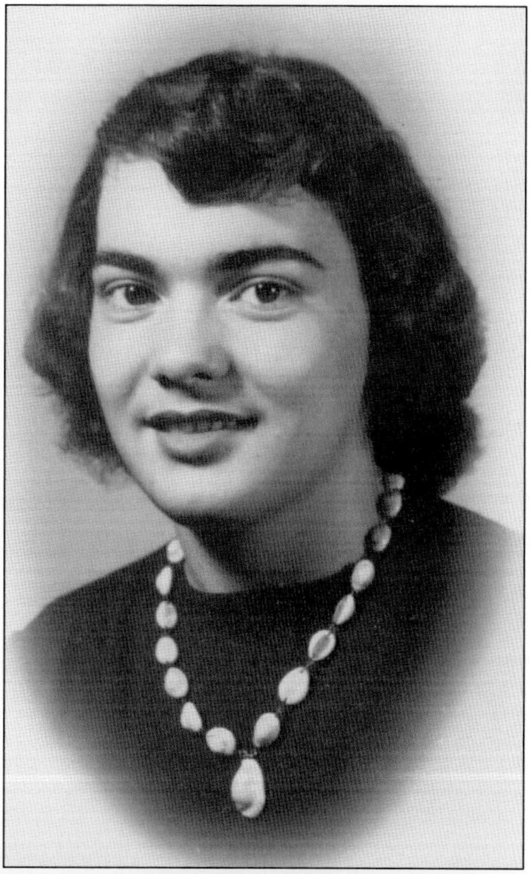

Iva Ward Whaley, left, and Betty Sue Whaley Gibson pause from their drive through the Smokies sometime in the 1950s for this photograph. (Courtesy of Sue Cruze Whaley Gibson.)

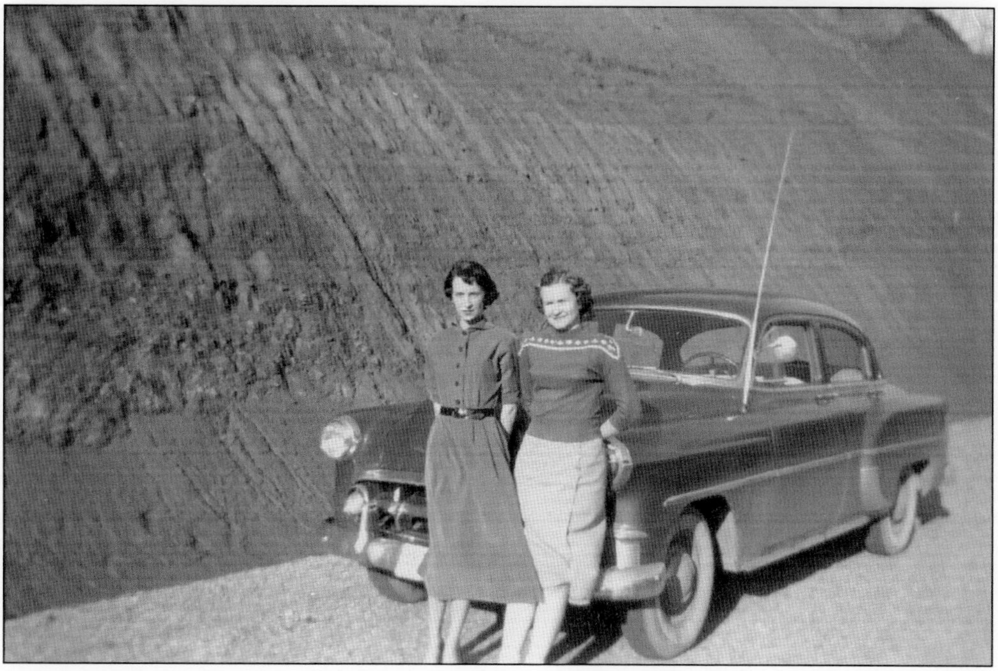

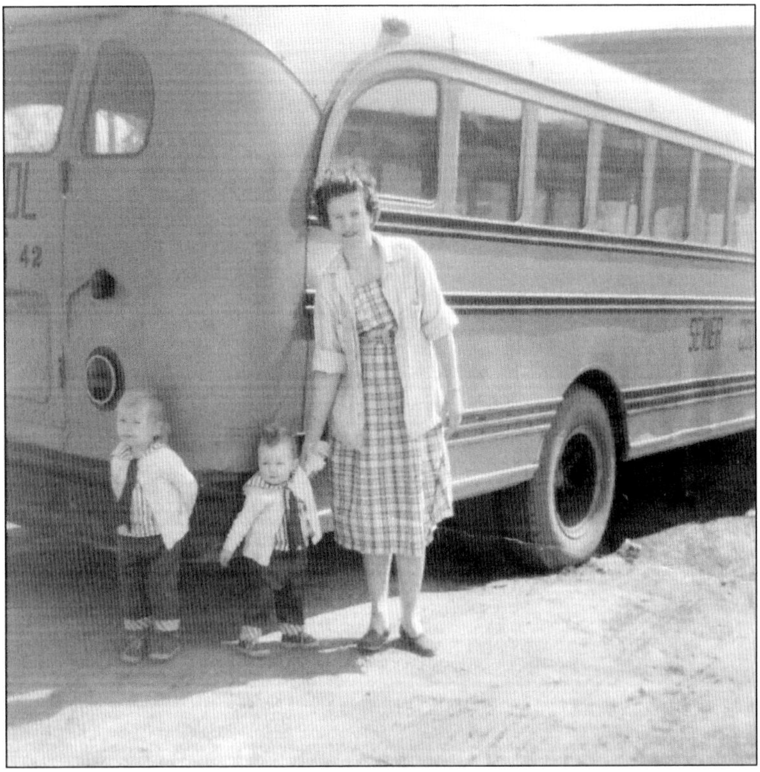

Betty Sue Whaley Cruze Gibson is pictured with two of her daughters, Janie (left) and Vickie. This photograph is dated March 1959. (Courtesy of Sue Whaley Cruze Gibson.)

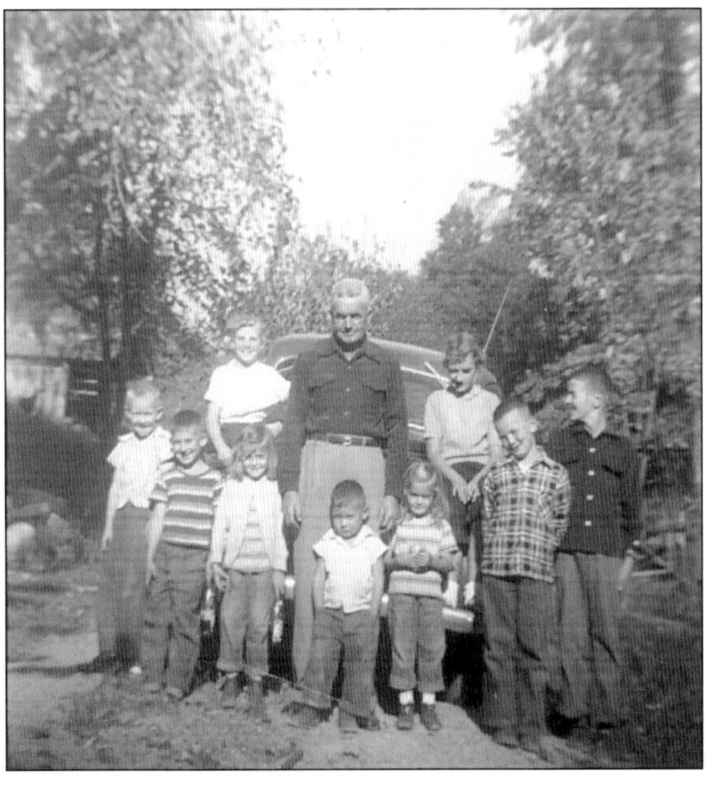

Lloyd "Dock" Whaley stands with his grandchildren at his home in Possum Holler sometime in the 1950s or 1960s. The group pictured is, from left to right, the following: (first row) Pete Trotter, Ralph L. Whaley, Judy Webb, Ronnie Ray Whaley, Gail Webb, and Tommy Miller; (second row) Martha Raye Trotter, Dock Whaley, Dorothy Whaley, and Billy Ray Whaley. (Courtesy of Sue Whaley Cruze Gibson.)

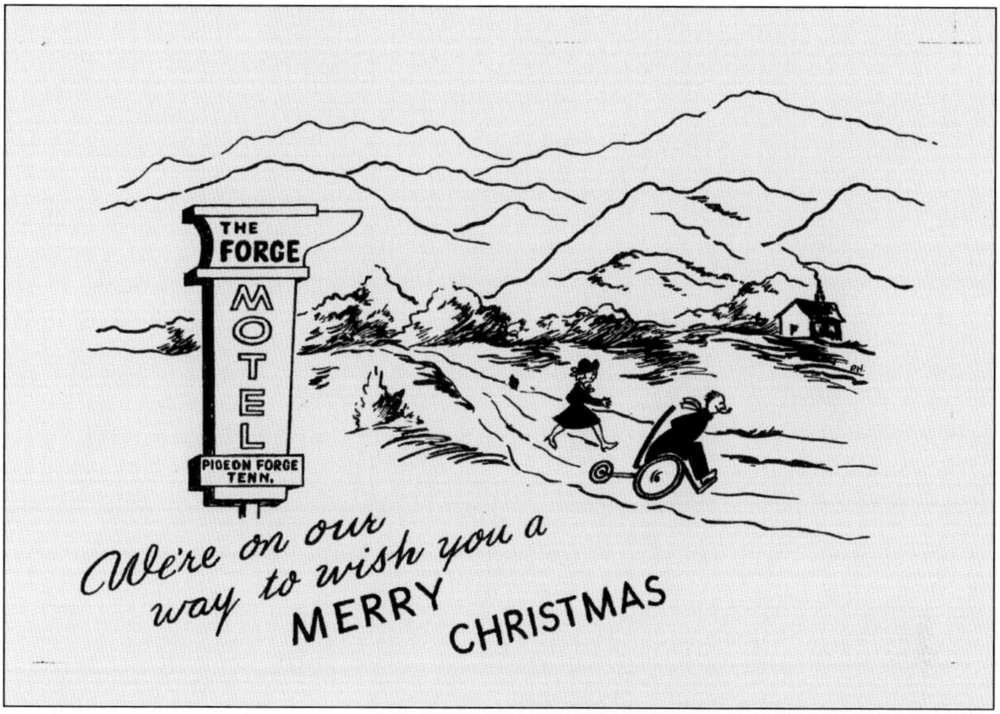

The Forge Motel Christmas card welcomed vacationers to the area. This was at a time in the 1950s when owners worked hard to entice visitors to stop in Pigeon Forge when so many only knew of Gatlinburg. (Courtesy of Janice M. Crowe.)

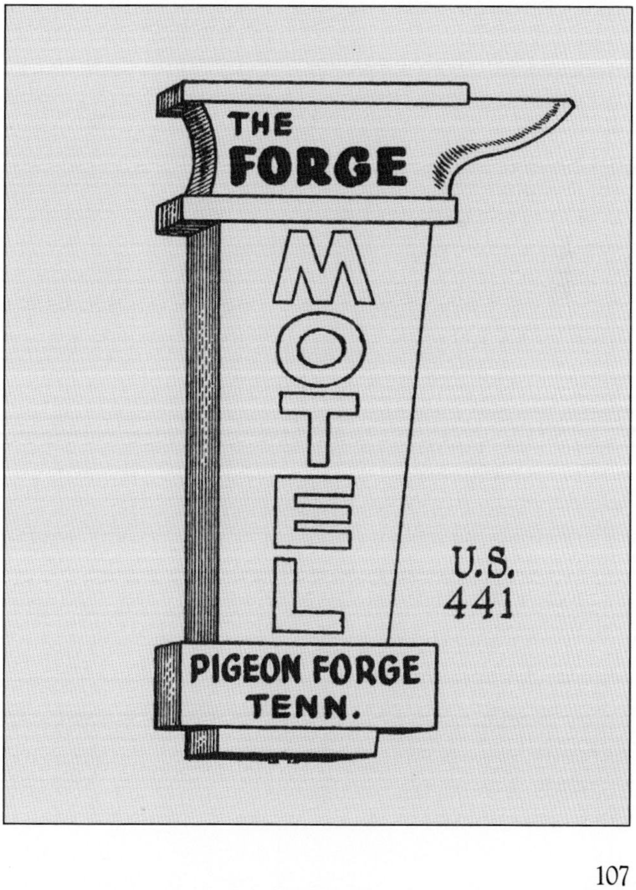

The Forge Motel was previously Lawson Lodge. It was purchased in the late 1950s by Tom and Sally Morrisey. The Morriseys promoted their motel by publicizing the area's four restaurants, golf at the Green View Driving Range, movies at the Mid-Way Drive In, a zoo, churches, pottery, crafts, the Old Mill, and the Pigeon Forge Art Gallery. (Courtesy of Janice M. Crowe.)

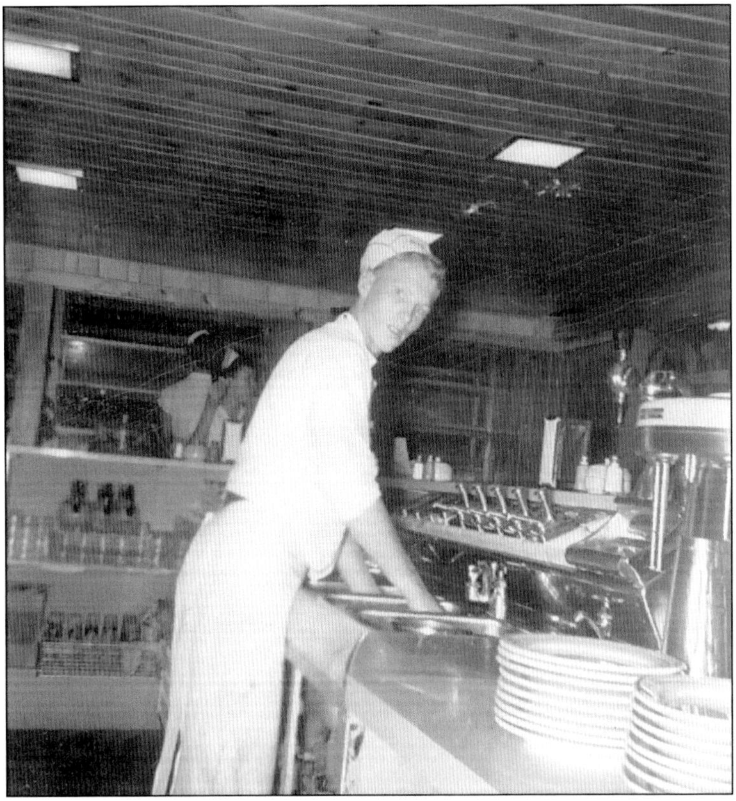

Charles Stamey is at work in the Green Pigeon Restaurant, owned and operated by his uncle, Charles Conner. The Green Pigeon was a forerunner of the Green Valley, a family-style restaurant owned and operated by Ralph and Ella Reagan for many years. (Courtesy of Bob and Jackie Barnes.)

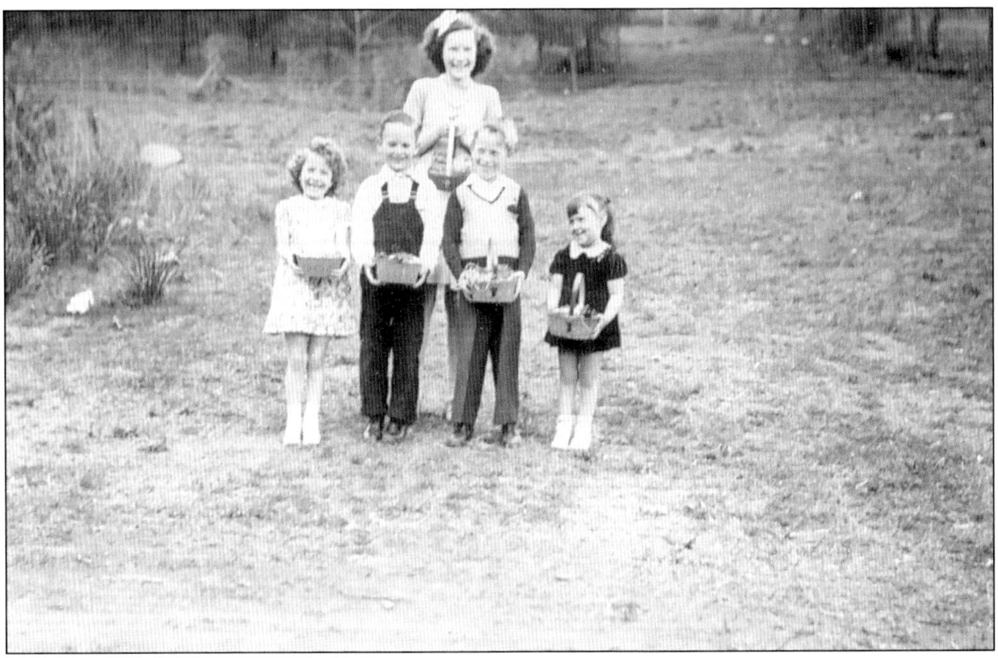

Wanda Barnes (back) is pictured here with, from left to right, Barbara Stamey, Doug Conner, Charles Stamey, and Carolyn Sheffer. The younger children are all grandchildren of Charles and Ella Conner. (Courtesy of Bob and Jackie Barnes.)

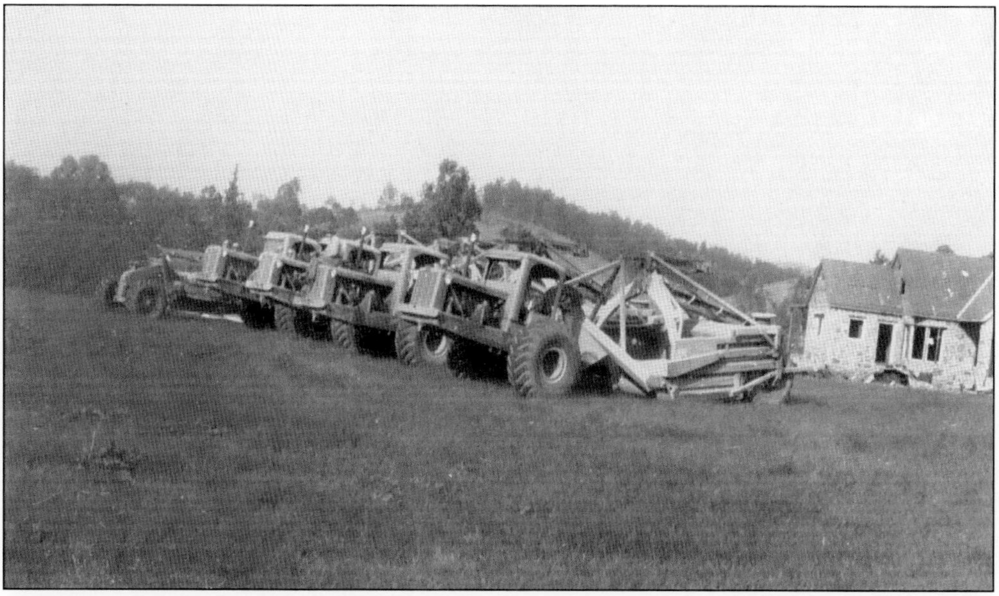

This photograph was taken in Charles W. Conner's yard at the south end of Pigeon Forge just after the heavy equipment pulled in. The equipment would be used to build a new divided highway through the community for future national park visitors. It would cut Conner's farm in two, taking 300 feet for the right-of-way. Charles' father, Dock Conner, had purchased 130 acres in 1920 at a price of $15,000 when he learned that his family would be relocated from the Smokemont area of the Great Smoky Mountains. (Courtesy of Bob and Jackie Barnes.)

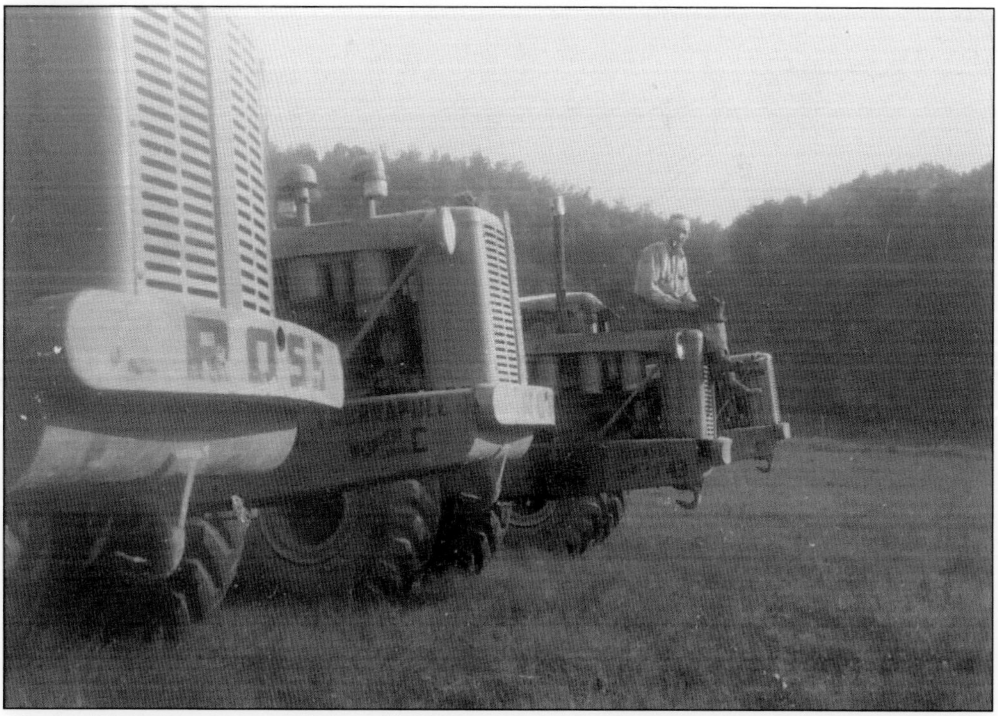

Charles W. Conner rests on the road building equipment that sat in his yard in preparation for construction of the Parkway, or U.S. Highway 441. (Courtesy of Bob and Jackie Barnes.)

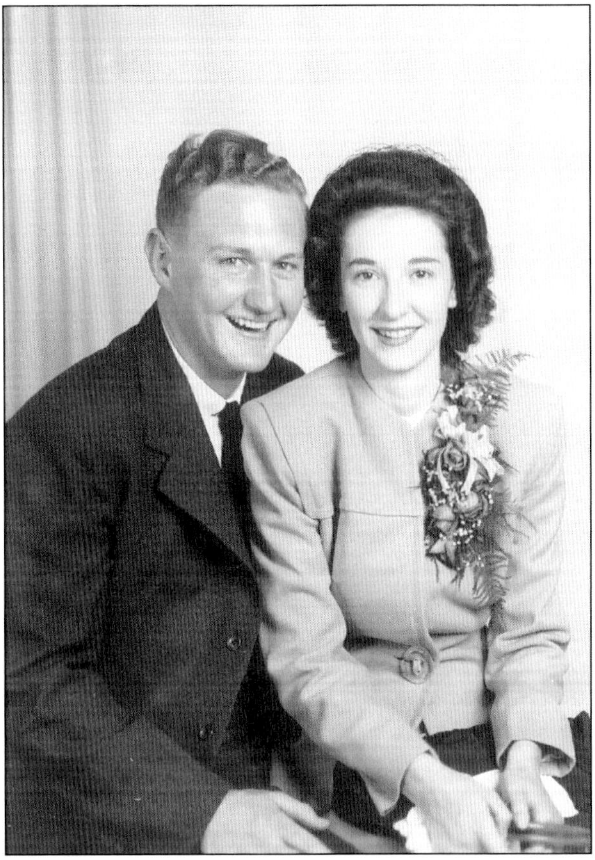

Dan and Norma Conner pose for a wedding photograph in the late 1940s. They met while living in North Carolina when Dan's father, Jehu Conner, operated a store at Smokemont. The two moved to Pigeon Forge and operated Norma Dan Motel, which continues to offer lodging today. (Courtesy of Dan Conner.)

This Pigeon Forge Grammar School photograph was taken in the 1940s. The students pictured are, from left to right, (first row) Ray Farr, C. L. Fleming, Mary Sue Campbell, Sarah Ferguson, Mary Helen Barnes, Betty Sue Myers, Ora Jean Parton, Junior Finchum, and Charles Ray Lafollette; (second row) Jim Trotter, Douglas Conner, Bob Reagan, Jack Duggan, Mike Rolen, Jimmy Owens, and Claude England. (Courtesy of Bob and Jackie Barnes.)

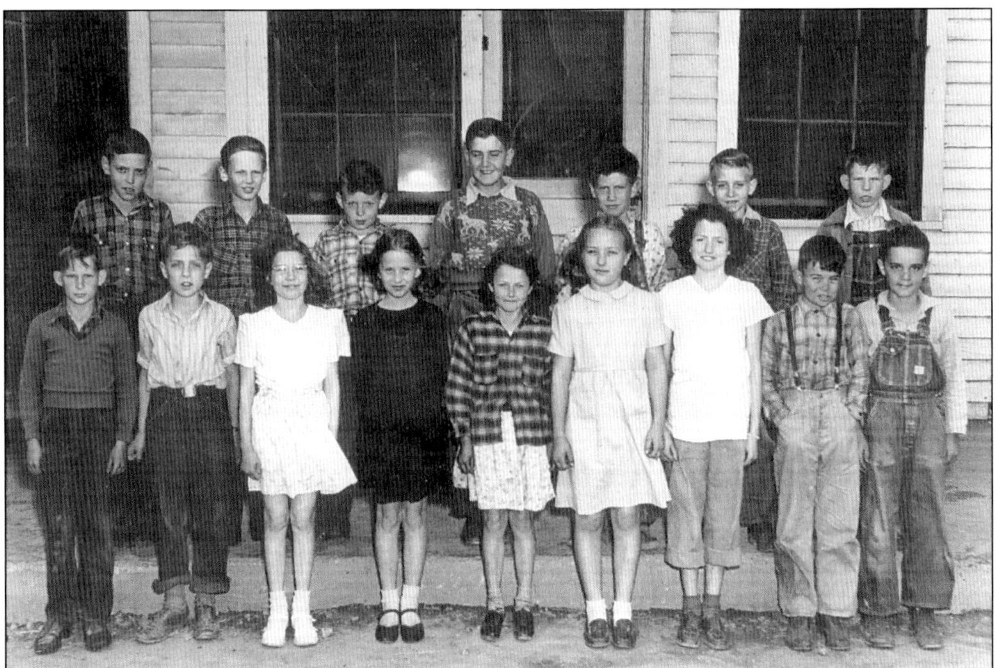

Wanda and Doug Conner were the children of Charles and Ella Conner, who lived at the south entrance to Pigeon Forge. Members of the Conner family operated businesses in the town's early tourism development years and have witnessed many changes over time. (Courtesy of Bob and Jackie Barnes.)

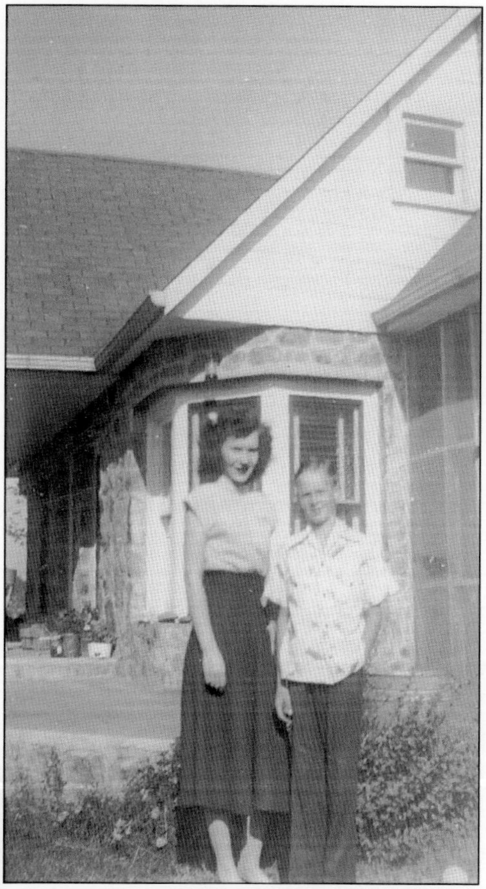

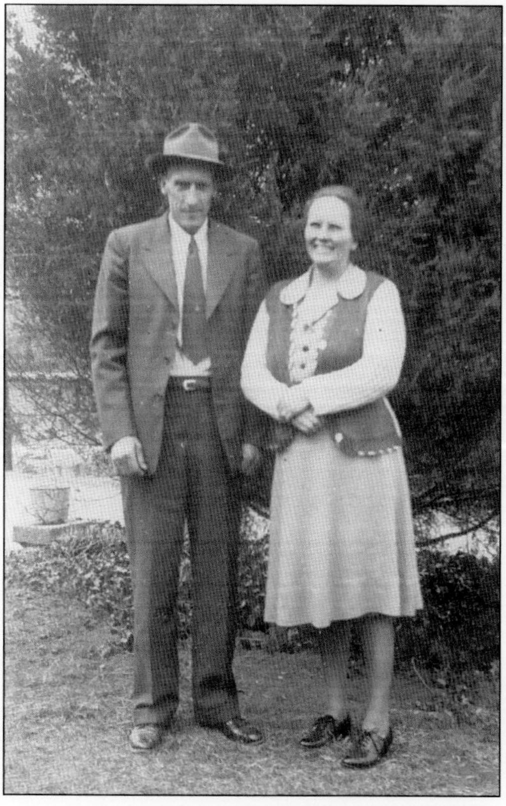

Charles W. Conner is pictured with his wife, Ella Beck. Charlie's Bunion, a mountain peak in the Great Smoky Mountains, was named for him. He trekked the Smokies with Horace Kephert and served as a guide when many of the park locations were mapped. (Courtesy of Bob and Jackie Barnes.)

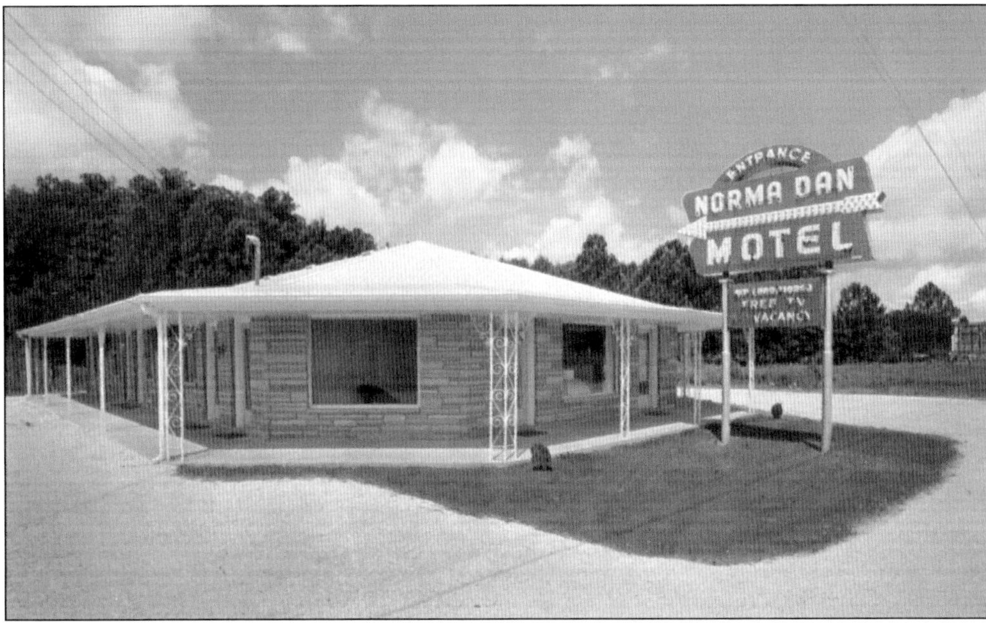

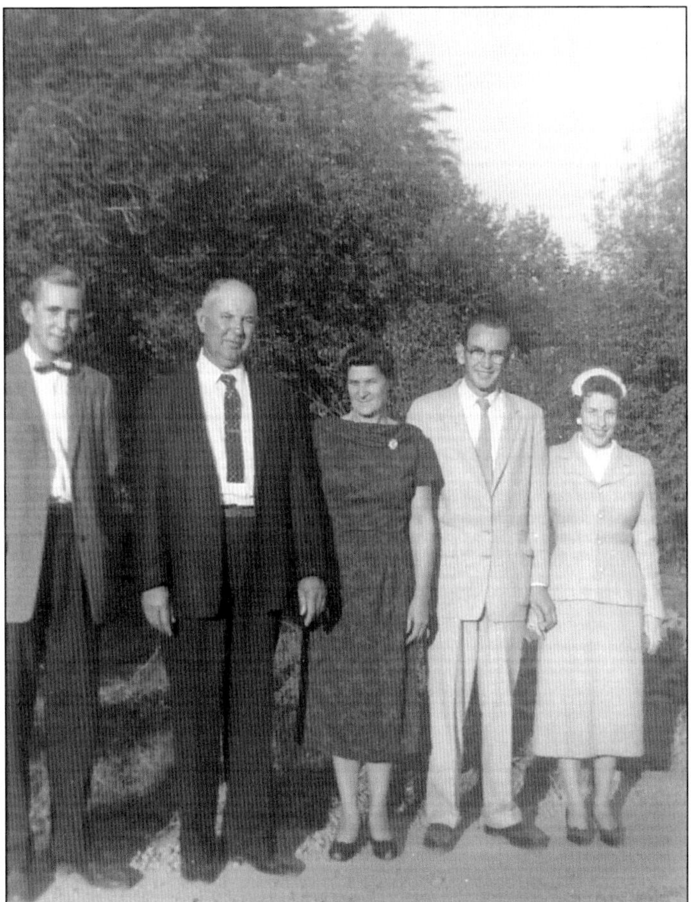

Norma Dan Motel is pictured as it was in 1958 when it opened. This small property is one of only a handful of motels still owned and operated by the same family who built the original business. Dan and Norma Conner left their home on the other side of the Great Smoky Mountains and came to Pigeon Forge in 1948; they were later joined in the operations by daughter Danette. Photography by Thompson Photo Products, Knoxville.)

Wayne L. and Rena Sue Ogle were among the first to operate motels in Pigeon Forge. The Ogle family is pictured here. They are, from left to right, Wayne Dale, Wayne L., Rena Sue, James David, and his wife, Sue Jane Tipton Ogle. (Courtesy of Rena Ogle.)

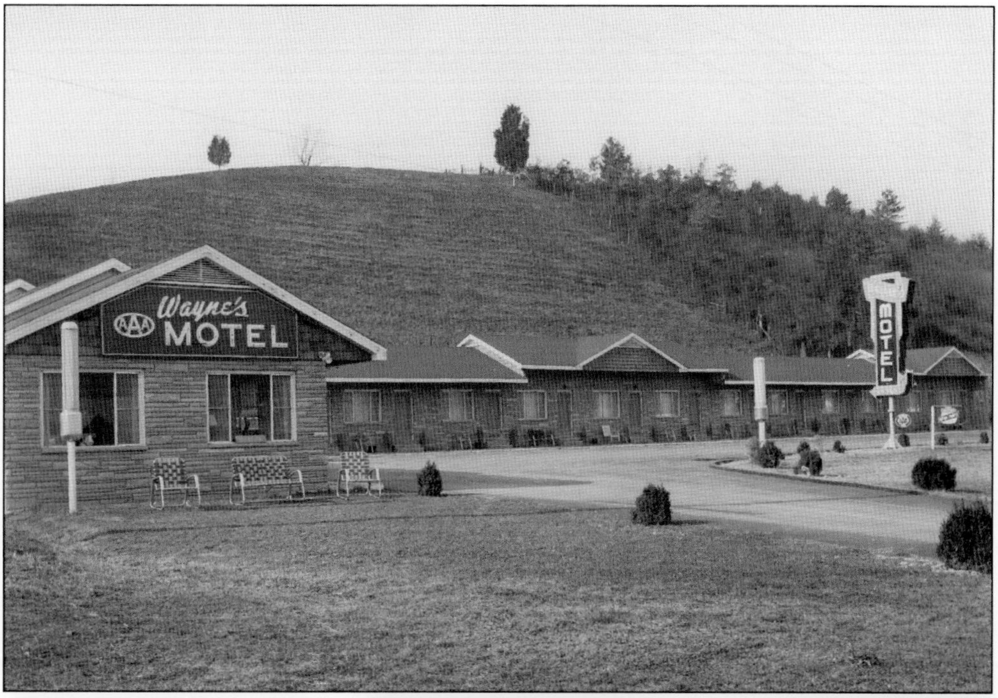

Wayne's Motel was one of the first to arrive after the roadside cottages had opened the doors to lodging establishments in Pigeon Forge. Wayne and Rena Ogle operated this motel before purchasing Red's Motel from Red Clevenger and renaming it Mountain Breeze Motel. Mountain Breeze remains in the Ogle family yet today. The couple sold Wayne's Motel to George and Helen Worsham, who renamed it Vacation Lodge. (Courtesy of Rena Ogle.)

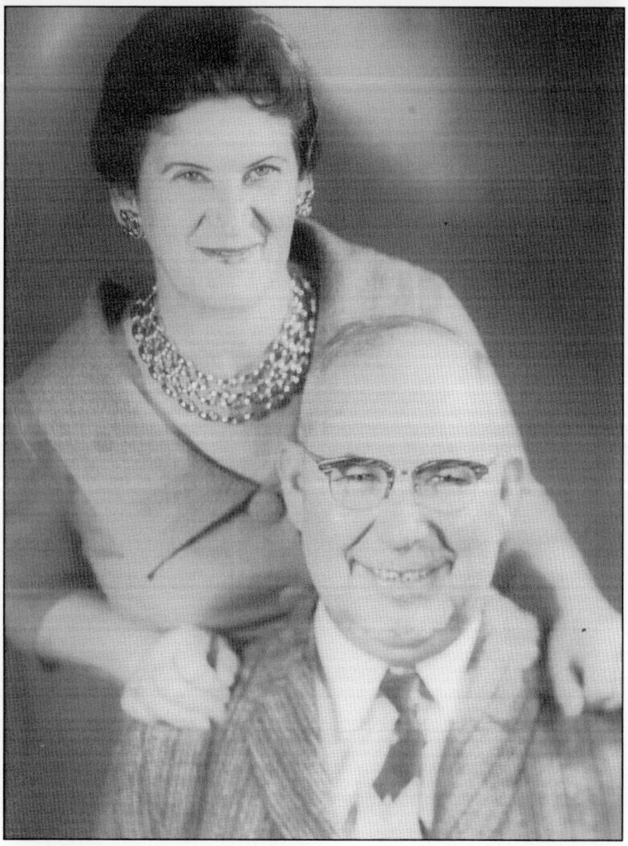

Wayne L. and Rena Ogle operated the Mountain Breeze Motel in Pigeon Forge for many years. His family had moved from the Sugarlands in the Great Smoky Mountains, and her family was from Greenbrier. (Courtesy of Rena Ogle.)

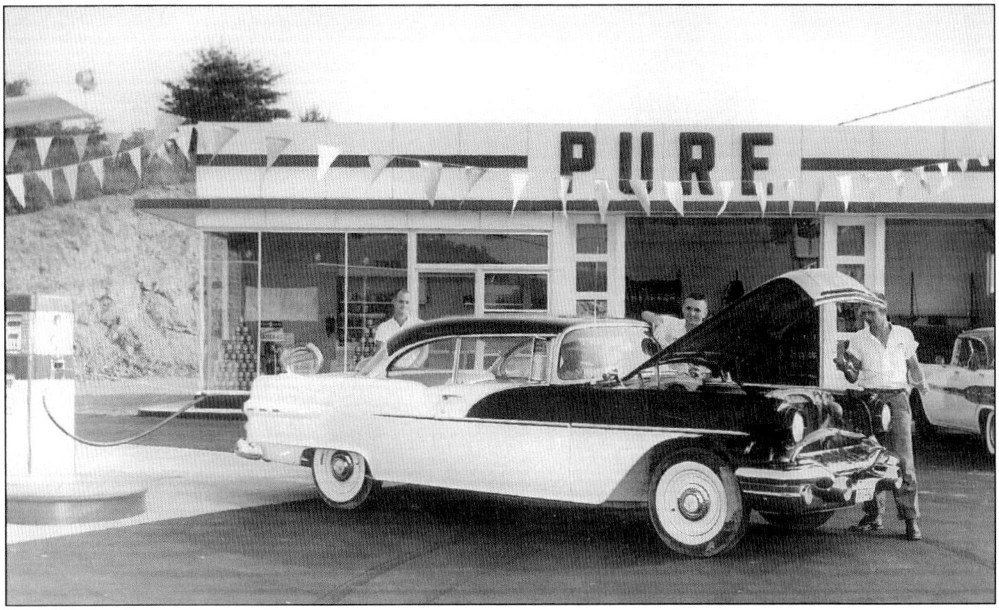

George Worsham's Pure service station operated in Pigeon Forge near the First Baptist Church. He is pictured here (center) with Bill Maples (left) and an unidentified man at right. Maples later purchased the station from Worsham. (Courtesy of Peggy Worsham Palmer.)

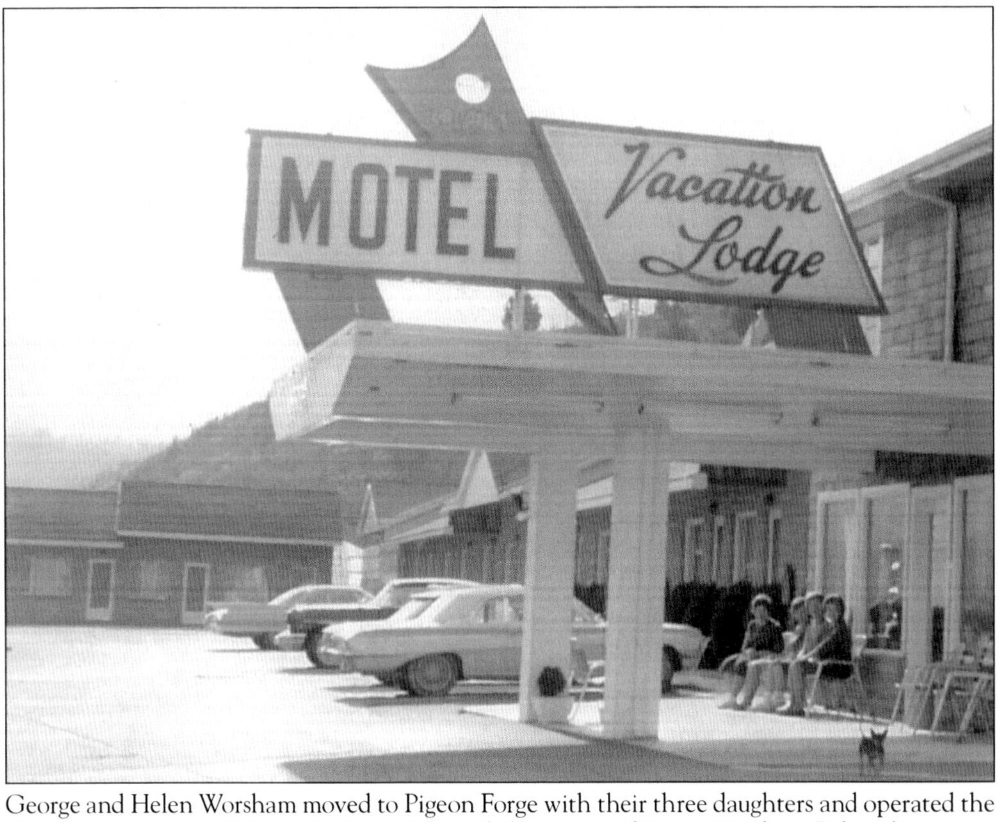

George and Helen Worsham moved to Pigeon Forge with their three daughters and operated the Vacation Lodge Motel, formerly Wayne's Motel. (Courtesy of Peggy Worsham Palmer.)

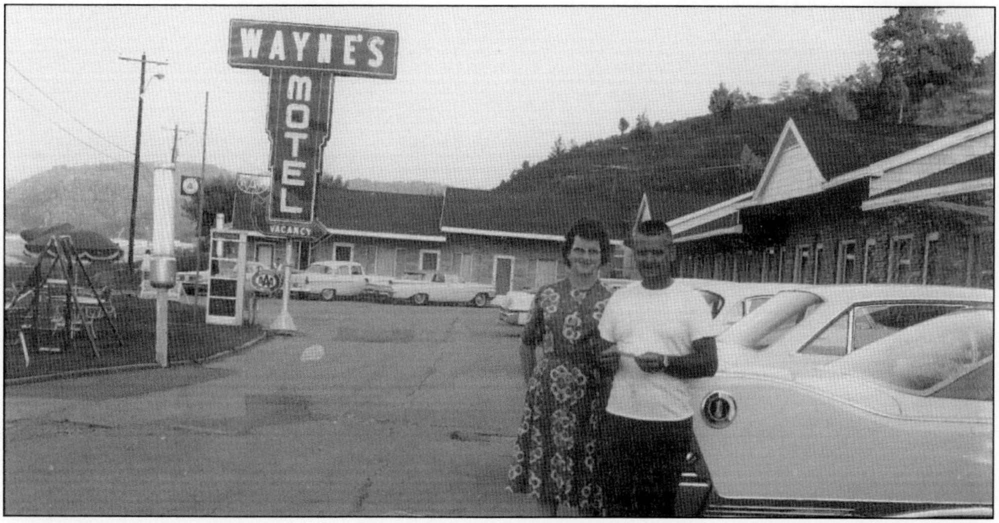

George and Helen Worsham are pictured in front of their new motel, Wayne's Motel, which later was named the Vacation Lodge. This lodging facility remained in the Worsham family for several years; it continues to operate under the Vacation Lodge name. (Courtesy of Peggy Worsham Palmer.)

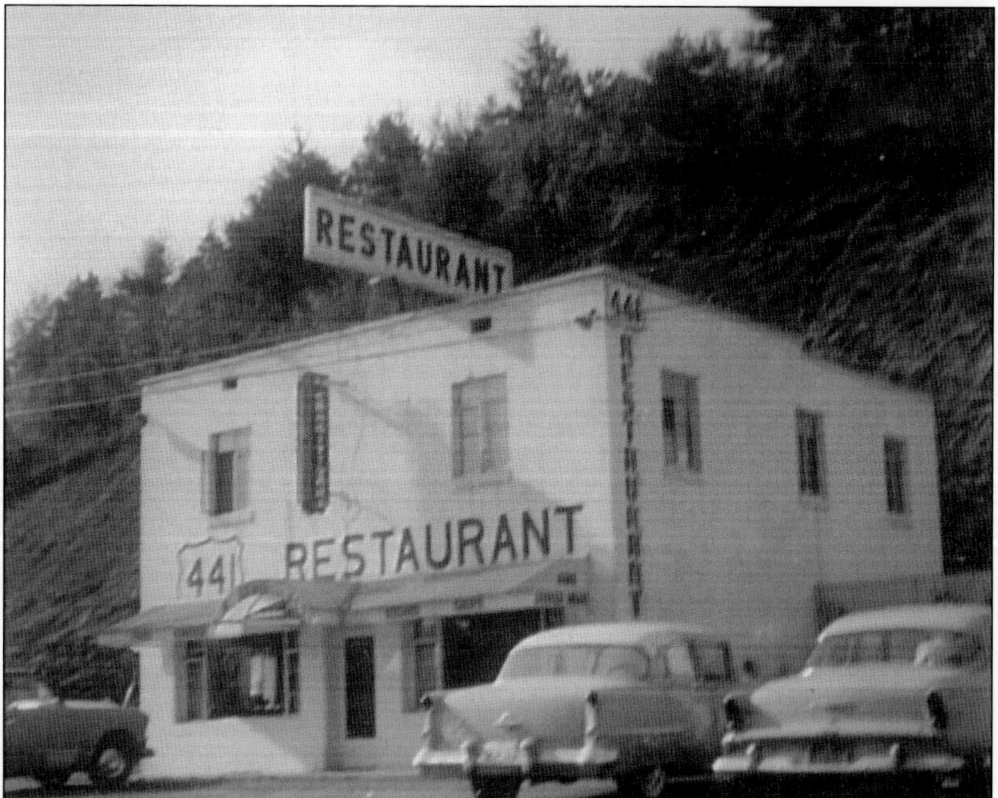

Pigeon Forge's 441 Restaurant opened soon after the town's new section of U.S. Highway 441 was constructed in the 1950s. George and Helen Worsham owned the business, and Helen operated it with assistance from Wilda Lamon. (Courtesy of Peggy Worsham Palmer.)

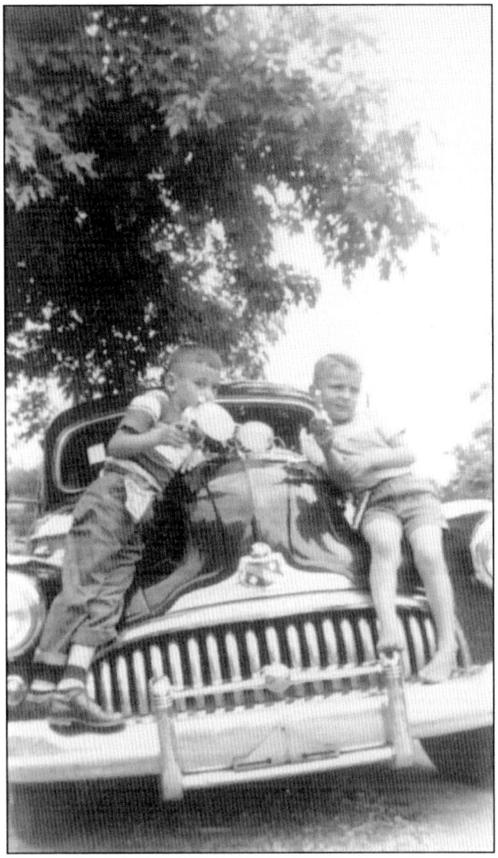

Jerry Wear (left) and Bert Ogle lived in the carefree days just as Pigeon Forge residents were considering their destiny as a tourism village. (Courtesy of Rena Ogle.)

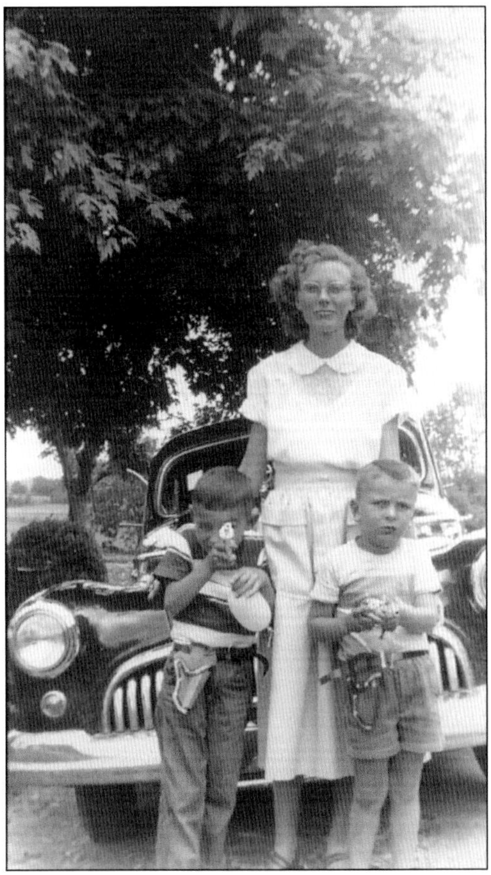

Jerry Wear (left) is pictured with his mother, Lorene Ogle Wear, and Bert Ogle. Jerry Wear is an avid historian whose ancestors include Col. Samuel Wear, a Pigeon Forge native who helped to write the Tennessee Constitution and was instrumental in organizing the state of Franklin. (Courtesy of Rena Ogle.)

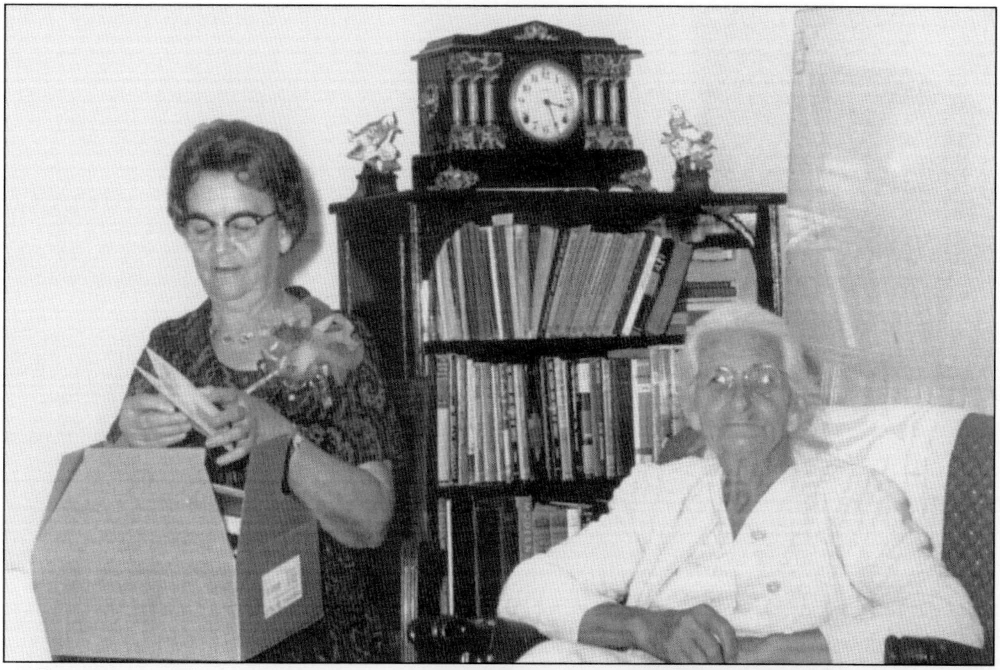

Mollie Ogle (right) attends the 50th wedding anniversary celebration of Lillie Whaley Ownby (left) and Walter Ownby (not pictured). This photograph was taken on September 3, 1965. (Photograph by Bashor's Photos, Sevierville; courtesy of Rena Ogle.)

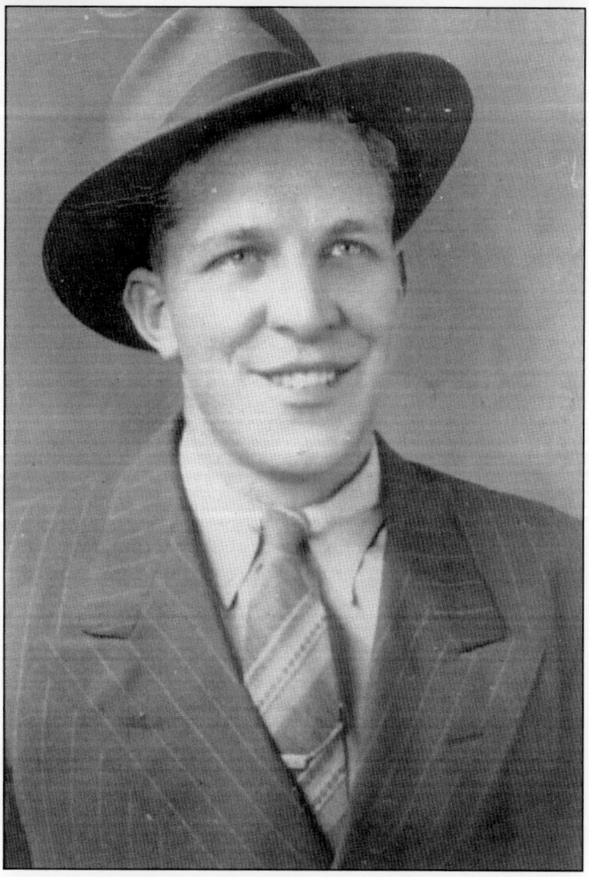

Kyle Cole, son of Joe and Callie Ramsey Cole, lived in Pigeon Forge near the Gatlinburg Country Club. He and his wife, Garnett, owned the Apple Tree Inn restaurant. (Courtesy of Bill and Jody Allen.)

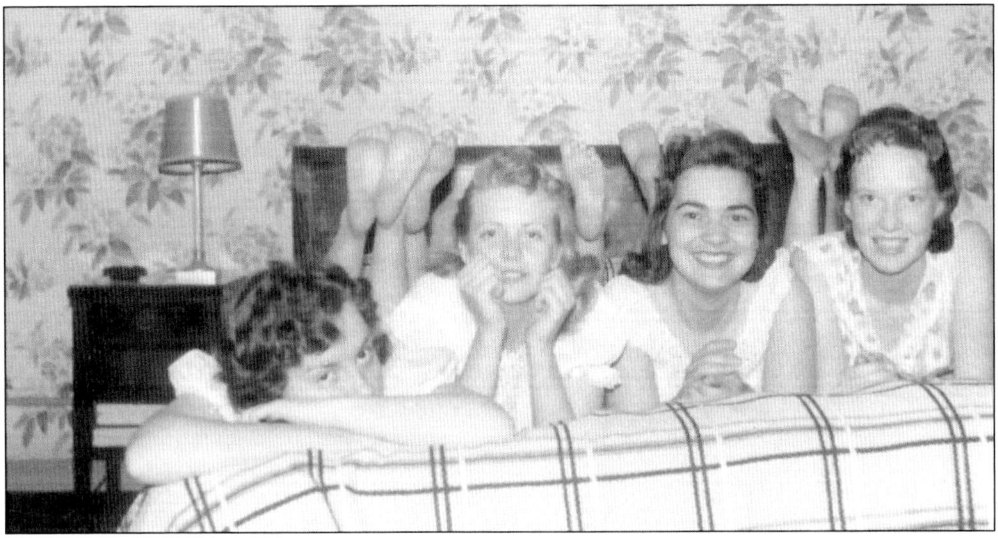

Sevier County High School senior girls from Pigeon Forge enjoy a break from sightseeing on their June 1959 senior class trip in Washington, D.C. They are, from left to right, Earlene McClure, present-day city manager; Jody Cole; Charlotte Myers; and Helen Clevenger. (Courtesy of Charlotte Myers McClure.)

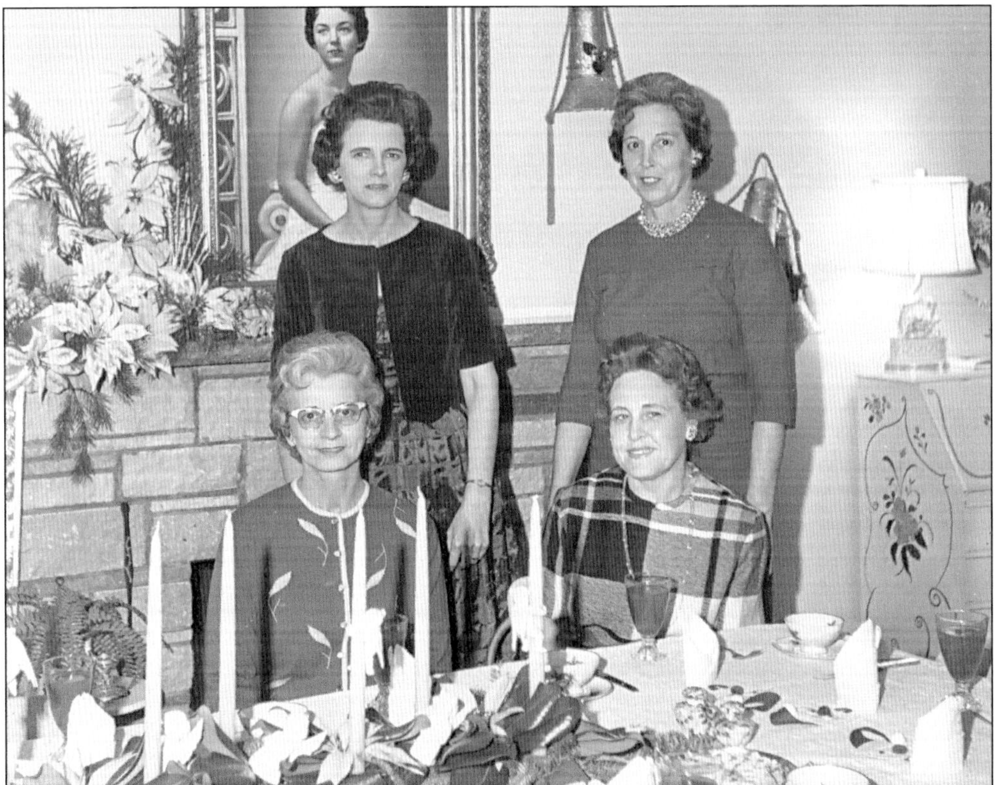

Pictured here are early members of the Pigeon Forge Garden Club, from left to right, (seated) Mildred Lowe and Pauline Ingle; (standing) Beulah Lowe and Ruth Quarrels. (Courtesy of Clara Quarrels Killian.)

This wedding photograph of Gerald and Lib (Elizabeth Ann) Cole Glandon was taken in 1958. (Courtesy of Bill and Jody Allen.)

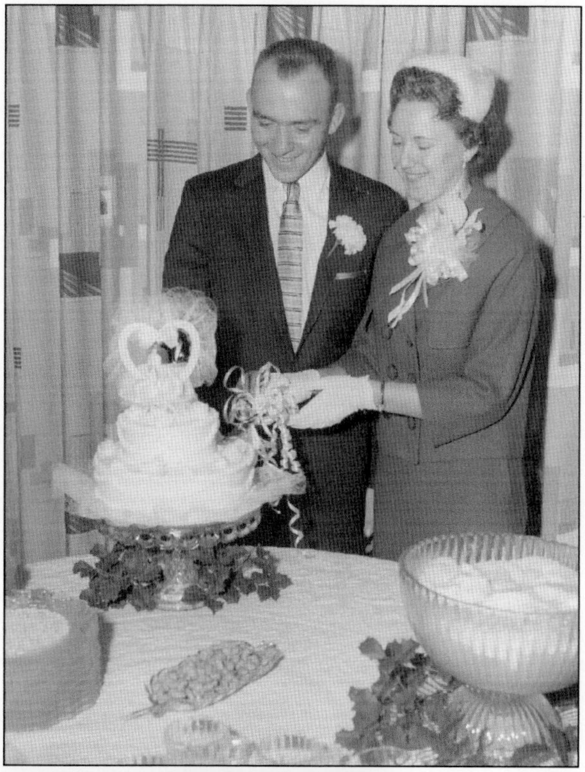

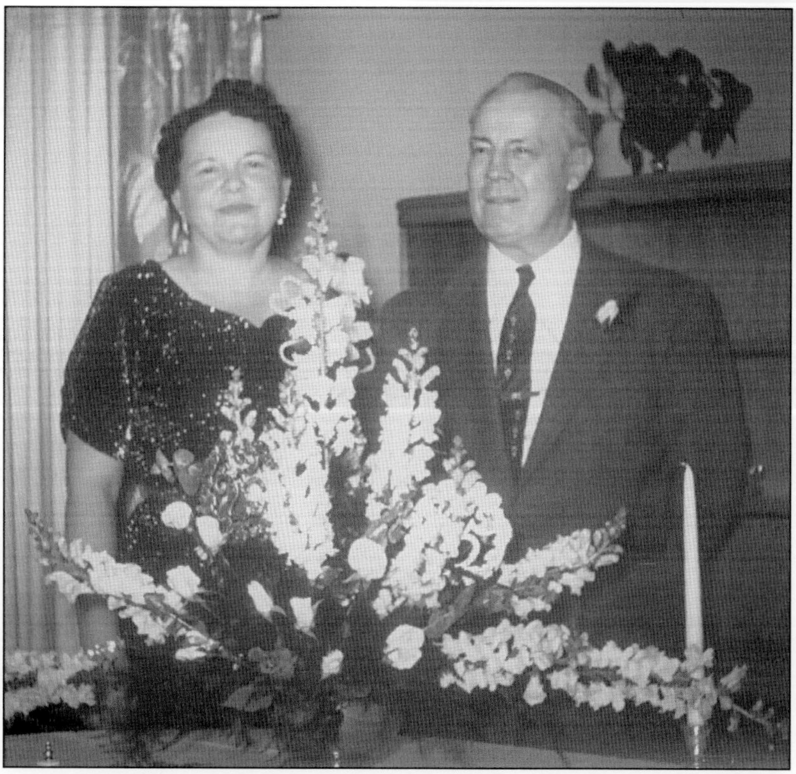

Victor V. Allen is pictured with his wife, Ruby Wynn Allen. Both loved to tend vegetable and flower gardens. They lived on River Road in an old white farmhouse with wide porches and gingerbread trim. (Courtesy of Bill and Jody Allen.)

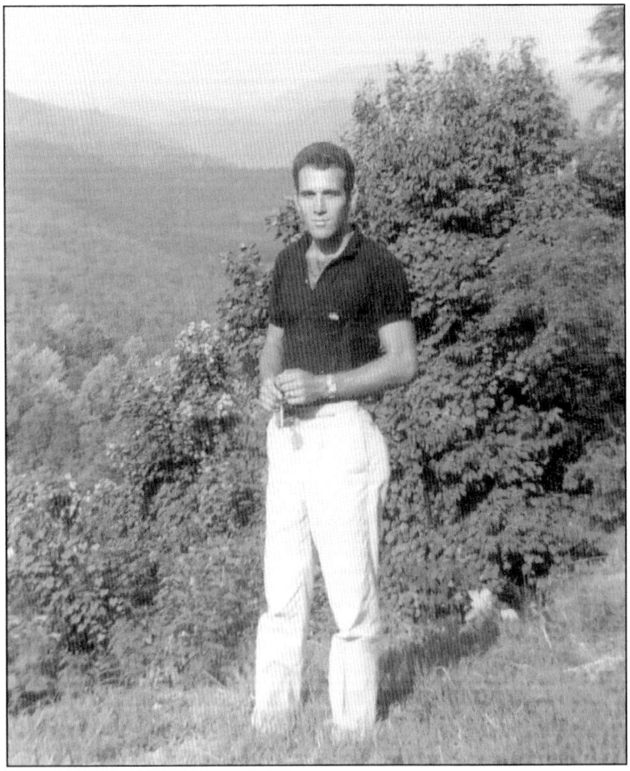

Kenneth Seaton and his first wife, Barbara, loved to drive through the Great Smoky Mountains in their younger years. Seaton owns and operates a large number of hotel facilities in Pigeon Forge and other surrounding areas. (Courtesy of Barbara Seaton.)

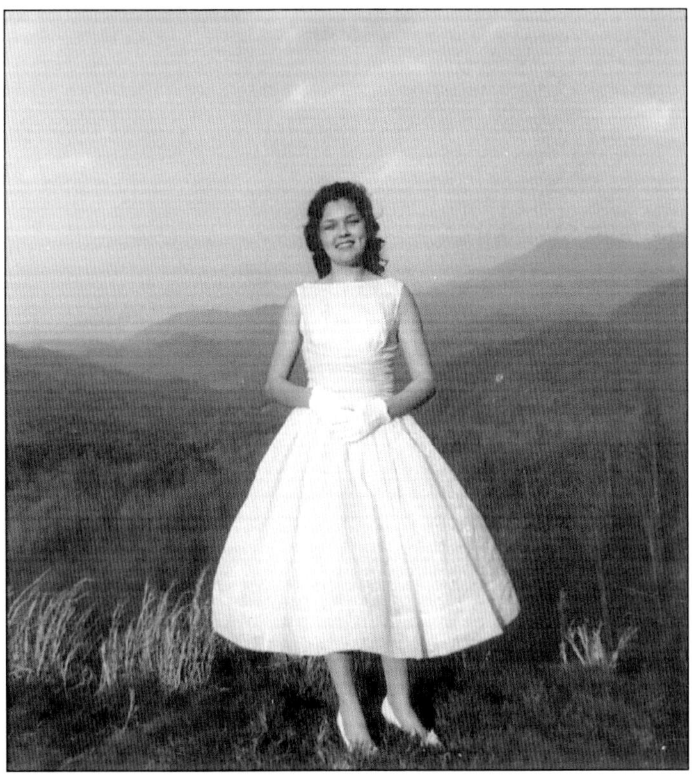

The majestic Great Smoky Mountains provide the perfect backdrop for Barbara Reagan Seaton on her Sunday drive after church. Barbara and Kenneth Seaton, now divorced, operated the Family Inns hotels in Pigeon Forge in the 1960s and 1970s while raising a family. He continues to operate the Family Inns parent company, KMS Enterprises, headquartered in Pigeon Forge. (Courtesy of Barbara Seaton.)

Kenneth and Barbara Seaton are pictured in Gatlinburg, her hometown. The two worked together to operate Valley Motor Inn in their early married years. (Courtesy of Barbara Seaton.)

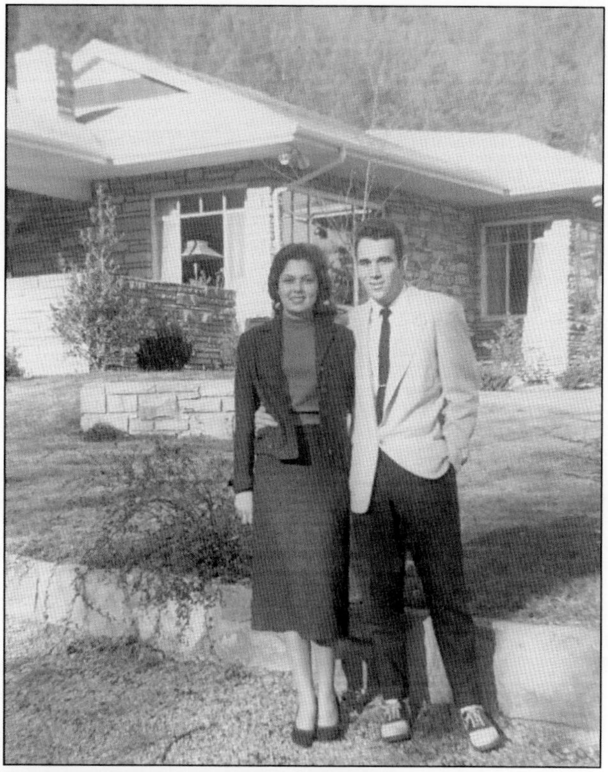

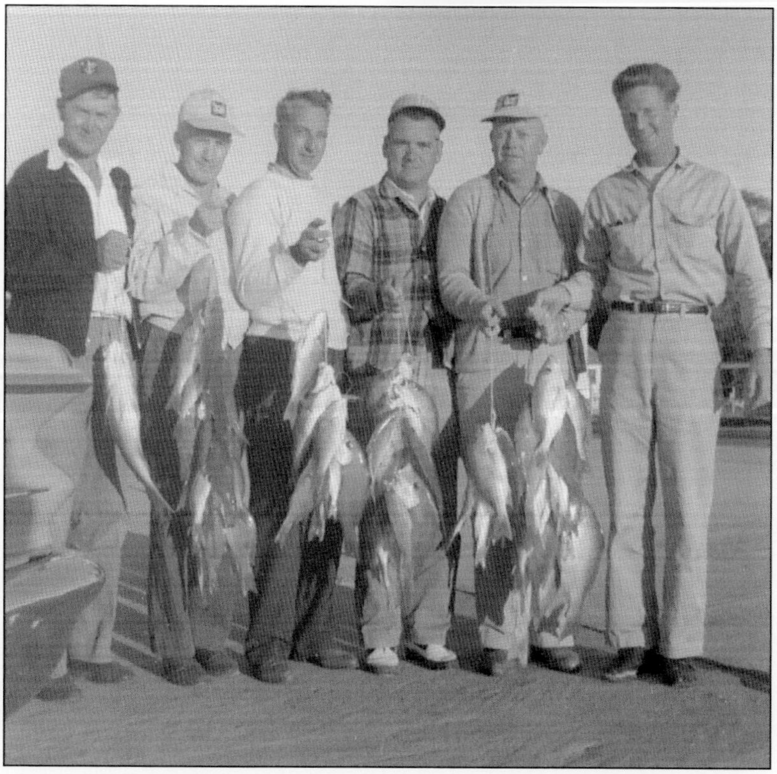

This fishing group photograph was taken in 1962. The group includes, from left to right, Wade McMahan, Estel Ownby, Charles Reagan, George Worsham, James Maples, and Clyde Maples. Three of these men, Wade McMahan, George Worsham, and James Maples, served on the city council for Pigeon Forge. (Courtesy of Pigeon Forge Public Library.)

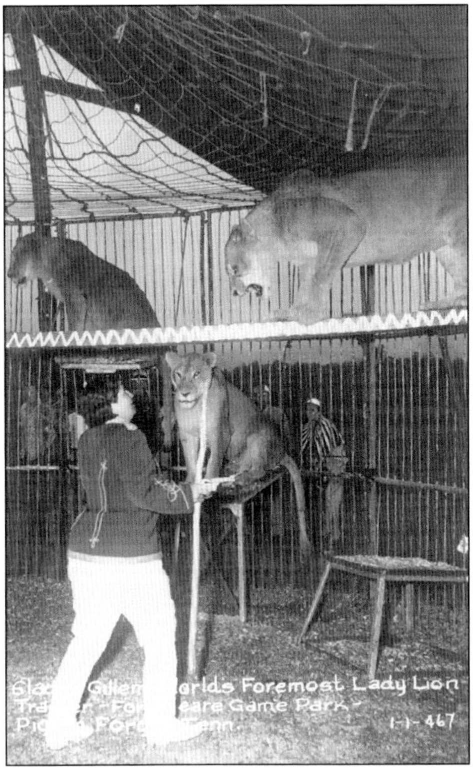

Gladys Gillem was billed as the world's foremost lady lion trainer. She performed at Fort Weare Game Park in the heart of Pigeon Forge. (Pauline Householder collection; courtesy of Jerry Loveday.)

Pigeon Forge's Fort Weare Game Park was a zoo that delighted families during the middle of the 1900s. Monkeys, lions, and elephants were among the animals here. Schoolchildren ran to the windows to watch every time the elephant decided to escape for the river and a cool bath. (Photograph by Thompson Photo Products, Knoxville.)

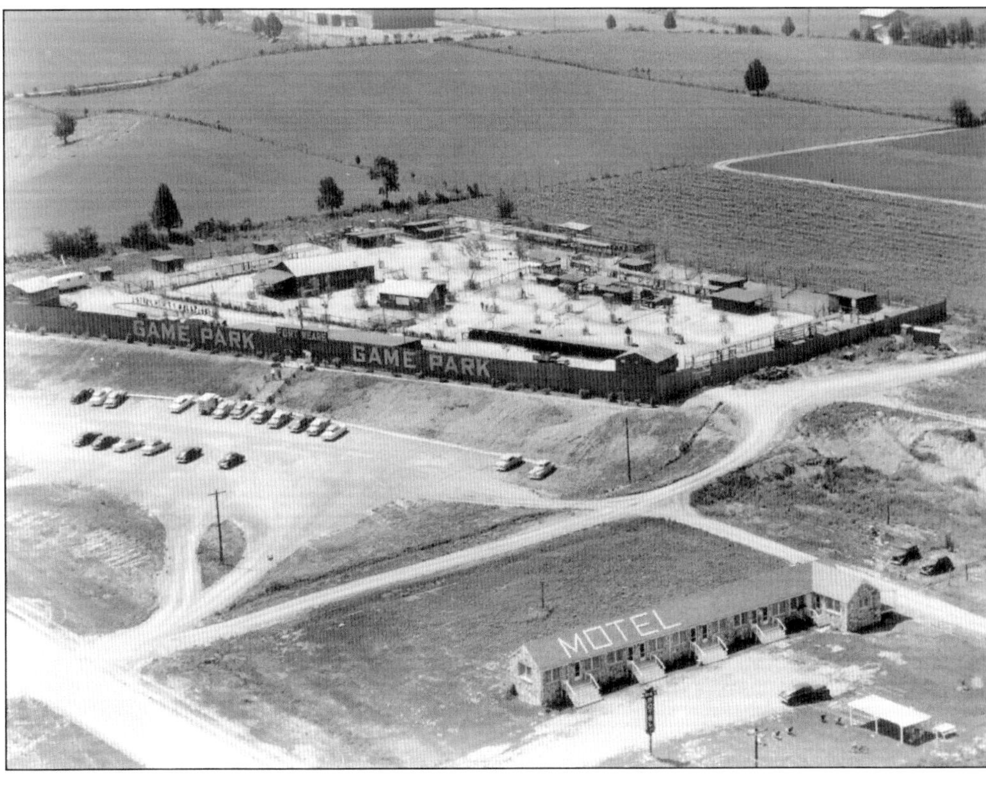

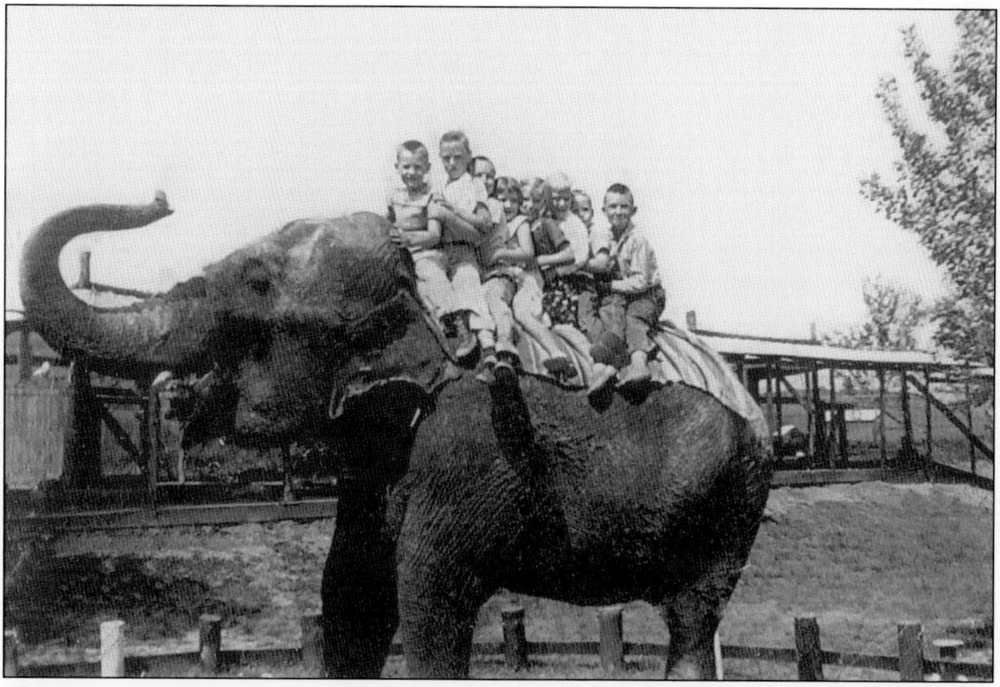

This group of students from a nearby school is pictured on a field trip to Fort Weare Game Park zoo in 1958. Pictured from left to right are Lowell Wilson, Wayne Cantrell, Danny Watson, Phyllis Watson, Linda Watson, Don Watson, Eugene Wilson, and Ben Parton

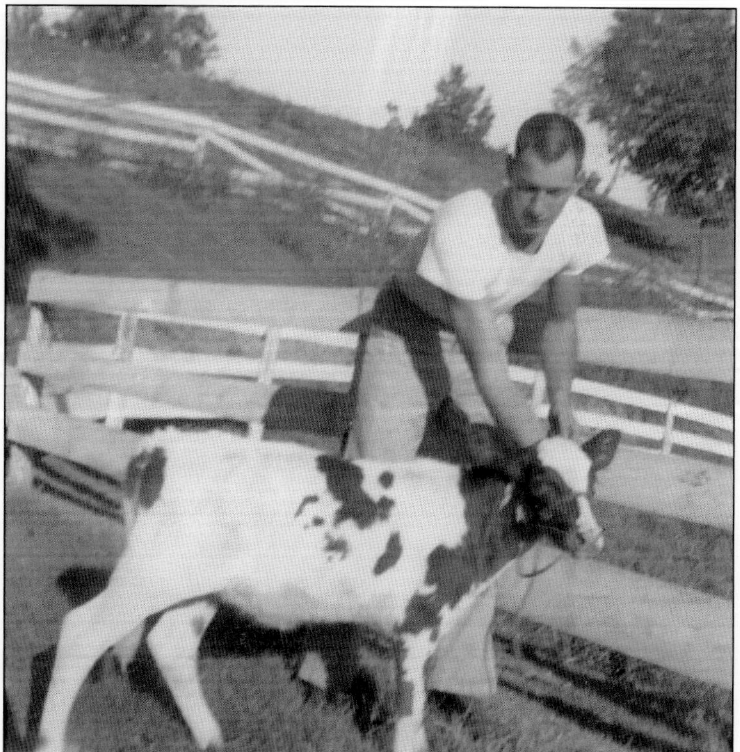

Bill Broady works with a calf on his family's dairy farm at the south end of Pigeon Forge. Dr. R. A. Broady, an area physician, saw the need for fresh milk through working with families in his practice and opened this dairy. (Courtesy of Bill Broady.)

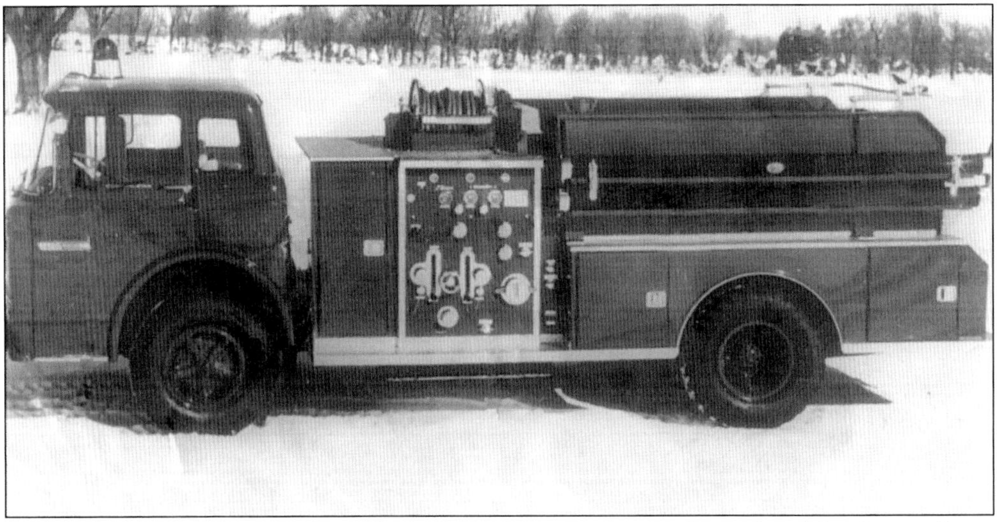

This is one of the Pigeon Forge Volunteer Fire Department's early trucks. After Pigeon Forge became a city in 1961, the first fire chief was Kyle Cole. (Courtesy of Carol Suttles King.)

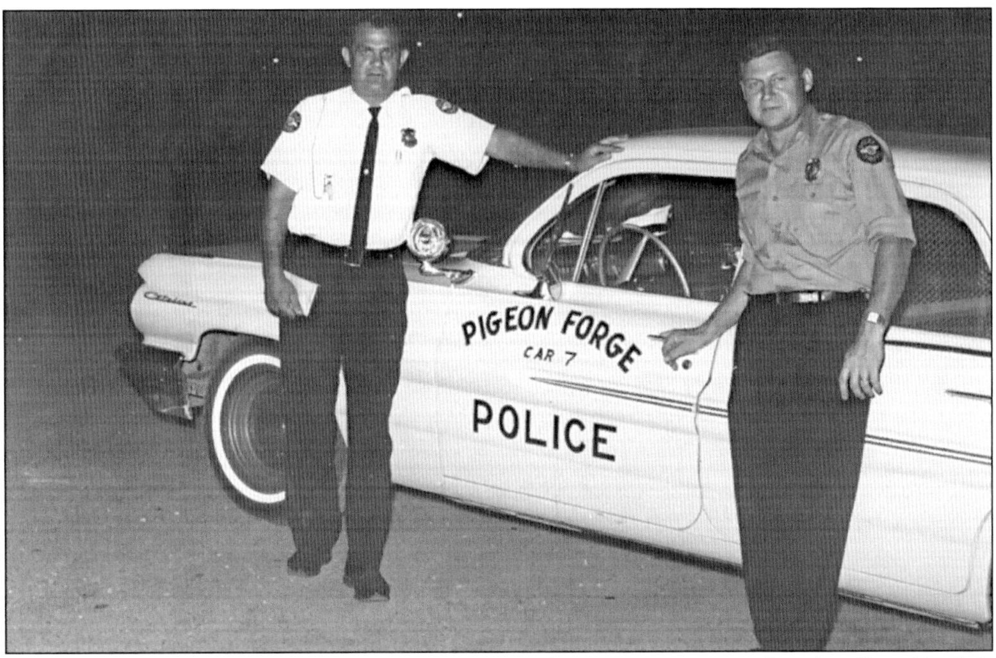

Lloyd Suttles (left), Pigeon Forge's police chief in the 1960s, is pictured with officer English McCarter. McCarter later became mayor of Pigeon Forge, and Suttles served as volunteer fire chief in the 1970s. The town's first police chief was Fred Pierce. (Courtesy of Carol Suttles King.)

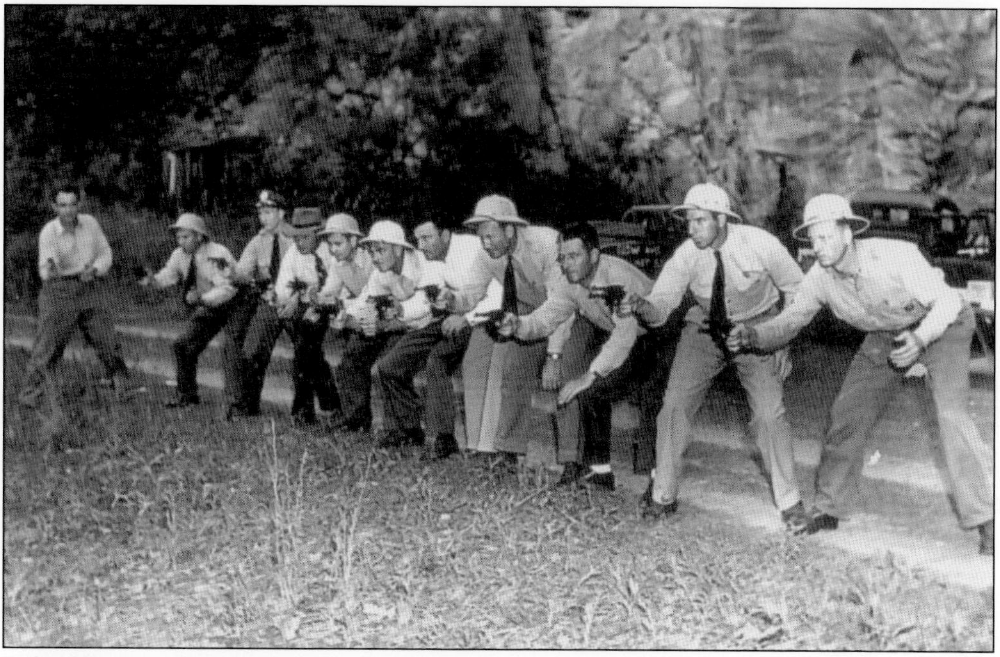

Federal Bureau of Investigation training exercises are being conducted for Pigeon Forge and Sevier County law enforcement officers in 1950. Ray Noland, a former Sevier County sheriff who lived in Pigeon Forge, is pictured in the group. From left to right are Agent Frank Alden, instructor; E. Edwards, ranger; Wib Ogle, Gatlinburg officer; Major Carr, Gatlinburg officer; Harold Edwards, ranger; Gerald Mernin, chief park ranger; Ray C. Noland, former county sheriff; Audley Whaley, ranger; John Noland, Gatlinburg officer; Boyd J. Stokes, county conservation officer; and Lee Ownby, ranger and Pigeon Forge minister. (Courtesy of Ersa Rhea Noland Smith.)

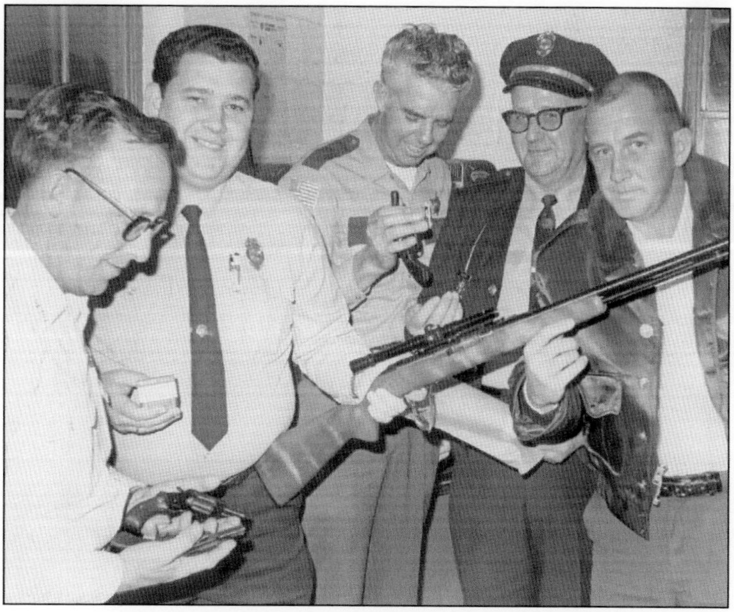

These officers inspect a new gun purchase. These were the days when one or two officers patrolled an entire city. Pictured are, from left to right, Buddy Seals, Pigeon Forge police chief; D. J. Kirby, Sevierville officer; James Ownby, Pigeon Forge officer; Paul Finchum, assistant police chief of Sevierville; and Max Trotter, assistant chief at Pigeon Forge. (Courtesy of Pigeon Forge Public Library.)

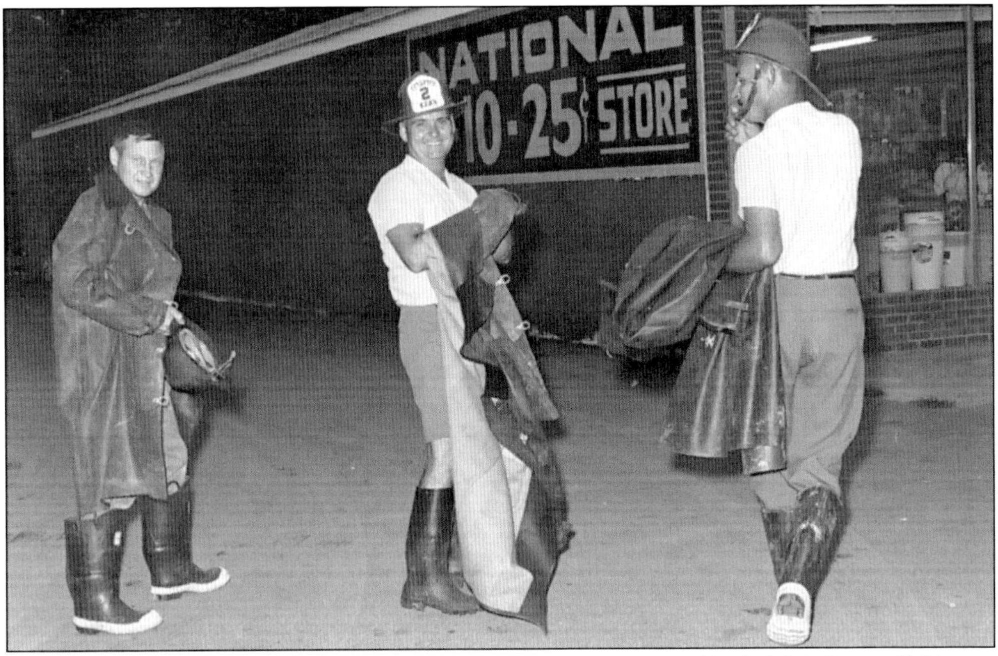

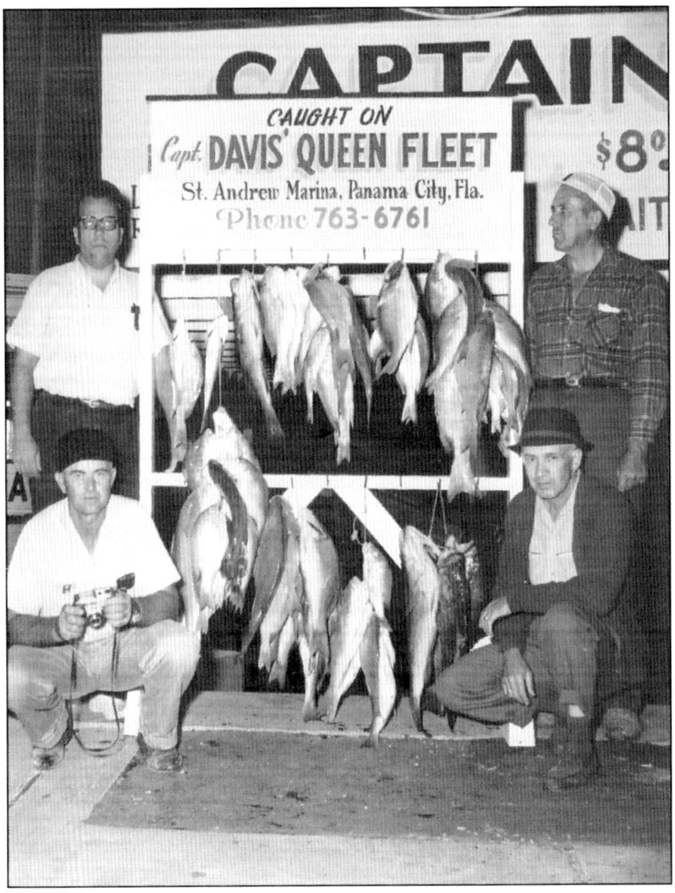

English McCarter (left), George Worsham (center), and Garland Harmon return from working a fire with the Pigeon Forge Volunteer Fire Department. The department was located next-door to the National Five and Dime, seen here. McCarter would later become the town's mayor, Worsham a city commissioner, and Harmon the assistant city manager. (Courtesy of Peggy Worsham Palmer.)

Men from Pigeon Forge take a fishing trip to Panama City, Florida, in the 1960s. They are, from left to right, (first row) Reford Lamons and Estel Ownby; (second row) Rev. W. W. Cope, former pastor of First Baptist Church of Pigeon Forge, and Charles Pickel. (Courtesy of Sarah Ball.)

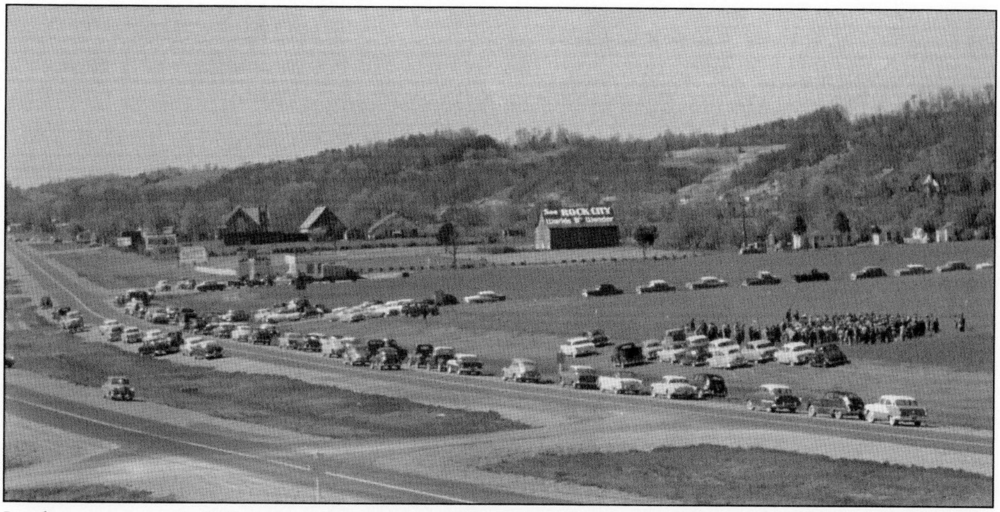

In the summer of 1956, Jehu Conner hired Water's Auction Company to sell 36 lots along the Parkway by present-day Dixie Stampede. The sparsely developed Parkway shown here is far different than the major park access road lined with resort industry businesses today. By the Methodist church is Sam Robertson's home and barn. Flower Garden Cottages are to the right of Judge Ben Robertson's barn advertising Rock City. Along the Parkway to the left of the crowd is Dan Conner's Gulf service station (built in 1952). (Photograph by Water's Auction Company; courtesy Dan Conner.)

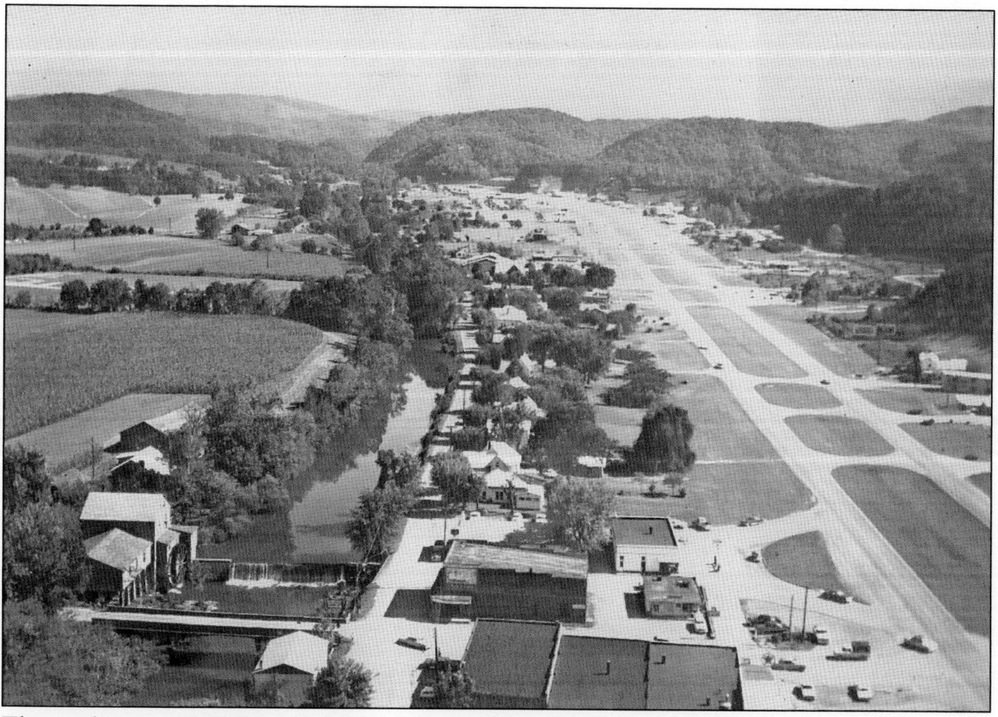

The predictions of William R. Montgomery, editor of *Montgomery's Vindicator*, were becoming realized. He wrote in 1921, referring to the new railroad, that someday the people of Pigeon Forge would not have to go to see the world but that the world would want to come see Pigeon Forge. (Courtesy of the *Mountain Press*.)